Korzenie Polskie

POLISH
ROOTS

These knights guarding their king are carved from tree trunks twenty feet tall. The figures stand at the entrance to a park in Great Poland near Gniezno.

Korzenie Polskie

POLISH ROOTS

Rosemary A. Chorzempa

Published by Genealogical Publishing Co., Inc.
1001 N. Calvert Street, Baltimore, MD 21202
Second printing 1993
Third printing 1994
Fourth printing 1995
Library of Congress Catalogue Card Number 93-77159
International Standard Book Number 0-8063-1378-1
Made in the United States of America

DEDICATION

This book is dedicated to Anastasia Rose Chorzempa, named after many of my ancestors, and the first of my descendants to join them.

CONTENTS

Part One: Research in America

List of Illustrations

List of Maps

ACKNOWLEDGMENTS

No one can write a book that contains this much information without the assistance of a number of specialists in the field of Polish genealogy. I would therefore like to express my appreciation to the following individuals for their assistance in preparing this book: Stephen S. Barthel, Joseph A. Borkowski, Anna Borski Campo, Michael Drabik, Clare Ann Gaouette, John J. Grabowski, Thomas L. Hollowak, Antek Jakubowski, Dr. Zygmunt Klimek (Kraków), Edward J. Mendyka, Thaddeus J. Obal, Gerald A. Ortell, Edward A. Peckwas, Jacque Penstone, William A. Radlinski, Jonathan D. Shea, John F. Skibiski, Jr., Antoni W. Szachnowski, Gene Szymarek, Reverend Peter Waslo, Bronisława Witkowska (Warsaw), Frank A. Zabrosky, and Jan Steven Zaleski.

Special thanks also to: the Polish Genealogical Society of America and its officers and board of directors for their permission to use material from articles appearing in the society's *Newsletter,* and for other information provided by the society; Stanley R. Schmidt for the use of his photographs of parish registers which were used for some of the illustrations, and for his many other suggestions; Dr. David G. Chełmiński for proof-reading the Polish words and offering a great deal of additional information and suggestions; my brother Mark D. Dembinski for drawing the maps; William F. (Fred) Hoffman for translating several difficult records; Daniel M. Schlyter and the Church of Jesus Christ of Latter-day Saints for permission to reprint the "Polish Genealogical Letter-Writing Guide," for the use of photographs of parish registers, and offering additional information; and my husband Larry and our children Rebecca, Nancy, Timothy, and Andrew.

INTRODUCTION

Wouldn't you like to go back in time and see what life was like for your ancestors? I have a photograph of a Polish housewife standing in the doorway of a nineteenth-century timber cottage. She is wearing a long petticoat, white lace apron, black shawl, and a white lace cap. The cottage is typical of many found in Kuyavia a hundred years ago—it has a thatched roof and flowers blooming near the doorway.

But something is not quite right—the housewife is wearing sneakers! Yes, I confess, you were tricked. The photograph is one of me taken in 1985 on a trip to Poland. My cousin took us to an ethnographic museum, an outdoor museum with farm buildings equipped with nineteenth-century furnishings, in Toruń. He proudly told the tour guide that we were his cousins from America. The guide smiled and called me towards her. She opened a trunk, pulled out the clothing, and dressed me in peasant finery of the last century. I could almost feel my ancestors moving around that house with me. That was the ultimate in family history research.

SILVA RERUM—"A FOREST OF THINGS"

The family home in Poland was called a "nest," alluding to the Polish eagle, symbol of the Polish nation. Regardless of his degree of wealth, every nobleman kept a collection of mementoes, documents, and personal notes in his nest, or manor house.

This collection was usually kept in a book, often called *Silva rerum*, Latin for "a forest of things." Included in the book were kitchen recipes, directions for making soaps, sealing wax for bottles, and pharmaceutical recipes for homemakers, such as herbal teas and salves for sunburn. Christenings, marriages, and deaths were entered on the pages, as well as world and local political events. According to one authority, even proverbs, family tales, and speeches made by the master of the house on holy days or at family celebrations were preserved (Eugeniusz Szczepaniak, "Silva Rerum, Or Don't Get This on Your Fingers or—God Forbid—Anything Else!," *Polish Genealogical Society Newsletter* VIII (Spring 1986), translated by William F. Hoffman).

The Polish *Silva rerum* was actually a forerunner of the modern scrapbook, and a tradition you may want to begin in your own family.

WHAT IS "FAMILY HISTORY"?

Family history—genealogy—means more to me than the names and dates on a piece of paper. It means Busia (Grandma) Chorzempa's lard and vinegar pie crust recipe; learning how to make *pisanki* because they are so beautiful, and then teaching others how to make these Polish Easter eggs; the four generations of china baby cups, the oldest one over a hundred years old, and the tradition of naming those baby girls "Rose"—grandma Rose Martha, mother Irene Rose, me—Rose Mary, and now my daughters Rebecca Rose, Nancy Rose, and Anastasia Rose; and finding a tradition and continuing it or starting one of your own.

Family history is the story of "Grandpa Dembinski and the Ghost," a dark shape that followed him home after he served Mass and passed by the cemetery, when grandpa was a boy in Poland. Stories such as this are a part of oral history, family history passed on by word of mouth, which sometimes is the only source of information to survive.

And then there are the photographs. The first one I received when I was fourteen, after grandpa Boczkowski's death: grandpa with a mustache, taken in Warsaw, Poland in 1900. Grandma made him shave off the mustache just before their wedding and he never had one again. The old lady who gave me the picture said, "Your grandfather loved you very much. He would have wanted you to have this." I asked her who she was and she said she was a relative, but did not know how she was related to my grandfather. I thought that was so sad. That was when I decided to find out who my relatives were and how we were related.

Ever since then I have collected photographs, mementoes, clippings, recipes, and stories, and filled up several scrapbooks and photo albums. I had my own *Silva rerum* and didn't even know it was a Polish tradition.

HOW TO BEGIN

Begin at the beginning. You have probably heard that phrase many times. In family history the beginning is *you!* We work backwards—from ourselves to our parents, to grandparents, and on to more distant ancestors. Gather information about yourself, perhaps writing an autobiography. Gather information about your parents and siblings and write down important events in each person's life. This is what you will be doing for all of your ancestors.

You will need documents—records to substantiate the information you have been given by your relatives. People have been known to make mistakes when they depend only on their memories. An 88-year-old lady's obituary gave her birthplace as Toledo, Ohio, according to information supplied by her daughter. I know this woman was born in Poland and came to America as an infant; I saw a copy of a ship's passenger list with her name on it.

Many genealogists work only on their direct lines of ancestry—parents, grandparents, great-grandparents—and disregard their collateral lines, the sisters and brothers of their ancestors. You may choose to pursue this either way, but there are benefits from spending a little extra time and searching for siblings. Besides getting a good picture of family life in past generations, a sibling's record may provide a clue in a situation where your direct ancestor's record is missing or lacking the information you need. For example, if your grandfather's birth record does not give his mother's maiden name, it might be found on a sibling's birth or marriage record.

The first records you will need to search will be those here in America which may give you your ancestor's date of arrival and port of entry, as well as his birthplace and place of residence in Europe. Next you will need to determine the exact location of your ancestor's village(s) on a map or in a gazetteer, and only then will you need to search the local civil and church records in Europe.

Record-keeping

Use a system—don't get into the shoe box-and-closet routine. Make a pedigree chart by drawing your family tree on a large sheet of paper, writing in pencil so that you can change information if necessary. Later you can use printed pedigree charts and family group sheets.

Begin a loose-leaf notebook file. Make a master copy of an information sheet that shows all the information you want to collect for each ancestor. Illustration 1 is an example of the one that I use.

Photocopy the original information sheet as many times as necessary. Using a loose-leaf binder you can add sheets to your alphabetical file as needed.

Organize your information in a file cabinet, using folders or large envelopes (used ones are fine). Label the contents of each folder or envelope. Record information in a spiral notebook when you are doing research in a library or interviewing relatives.

Use abbreviations for frequently used words, such as *MA* for Maryanna, *bp* for baptized, *bd* for buried. Carefully transcribe the material onto a computer file, or by typewriter or by hand into a permanent notebook or file, spelling out your abbreviations. You may wish to review the original transcriptions at some future time, and may find a copying error, so do keep your original notes. Always note the source of information on each sheet, including the date and place.

NAME _____

           (Last)   (First)   (Middle)   (Maiden)

BORN _____

           (Date)   (Place)   (Registration No. & Place)

DIED _____

           (Date)   (Place)   (Reg. No. & Place) (Age)   (Cause)

BURIED _____

           (Date)   (Cemetery)   (Grave Location)

BAPTIZED _____

           (Date)   (Place: Church & Town)   (Godparents)

MARRIED _____

           (Date)   (Place: Church & Town)   (Witnesses)

SPOUSE _____

           (Name)   (Born)   (Died)   (Parents)

CHILDREN:

NAME   BORN   DIED   MARRIED (Person & Date)

PARENTS: Father: _____

          Mother: _____

ADDRESSES _____

IMMIGRATED TO U.S. _____

           (Date)   (From)   (To)   (Ship)

MILITARY SERVICE _____

           (Country)   (Dates)   (Branch)

SCHOOLS ATTENDED _____

PUBLIC & CHURCH RECORDS &
MISCELLANEOUS RECORDS—see reverse
(city directories, censuses, gravestones, newspaper clippings, etc.)

Illustration 1. Sample of Personal Information Page from Notebook Filing System. (Devise one yourself using categories that you think are important.)

Make a research log in table form listing the place, date, and person interviewed, or the library where you did the research, and the results. Also keep a log of your genealogical correspondence, noting to whom you wrote, information requested, address, date, and the date you received a reply. The current edition of *The Genealogist's Address Book* by Elizabeth Petty Bentley (Baltimore: Genealogical Publishing Company) contains most of the addresses you will need for correspondence in the United States, including addresses to write to in order to obtain civil vital records (birth, marriage, and death records).

A *SASE* is a self-addressed stamped envelope, a must for most of a genealogist's correspondence. Address an envelope to yourself and put one first-class postage stamp on it. Put a SASE in each letter that you send to anyone from whom you expect a reply. If you are requesting a document or service provided by a government agency you usually do not need a SASE because you will be paying a fee for the service provided.

When writing to a person or agency outside the United States do not use a SASE. Purchase one or two International Reply Coupons (IRCs) from the post office. The person to whom you are writing will exchange the coupons for return postage.

Fold your letters as little as possible. Use standard #10 envelopes for your correspondence. Number 9 envelopes will fit inside a #10 without being folded and are ideal for use as a SASE. Eight-and-a-half by eleven-inch sheets (standard typing paper) can be folded in thirds and mailed back in a #9 envelope. Both sizes are available at discount and regular office supply stores.

Sending a thank-you or follow-up letter after exchanging information is usually appreciated by the recipients and may encourage them to be more generous with your future requests.

Helpful Hints

Always use complete names of people, including maiden names, aliases, and nicknames.

Use a pencil to record information if you are not certain that it is correct, then write in ink when you have proof that the information is correct.

Use the genealogist's system for writing dates: day—month—year. When someone writes "7-6-77" do they mean "July 6, 1977" or "July 6, 1877," or "7 June 1877" or something else? Never use numbers alone—write the month and century also: 7 Jun 1877. If you want to abbreviate the months, use the first three letters of the month. You will often see months written in roman numerals in Polish records: "7 VI 1877" for "7 June 1877."

Make photocopies of all your original documents. Take the copies with you when you go to do research and leave the originals at home. The most accurate records are those in the native language of both the record-keeper and the person reporting the event, as opposed to a record-keeper who is unfamiliar with the language. A Polish-speaking pastor recording his parishioners' marriages is more likely to record the information correctly than an English-speaking census-taker trying to understand a recently immigrated Pole.

Records made closer to the date of the event are also more likely to be accurate than those made at a later time. For example, on the 1900 census a person's age may be given as 33 years, but a passenger arrival list gives his age as 10/12 year (10 months) in 1871. An older record *should* give more accurate information.

During the last partition period, 1795 to 1918, Poland as a nation did not exist. On most records such as censuses, passenger lists, and naturalization papers, the countries of Prussia (or Germany), Russia, and Austria will be seen as the "national origin" of people who were ethnically Polish. Prussian-Poland, Russian-Poland, and Austrian-Poland are also found in American records, but these designations merely indicate the governing administration of an immigrant's former place of residence.

Polonia is a term that refers to Polish communities of the past or present beyond Poland's historic borders, including those in America.

A *bibliography* is a list of books or other publications. If you would like to read more about a certain topic, select one of the publications listed at the end of a section or one of those listed as a source for that topic. If a book or publication is not available from your public library or from the publisher or society that issued it, ask your library to obtain it through the inter-library loan program.

Throughout the text addresses are provided for most small publishers so that you can obtain publications from them if you wish to do so. Addresses of major publishers are available at your local public library. The address for the Polish Genealogical Society of America can be found in the section about genealogical societies.

In Polish genealogical research the knowledge of many subjects is often required: languages, geography, European history, Polish history, and local history. This book attempts to provide enough information in these areas to start you on your way. When your time permits and your interest is aroused, you may want to learn more about various aspects of Polish history, culture, and language.

Although the main focus of this book is genealogical research, remember always that your family's stories, traditions, keepsakes, and photographs are just as important as names and dates on paper.

Part One:

RESEARCH IN AMERICA

Chapter One:

VALUABLE RECORDS

The records discussed in this chapter generally provide the most useful information to genealogists working on Polish-American research. The records closest at hand, however—those kept by your family—should be examined first.

THE TRUNK IN THE ATTIC

Many genealogists have searched in vain for a family Bible, probably because one never existed. A Bible was a fairly expensive investment, more than most peasants in Poland could afford. Catholics, the predominant religious group in Poland, did not read and quote the Bible as much as some of the other religious denominations. Polish language and culture, and schooling in general, were suppressed by the partitioning powers during the time our ancestors emigrated, thus most Polish peasants could not read or write.

However, many other sources of genealogical information may be found in your possession or that of your relatives. Many sentimental articles were brought from the old country—baptismal and marriage certificates, photographs, prayer books, jewelry, and personal mementoes. Passports were sometimes required by the government in control of the area from which your ancestor came.

Family members who could write frequently did so in diaries or short declarations. My paternal grandfather wrote a short "Statement of My Life" at age 78, which included the name of the village in which he was born, his birth date, parents' full names, and the year of his arrival in America.

Letters were sent back and forth between the immigrants and their relatives left behind; those who could not read or write sought help from those who could. These letters may yield clues to relatives who remained in Poland and the location of your ancestors' old home.

Old letters can even rekindle a correspondence terminated long ago. The mother of my cousin Romualda in Poland corresponded with my grandfather Dembinski here in America before World War II. In 1980 Romualda wrote to grandfather's old address in Toledo where his daughter now lives. Grandfather died in 1960, so my aunt gave me the letter because I was interested in family history. I began a correspondence with Romualda that led to my staying at her apartment in Toruń when I went to Poland in 1985.

Photographs also are a very important source for family history research. You can learn many facts from studying old photographs. Brides often wore colored dresses, not always white. Is everyone in the picture dressed in black? It was probably taken shortly after a funeral. Whose funeral? The family member who is missing from the setting, possibly one who died in Poland even though the photograph was taken in America. Do you know that person's date of death? If you do, you have probably just dated that photograph.

If there are no names or dates on your old photographs, label them on the back (if the photo is mounted on heavy cardboard) or as a caption under the photograph. If you don't know who the people are, ask your older relatives *soon*—before they forget or are not around to help you.

CIOCIA KASIA

One of your most valuable resources is your own family. Talk to your relatives, especially the older ones, and always take notes and date them. Use a tape recorder, if possible, but always ask permission first; some people do not like being recorded.

Ask your relatives about family stories and traditions, and what they remember about their own childhood and ancestors. Ask to see Bibles, birth and marriage certificates, scrapbooks, diaries, letters, and photo albums. Copy important information and note the source. Make photocopies of written documents if permission is granted. If you copy photographs, promptly return the originals and ask if the owner would also like a copy.

Share information, don't just *take* it. People will be more willing to show you their prized possessions and talk to you if you share something of your own with them.

CHURCH RECORDS

The most accurate documentation for Polish-American research is often found in church records. The parish priest usually spoke the same language as the parishioners and, therefore, could give more factual information than a civil registrar who may never have heard the Polish language before.

Some marriage and funeral records listed the place of birth in Poland or the parents' names or survivors. Ask to see the original entry or have *all* the information, including all notations, copied if you are corresponding. Some of the additional information may seem unimportant to the secretary or parish priest extracting the record for you, but may in fact be very important. Send a thank-you letter with a monetary donation to the parish or for a Mass offering for your deceased ancestors.

CEMETERY AND GRAVESTONE RECORDS

Do not overlook cemetery records and gravestone inscriptions. Many genealogical societies have copied gravestone inscriptions and bound them in book form. Some are for sale through the societies, or are available at local libraries.

You may not find gravestones for all of your ancestors. Some have been vandalized, some have deteriorated over time, or the survivors may not have been able to afford one.

Check the records in the cemetery office—not only the index cards with grave locations, but also the *original* record books with handwritten entries. The staff may be reluctant to pull out these large dusty volumes, but be tactful and inform them that you are willing to pay for this service; some cemeteries do charge for searching records.

Information usually recorded includes name, address, age, date of burial, church affiliation, cause of death, and name of the funeral home. Find out if the grave site was a family plot—who else is buried there? The office staff or groundskeeper can give you directions to find the grave.

FUNERAL HOME RECORDS

Many funeral homes keep their old records. The director of one funeral home showed me an original record book in Polish from the year 1895 showing the cost of the casket, white gloves for pallbearers, flowers, and horse and carriage rental. At that time people were not "laid out" at a funeral home, but in the parlors of their own homes. Personal records, such as address, age, and cause of death, may also be included in funeral home records.

Memorial cards from funerals can also give useful information: birth date (caution: not always accurate), age, death and burial dates, and the names of the funeral home, church where services were held (and where you may find more records), and the cemetery. Look over the remembrance book given to the deceased person's family by the funeral home; it is the one visitors sign at the visitation.

OBITUARIES

Obituaries can be found in English-language, Polish-American, or Polish-Catholic newspapers. Before the community had a Polish-language newspaper, German-speaking Poles from the Prussian- and Austrian-held regions might have been mentioned in local German-American newspapers. Genealogical societies, libraries, government programs, and individuals have prepared indexes of obituaries for some of these newspapers.

For example, the Toledo (Ohio)–Lucas County Public Library continues a project started by the W. P. A. of indexing the names of all the people whose obituaries appeared in all Toledo newspapers since the 1830s, giving their addresses and ages and dates of publication of the paper. To find out more about a person in the index, simply find the obituary in the appropriate newspaper, all of which are on microfilm.

Most libraries do not index every obituary, but they usually have information on the more prominent people in the community. Check the libraries in the vicinity of your ancestor's home for the availability of obituaries.

The Polish Genealogical Society of America has published several books dealing with obituaries and indexes:

Golembiewski, Thomas E. *The Study of Obituaries as a Source for Polish Genealogical Research*. Chicago: Polish Genealogical Society, 1984.

Hollowak, Thomas L. *Index to the Obituaries in the Jedność-Polonia, 1926–1946*. Chicago: Polish Genealogical Society, 1983.

Hollowak, Thomas L. and William F. Hoffman. *Index to the Obituaries and Death Notices Appearing in the Dziennik Chicagoski* (a Polish daily newspaper in Chicago). Vol. I (1890–1899); Vol. II (1900–1909); Vol. III (1910–1919); Vol. IV, surnames A–L (1920–1929); Vol. V, surnames M–Z (1920–1929). Chicago: Polish Genealogical Society, 1984–1991.

The Polish Museum of America, 984 N. Milwaukee Avenue, Chicago, Illinois 60622, has a large microfilm collection of Polish-American newspapers from various cities. If you know your ancestor's date of death, you may find his obituary in a hometown newspaper. Check local libraries for Polish-American newspapers published in the area.

CHURCH ANNIVERSARY BOOKS

Anniversary and historical publications from churches and societies, sometimes called jubilee books, contain much information about members and founders. One of the largest such collections is found at the Polish Museum of America Archives. Local libraries and the Church of Jesus Christ of Latter-day Saints (LDS) Family History Library also have some anniversary books. (More about the LDS later.)

FRATERNAL SOCIETIES

Polish fraternal benefit societies were formed when the Poles first began to arrive in America. Their primary purpose was to provide life insurance benefits to Poles, but after a while the societies also became known for their social gatherings and benevolent works.

Many of these societies have kept their death claim files, which include the insurance applications containing the applicant's name, place and year of birth, street address, physical description, and medical history. Some also may have information about the names, ages, health status, or cause of death of the applicant's parents.

Be sure your ancestor was a member of such a society before you request a search of its records. Obituaries usually listed the organizations of which the deceased was a member. Other clues to membership are dues books, rings, medals, pins, badges, sashes, and caps.

The following is a list of Polish fraternal benefit societies and their addresses. The founding year of each society, if known, is given in parentheses.

Alliance of Poles of America (1895)
6966 Broadway Avenue
Cleveland, Ohio 44105

Association of Polish Women of the United States
7526 Broadway Avenue
Cleveland, Ohio 44105

Association of Sons of Poland (1903)
665 Newark Avenue
Jersey City, New Jersey 07306

Polish Alma Mater of America (1897)
4842 West Fullerton Avenue
Chicago, Illinois 60639

Polish Association of America (1895)
1202 West Oklahoma
Milwaukee, Wisconsin 53215

Polish Beneficial Association of St. John Cantius (1900)
3131 Richmond Street
Philadelphia, Pennsylvania 19134

Polish Falcons of America (1887)
97–99 South 18th Street
Pittsburgh, Pennsylvania 15203

Polish National Alliance of Brooklyn
155 Noble Street
Brooklyn, New York 11222

Polish National Alliance of the United States of North America (1880)
6100 North Cicero Avenue
Chicago, Illinois 60648
(Early records were destroyed; death claim records start at 1948.)

Polish National Union of America
1002 Pittston Avenue
Scranton, Pennsylvania 18505

Polish Roman Catholic Union of America (1873)
984 N. Milwaukee Avenue
Chicago, Illinois 60622

Polish Union of America (1890)
771 Filmore Avenue
Buffalo, New York 14212

Polish Union of United States of North America
53–59 North Main Street
Wilkes Barre, Pennsylvania 18701

The Polish White Eagle Association
1302 Second Street N. E.
Minneapolis, Minnesota 55413

Polish Women's Alliance of America (1898)
205 S. Northwest Highway
Park Ridge, Illinois 60028

Union of Poles in America
6501 Lansing Avenue
Cleveland, Ohio 44105

Union of Polish Women in America (1921)
2636–38 East Allegheny Avenue
Philadelphia, Pennsylvania 19134

United Polish Women of America
1200 North Ashland Avenue
Chicago, Illinois 60622
(Death claim records start at 1966.)

Source: Peckwas, Edward A. "Century Old Records Saved." *Polish Genealogical Society Newsletter* II (January 1980), 1–2.

VITAL RECORDS

Vital records are civil records (not church records) of births, deaths, marriages, and divorces. In the United States vital records are kept by the individual states. The first states to begin vital registration were Massachusetts (1842) and New Jersey (1848), and a few large cities also began vital registration in the mid-1800s. However, it was not until the decade 1910 to 1919 that the last seventeen states adopted statewide birth and death registration.

The principal reason for collecting information was to record the causes of death in order to combat diseases, such as cholera, caused by unsanitary conditions. The first recorded vital records, therefore, were death records. Birth records were developed next, then marriage records.

The content of the records varied by locality until fairly recently, when registration forms became standardized. The earliest registers consisted of handwritten entries recorded in books, but not all events were recorded, or recorded near the time of the event. For instance, a man might come to town on business and while there pay a visit to the courthouse to report the births of his last two or three children, even though the births occurred months or even years earlier. I found many such cases several years ago when I got a chance to look at the *original* pre-1900 handwritten registers that had been banished to the damp basement of the Lucas County courthouse in Toledo, Ohio. (The courthouse, and much of downtown Toledo, sat on a swampy area at the time it was built.) Currently, copies of these older records are available on microfilm at the Toledo–Lucas County Public Library. Undoubtedly there are other records elsewhere that have suffered the same fate.

To illustrate other problems that can arise, I will use an example taken from one of the above-mentioned registers: the birth of one of my great-grandfather Izydor (Isadore) Komorowski's children. An entry in the birth register reads, "Kamerasky (daughter of Theodore), born October 1, 1873." However, there is a baptismal entry for this daughter in St. Mary's Roman Catholic (German) parish that reads, "Rosa Comurasca, born August 19, 1873, baptized August 24, 1873, daughter of Isadore and Maryanna . . ." Which record should I trust to be the most accurate? Neither spelled the surname correctly. However, Izydor did speak German and Polish but not English at that point, so I trusted the church records more. Another reason for believing the church register: St. Rose's feast day is (and was in 1873) August 30. By comparing his other children's birth and baptismal dates with saints' feast days, I knew Izydor named his children for saints whose feast days were about the same time as his children's birth and baptismal dates—a common tradition in Poland that many immigrants brought to America (see chapter 12).

The more recent a death record (or any other vital record) is, the more information is usually provided, and the more likely it is that the information will be correct. The age, birth date and place, and parents' names of the deceased can be found in death records; however, sometimes the informant may not have known the information (in which case the space will be marked "unk" or "unknown") or even have given incorrect information. An informant for a death record could have been a spouse, son- or daughter-in-law, grandchild, or mortician, and may not have known much, if anything, about the deceased person's background.

Now that I have cautioned you about vital records, I can give you one good reason why you *should* use them—because they are there. Sometimes a vital record may be the only document you can find that contains needed information. Sometimes it can confirm information found in another source, such as a church register or family story. And sometimes it can just be confusing—but record the information anyway. Perhaps years later you will untangle the puzzle and be grateful that you copied it so long ago.

Vital records for a specific locality are available from the vital records office in that state. Addresses for these offices can be found in *Where to Write for Vital Records*, which can be ordered from the U.S. Government Printing Office or found at your local library. They are also listed in such books as Elizabeth P. Bentley's *Genealogist's Address Book* and Thomas Kemp's *Vi-*

tal Records Handbook, both published by the Genealogical Publishing Company. Microfilm, copies, and/or abstracts of vital records can also be found at local records offices (department of health, city hall, courthouse, etc.), the LDS Family History Library, and local libraries and research centers.

UNITED STATES FEDERAL CENSUS RECORDS

The Constitution directed that a federal census be taken every ten years, beginning in 1790, for tax purposes and to apportion congressional representation. Not much personal information was included in the early records, and before 1850 only the names of the heads of families were listed. With each successive census, however, more information was requested. The most useful census records for Polish-American genealogical research are those of 1880, 1900, and 1910. Almost all of the 1890 census records were destroyed by fire.

The following information of genealogical value on the 1880, 1900, and 1910 censuses was requested for *each* person: name, age (the 1900 census gives the month and year of each person's birth), sex, occupation (includes "housewife" or the name of the woman's occupation, and "student" or blank for each child), place of birth (state, territory, or country), place of birth for each person's father and mother, relationship of each person to the head of the family, and marital status. In addition to the preceding, the 1900 and 1910 censuses also asked the length of time in the U.S. and whether naturalized, the number of years of the person's present marriage, whether the person spoke English, how many children a mother had given birth to and how many were still alive.

There is less genealogical information found in the 1920 census: name, age, sex, marital status, occupation, year of immigration to the U.S., whether naturalized and year of naturalization, place of birth for each person and parents, and relationship to head of the family.

The census data was recorded on June 1 in 1880 and 1900, April 15 for 1910, and January 1 in 1920.

Soundex indexes are available for the censuses of 1880, 1900, and 1920. A Soundex is a code that uses the first letter of a surname followed by numbers representing other letters in the surname; each number represents similar sounding consonants but vowels are not given a number. The 1910 census is indexed, but only for twenty-one states, and is called a Miracode index, a variation of the Soundex.

Although there are indexes, it is a good idea to know at least the county and state of the person's residence, as there may be many people with the same or similar names. It also is possible to search for a person in census records without using an index, provided you know the street address and can find it on a city map that shows wards or on a census enumeration district map.

Census records may not contain accurate information for recent immigrants because the language barrier between the English-speaking census-taker and the Polish resident often caused many problems. My great-grandfather Izydor Komorowski could not be located in the 1900 Soundex of the census. I tried every possible spelling and pronunciation variation, and then I searched the entire Bedford Township enumeration district in Monroe County, Michigan, name-by-name. Finally, I located him—the census-taker had spelled his name *Isadore Momoraski*! There should not have been too much of a language problem because Izydor came to America *thirty* years before the 1900 census.

Federal census records from 1790 to 1920 are available for use by the public at various locations: the National Archives in Washington, the regional branches of the National Archives, which are located throughout the country (see pages 31–32), and LDS family history centers. Most libraries have census records for the states or counties in their own areas, although some libraries, such as the Allen County (Indiana) Public Library, have census records for every state.

UNITED STATES NATURALIZATION RECORDS

You may hear opposing views on whether the majority of Polish immigrants intended to stay in America and quickly become naturalized citizens, or intended to return home after earning a large sum of money. In either case, many immigrants filed their naturalization papers as soon as the required waiting period was over. Some employers required that their employees at least file a declaration of intention, and there also may have been other incentives to file their naturalization papers.

There are several types of "papers": declaration of intention, petition for naturalization, certificate of naturalization, and records of the court. The certificate of naturalization was the only paper given to the immigrant, and one of his relatives may still possess it. There is often more information available on the declaration and petition than on the certificate, and thus it is worth the time to check out the other papers.

The immigrant went to a court of record (in any one of several possible jurisdictions) to fill out forms for his "first papers," the declaration of intention, stating his desire to become a citizen of the United States. Sometimes other documents related to his first papers were also filed at this time. These first papers usually preceded the subsequent papers by two years or more, and may have been filed in or near the port of entry or near the early residence of the immigrant. Early declarations asked for the applicant's name, country of birth or allegiance, date of application, and signature. Some listed the date and port of arrival.

On September 27, 1906, the Bureau of Immigration and Naturalization, under the Department of Commerce and Labor, took control of the naturalization process. Since then, only federal courts have handled naturalizations. The information requested on declarations was increased to include name, age, occupation, personal description, date and place of birth, previous citizenship, present address, last foreign address, name of vessel, port of embarkation, date and port of arrival, date of application, and signature.

After a compulsory residence period, usually five years, the immigrant returned to the court, bringing witnesses, to file a petition for naturalization. The immigrant took an oath of allegiance to the United States and had to prove that his residency requirement had been fulfilled. These "final papers" included the petition, oath of allegiance, proof of residence, witnesses' statements, and sometimes additional documents.

The petition form asked for the applicant's name, residence, occupation, date and place of birth, previous citizenship, personal description, date of emigration, ports of embarkation and arrival, marital status, names, dates, and places of birth and residence of applicant's spouse and children, date when U.S. residence commenced, time of residence in state, name changes, and signature. After 1930 a photograph of the applicant was often included.

Declarations, certificates of arrival, and certificates of completion of citizenship classes were often interfiled with the petitions. The certificate of naturalization was given to the new citizen, while the stub and order to issue a certificate of naturalization or citizenship were kept by the court. Other records of the court, called "journal" or "docket" records, and other records not listed above, may make up the remainder of the naturalization papers.

By law from 1855 until 1922, a woman automatically became a United States citizen by marriage to a citizen or through the naturalization of her husband. However, problems existed until modern times. My grandmother, Rose Boczkowski, was born in Ohio and married an immigrant in 1911. During World War II she lost her citizenship because she was married to an alien! My grandfather applied for citizenship, and my grandmother had to take the oath of allegiance to regain her lost citizenship. Women automatically became citizens by marriage to an American citizen, but men did not share the same benefit.

Children under sixteen years of age automatically became citizens through the naturalization of their parents. If the person was between sixteen and twenty-one when he arrived in America, he was required to wait until after his twenty-first birthday to become naturalized. The applicant's birthday and age on last birthday, and month and year of arrival, were also required on the form.

Naturalization records may be found in city halls and in city, police, county, state, and federal courts. The National Archives and its regional branches have many naturalization records for their districts, and some libraries have records from their vicinity on microfilm. Contact your local library (genealogy or local history department) or genealogical society to find the location of naturalization records in the area in which you are interested.

The Immigration and Naturalization Service (INS) has many records of naturalization after 1906. To extract information from the naturalization records held by the INS, request form G-639, Freedom of Information/Privacy Act Request, from the U.S. Department of Justice, Immigration and Naturalization Service, 119 D Street, N. E., Washington, D. C. 20536.

As of December 5, 1972, it is no longer illegal to reproduce (photocopy, photograph, etc.) any type of naturalization records. Uncertified copies, for genealogical purposes, can be made without restriction.

To learn more about naturalization records, read *Locating Your Immigrant Ancestor: A Guide to Naturalization Records*, by James and Lila Neagles (Logan, Utah: Everton Publishers, 1975), or *Guide to Genealogical Research in the National Archives,* rev. ed. (Washington, D.C.: National Archives and Records Administration, 1985).

ALIEN REGISTRATION RECORDS

For aliens alive after 1940, much of the same information can be retrieved from alien registration records as from naturalization records. To access the files you must have the Alien Registration Number. If you find an Alien Registration Card among your ancestor's possessions, that is precisely what you need. Send your inquiry to the above address for the U.S. Department of Justice, Immigration and Naturalization Service.

WORLD WAR I UNITED STATES DRAFT REGISTRATION RECORDS

All men, United States citizens and aliens alike, were required to register for the draft during World War I. Anyone born between June 6, 1886 and June 5, 1896 was required to register. Even if your ancestor was not born during this time period, a brother or an uncle may have been. The exact place of birth was required for the applicant and his father, along with other genealogical information. Near the end of the war, older men were also required to register. Draft registration (Selective Service) records can be found at local libraries and regional branches of the National Archives.

The Atlanta branch of the National Archives, National Archives–Southeast Region, has over 24 million World War I draft registration cards for men born between 1873 and 1900, and it serves the entire nation, not only the Georgia district. Records are arranged by state, then by local draft board. Ask for "World War I Registration Card Request" forms from: National Archives–Southeast Region, 1557 St. Joseph Avenue, East Point, Georgia 30344.

WORLD WAR I POLISH-AMERICAN MILITARY RECORDS

While these records are not civil records, they are listed here so that they follow the discussion of U. S. draft registration records. According to Dr. Joseph T. Hapak in his article "World War I Polish-American Military Records" (*Polish Genealogical Society Newsletter* X, Spring 1987), "*The Polish Army in France* was the formal name of the military unit better known in the United States as *Haller's Army*. It was also known as the *Blue Army* on account of the sky-blue uniforms issued to the volunteers upon their arrival in France."

The volunteers from America joined volunteers from France and German army prisoners of war of Polish origin. More than 20,000 volunteers came from America alone. U. S. Selective Service officials complained that men were being illegally inducted into the Polish Army, and many times demanded the discharge of the Polish-Americans, after which they were inducted into the U. S. Army.

The recruiting and medical records of Haller's Army (25,000 volunteers) are kept in the Polish Museum of America Archives and are currently being indexed.

OTHER MILITARY RECORDS

A fifteen-volume set of books printed by the State of Ohio lists every serviceman who enlisted from Ohio during World War I—*The Official Roster of Ohio Soldiers, Sailors and Marines in the World War, 1917–1918*. Each alphabetical entry gives the birth place (even in Poland), age (example: 21%₁₂ years) or birth date, and date of enlistment (from which you can compute the approximate birth date), address, and, of course, the enlistee's military history. No doubt similar books or records exist for other states.

U. S. military service records for the two world wars can be obtained from the National Personnel Records Center (MPR), G. S. A. (Military Records), 9700 Page Boulevard, St. Louis, Missouri 63132.

If any of your ancestors served in the military during the Civil War, you may find their records in books such as the *Official Roster of the Soldiers of the State of Ohio in the War of the Rebellion, 1861–1865* (Akron, Ohio: The Werner Printing and Manufacturing Company, 1887). Similar rosters were compiled for other states, but of course the largest body of records on Civil War participants is to be found among the Compiled Service Records in the National Archives. For a state-by-state breakdown of holdings see the *Guide to Genealogical Research in the National Archives*, rev. 1985.

As a matter of interest the following book was written specifically about the Poles who fought in the American Civil War, and lists over one thousand Poles according to the states under which they served: *Historja udziału Polaków w amerikańskiej wojnie domowej* (History of the Participation of Poles in the American Civil War), by Mieczysław Haiman (Chicago: Drukiem Dziennika zjednoczenia, 1928).

CITY DIRECTORIES

Many cities and large towns published directories containing alphabetical listings of most of the inhabitants, along with advertising and lists of policemen, firemen, churches, organizations, etc. Occasionally deaths that occurred during the past year were also listed (name and date of death). Many of these city directories began publication before the Civil War and have continued to the present. Later editions may also include an alphabetical listing of the streets, giving house numbers and occupants' names. You can learn a lot about the town as it was many years ago by reading the advertising and introductory material, but the most useful part of these directories is the list of inhabitants.

Each individual adult's name appears alphabetically, along with his or her occupation, occasionally the employer's name (helpful if you decide to check employment records), and home address. Wives employed outside the home have a separate listing; otherwise wives' names can usually be found in parentheses after their husbands' names.

Using the city directories you can trace your ancestor from one address or occupation to another. With the additional help of city maps, you can find your ancestor's correct enumeration district for a census. City directories are also a useful tool for following your ancestor between censuses. City directories are available in original book form and/or on microfilm at the public libraries in the area where your ancestor resided.

OTHER CIVIL RECORDS

Other civil records that may contain useful information are Social Security, insurance, employment, court records, and wills. While court records and wills are an important source of genealogical information to many American researchers, they usually do not benefit Polish-American researchers as much, due to the fact that the Poles arrived in America relatively recently and there are other important resources available.

SHIPS' PASSENGER LISTS

When the immigrant reached America's shore, his paper trail began with a record of his arrival. How much information was recorded depended on the year and port of arrival.

In the nineteenth century the U.S. government drew up passenger laws several times in order to place controls on immigration and relieve overcrowded and unhealthy conditions aboard passenger ships. No federal restrictions existed until 1875, when criminals and prostitutes were forbidden to enter the United States. Until that time, each state placed its own restrictions on the influx of mentally ill and handicapped people, criminals, and paupers.

The Passenger Act of 1882 ordered ships' captains to keep lists of passengers. Information to be recorded for each steerage passenger included name, age, sex, calling (occupation), native country, and intended destination. Previously, beginning in the year 1820, the lists were required to include only the passenger's name, age, occupation, and the country to which he owed allegiance (which was not necessarily his native country).

Two great series of ships' passenger lists, Customs Passenger Lists and Immigration Passenger Lists, have been placed on microfilm and are available for research at the National Archives. A table showing microfilmed passenger lists for the major ports of entry is shown opposite.

National Archives regional branches also have records of some passenger lists; however, all branches will not have all the lists. Microfilm rolls can also be purchased, but first request a copy of *Immigrant and Passenger Arrivals: A Select Catalog of National Archives Microfilm Publications* from the National Archives Trust Fund Board, P.O. Box 100793, Atlanta, GA 30384 (price $2.00). Make your check or money order payable to the National Archives Trust Fund and add $3.00 for postage and handling.

The National Archives staff can search the records for a specific passenger if you provide the passenger's full name, port of entry, and approximate date of arrival. They will search the indexes for Baltimore (1820–1952), Boston (1848–91 and 1902–20), New Orleans (1820–1952), New York (1820–46 and 1897–1948), Philadelphia (1800–1948), and minor ports (1820–74 and 1890–1924). The staff can then find the proper passenger list and send you a copy of the entry.

If you provide the passenger's full name, port of entry, name of vessel, and exact date of arrival, a copy of the entry on the passenger list can be made for you without searching the indexes.

If you have located your ancestor's name on a port of entry index yourself, copy all the information given in the index entry and send that information to the National Archives. They will find the correct record and send you a photocopy of your ancestor's record of arrival.

Requests must be made on NATF Form 81. To obtain copies of this form write to: Reference Service Branch (NNRS), National Archives and Records Administration, 8th and Pennsylvania Avenue, N. W., Washington, D. C. 20408.

The LDS Family History Library in Salt Lake City and many public libraries also have microfilm copies of passenger lists and/or indexes.

Not everyone who came to America entered through Ellis Island, which operated only from 1892 to 1954. Major ports of entry for Polish immigrants were New York and Baltimore, although some may have arrived at Boston and Philadelphia. Poles on their way to Panna Maria, Texas, or another southern or western destination, may have disembarked at the ports of New Orleans or Galveston.

Many immigrants entered the United States via Canada—about 40

PASSENGER LISTS AT THE NATIONAL ARCHIVES*

Customs Passenger Lists

Port	Passenger Lists Available	Indexes Available
Baltimore	1820–91 (with gaps)	1820–91
Boston	1820–74 (with gaps) 1883–99, 1912	1848–91
Galveston	1846–71	1820–71
New Orleans	1820–1903	1820–99
New York	1820–June 1897	No indexes yet for 1847–June 1897
Philadelphia	1800–1905	1800–1906

Immigration Passenger Lists

Port	Passenger Lists Available	Indexes Available
Baltimore	December 1891–1957	1897–July 1952 (Soundex)
Boston	August 1891– December 1943	1902–20 (Card Index) April 1899– September 1940 (Book Index)
Galveston (includes Houston and other Texas ports)	1896–1948	1896–1951
New Orleans	1903–45	1900–52 (Card Index)
New York	June 1897–1948	June 1897– December 1948 1906–42 (Book Index)
Philadelphia	1883–1945	1883–1948 (Soundex) May 1906–June 1926 (Book Index)

*Customs passenger lists are records of the U.S. Customs Service and begin in 1820. Immigration passenger lists begin around the 1890s and are records of the Immigration and Naturalization Service.

percent of all passengers arriving in Canada around the year 1895 eventually crossed the border into the United States. Canadian steamship and railway companies offered lower fares, which encouraged travel via Canada. Many immigrants arrived at the port of Gross Isle, thirty miles downriver from Quebec on the St. Lawrence River.

The first headquarters to document immigration across the Canadian–United States border was at Montreal, where immigration records for ports of entry along the entire border were kept. The facility later was moved to St. Albans, Vermont. Records of passenger arrivals at Canadian ports as well as passenger trains crossing the border into the United States have been micro-filmed. Filmed records from St. Albans for the years 1895 to 1954 are available at the National Archives.

The National Archives of Canada has records of arrival for the ports of Quebec (from 1865) and Halifax (from 1881). To obtain information from them you must provide the name of the passenger, port, and month and year of arrival. Write to: National Archives of Canada, 395 Wellington Street, Ottawa, Ontario K1A 0N3, Canada.

Millions of emigrants, including Poles, left Europe from the German ports of Hamburg and Bremen. Hamburg emigration lists (see page 153) are available for research, but those of Bremen, which handled more than twice as many emigrants as Hamburg, were destroyed due to a lack of storage space and by an Allied bombing raid during World War II. This makes the American passenger arrival lists much more important than they would have been had the Bremen lists survived.

A multi-volume publication that should interest the Polish-American researcher because it sometimes names Polish immigrants who came from German-occupied areas of Poland, or who sailed from German ports or had German-sounding names, is *Germans to America: Lists of Passengers Arriving at U. S. Ports, 1850–*, edited by Ira A. Glazier and P. William Filby (Wilmington, Delaware: Scholarly Resources, 1988–). *Germans to America* was created by extracting "German" names from U. S. passenger arrival records. The series begins with German passenger arrivals in 1850; the latest volume contains records from 1870. Each volume is indexed by passengers' names. If you suspect that you have found your ancestor on one of these lists, obtain a copy of the ship's passenger list.

Your Ancestor's Ship

If you are curious to know what the ship that carried your ancestor to America looked like, there are several maritime museums that can provide a photograph and/or print of the ship. Some of these museums can also look up the ship's name in maritime encyclopedias and send you a brief description of the ship, including its size, type of power, and date and place it was built. You might want to write or visit one of the following:

The Mariner's Museum
Museum Archives
Newport News, Virginia 23606

Mystic Seaport Museum
Museum Archives
Mystic, Connecticut 06355

Ocean Steamships
P. O. Box 8797
Universal City, California 91709

Peabody Museum
East India Square
Salem, Massachusetts 01970

Steamship Historical Society of America
415 Pelton Avenue
Staten Island, New York 10310

The Steamship Historical Society of America
University of Baltimore Library
S. S. H. S. A. Collection
1420 Maryland Avenue
Baltimore, Maryland 21201

National Maritime Museum
Greenwich Old Royal Observatory
London, SE10 9NF, England

Deutsches Schiffahrtsmuseum Archives
2850 Bremerhaven, Deutschland (Germany)

Hapag-Lloyd AG
Gustav-Detjen-Allee 2-6
2800 Bremen, Deutschland (Germany)

Maximilian-Verlagsgruppe
Postfach 2352
4900 Herford, Deutschland (Germany)

Historic Emigration Office
c/o Tourist Information am Hafen
Bei den St.-Pauli-Landungsbrücken 3
P.O. Box 102249
D-2000 Hamburg 36
Germany

Source: Peckwas, Edward A. "Finding the Ships of Your Ancestors." *Polish Genealogical Society Newsletter* X (Fall 1987), 30–31.

The following are sources for pictures and histories of ships:

Morton Allan Directory of European Passenger Steamship Arrivals for the Years 1890 to 1930 at the Port of New York and for the Years 1904 to 1926 at the Ports of New York, Philadelphia, Boston, and Baltimore. Baltimore: Genealogical Publishing Company, 1979 (reprint).

Anuta, Michael J. *Ships of Our Ancestors*, 1983. Published by Ships of Our Ancestors, Inc., RA 655 Westland 577, Menominee, Michigan 49859-9775.

Bonsor, Noel R. P. *North Atlantic Seaway: An Illustrated History of the Passenger Services Linking the Old World with the New.* 4 vols. New York: Arco Publishing Company Inc., c. 1975–.

Smith, Euguene Waldo. *Trans-Atlantic Passenger Ships, Past and Present.* Boston: George H. Dean Company, 1947.

UNITED STATES PASSPORT OFFICE

The National Archives has passport applications (and related records) for 1791–1925. If your ancestor ever returned to Poland, there might have been a passport record. Although passports were not required for travel outside the United States, many U. S. citizens obtained them to prove their citizenship so that, for example, they might not be conscripted into military service in Europe.

A passport application usually contains the name, signature, age, place of residence, personal description, names or number of additional travelling family members, date, and date and court of naturalization (if naturalized). Sometimes the exact birth date and place of the applicant, spouse, and minor children are given, as well as the date and port of arrival in the United States, and vessel (if naturalized).

To have a search made, you must provide the full name of the person, residence, and place and approximate date of the application. A charge is made for the search, and copies will be sent to you.

If the passport was issued before 1906, write to the Diplomatic Records Branch of the National Archives, Room 5E, Washington, D. C. 20408.

For passports issued after 1906 you may try writing to the Passport Office, Department of State, 1425 K Street, N. W., Washington, D. C. 20520.

RUSSIAN CONSULAR RECORDS

Many Americans and Canadians who were born or lived in Russian-occupied areas of Europe did business with the Russian consular offices in America. These people would have lived in America from 1862 to 1928. Information contained in these consular records includes ship arrival information, cancelled passports, visa applications, nationality certificates, certificates of origin, military service information, birth, baptismal, and marriage records, and photographs.

In 1933 the U. S. State Department removed these and other records from the consular offices. Most of the records were stored at the National Archives Records Center in Suitland, Maryland. The Jewish Genealogical Society sorted out and indexed the material. The LDS has microfilmed those records of genealogical value, and they are now available to researchers. Sallyann Sack and Suzan F. Wynne have published an index in book form using a Soundex code for these records: *The Russian Consular Records Index and Catalog* (New York: Garland, 1987).

The National Archives of Canada in Ottawa has the Russian consular records from Canada for the years 1900 to 1922.

For additional information about the Russian consular records, consult the following: Strouf, Dorothy S. "The Russian Consular Records Index and Catalog," PGSN, vol. XI, no. 2, Fall 1988, p. 32.

SOURCES AND ADDITIONAL READING

Bentley, Elizabeth P. *The Genealogist's Address Book*. 1992–93 Edition (or current year). Baltimore: Genealogical Publishing Company.

Greenwood, Val D. *The Researcher's Guide to American Genealogy*. 2nd ed. Baltimore: Genealogical Publishing Company, 1990.

Jamestown Pioneers from Poland. Jamestown: The Polish American Congress, 1958.

Kemp, Thomas J. *Vital Records Handbook*. Baltimore: Genealogical Publishing Company, 1988, 1990. Provides addresses of vital records offices, dates for which records are available, fees, and copies of request forms.

National Archives Trust Fund Board. *Guide to Genealogical Research in the National Archives.* Washington, D.C.: National Archives and Records Administration, 1985.

Ortell, Gerald A. "The Draft Registration Records of World War I." *Polish Genealogical Society Newsletter* VII (Fall 1985), 25, 31.

Tepper, Michael. *American Passenger Arrival Records: A Guide to the Records of Immigrants Arriving at American Ports by Sail and Steam.* Updated and enlarged edition. Baltimore: Genealogical Publishing Company, 1993.

United States Department of Health and Human Services. *Where to Write for Vital Records.* Available from the Superintendent of Documents, U.S. Government Printing Office, Washington, D. C. 20402. (DHHS Publication No. (PHS) 87-1142.)

Chapter Two:

POLISH
GENEALOGICAL RESEARCH
IN AMERICA

Before World War I the following American cities had the largest Polish populations, according to *The Historical Atlas of Poland*.

Cities with over 100,000 Poles: Chicago, Illinois; Detroit, Michigan; New York, New York.

Cities with 50,000 to 100,000 Poles: Buffalo, New York; Cleveland, Ohio; Milwaukee, Wisconsin; Philadelphia, Pennsylvania.

Cities with 25,000 to 50,000 Poles: Baltimore, Maryland; Bay City, Michigan; Hamtramck, Michigan; Jersey City, New Jersey; Newark, New Jersey; Pittsburgh, Pennsylvania; St. Louis, Missouri; Toledo, Ohio.

Cities with 10,000 to 25,000 Poles: Boston, Massachusetts; Chicopee, Massachusetts; Gallitzin, Pennsylvania; Grand Rapids, Michigan; Minneapolis, Minnesota; Nanticoke, Pennsylvania; New Britain, Connecticut; Omaha, Nebraska; Rochester, New York; Scranton, Pennsylvania; Shenandoah, Pennsylvania; South Bend, Indiana.

Cities with under 10,000 Poles: Bayonne, New Jersey; Erie, Pennsylvania; Kosciusko, Mississippi; Lublin, Wisconsin; Passaic, New Jersey; Paterson, New Jersey; Poland, New York; Wausau, Florida; Wausau, Wisconsin; the cities of Pulaski in Georgia, Illinois, Iowa, New York, Tennessee, Virginia, and Wisconsin; the cities of Warsaw in Alabama, Georgia, Indiana, Illinois, Kentucky, Missouri, New York, North Carolina, Ohio, and Virginia.

Following is a list of U.S. cities that currently have the greatest number of residents who have at least one parent of Polish descent, followed by the number of these "Poles" in each city:

Chicago	797,402
Detroit	511,829
New York	478,138
Philadelphia	284,881
Buffalo	230,309
Pittsburgh	213,880
Milwaukee	207,516
Nassau-Suffolk, New York	196,209
Los Angeles	168,654
Cleveland	166,477

Source: *Polish-American Journal*, June 1989, from *USA Today* research.

The cities cited above would be a good starting point for your research involving Polish-American genealogy; libraries in these areas should have information on Polish-Americans who lived in the locality.

RESEARCH LIBRARIES WITH POLISH MATERIALS IN THE UNITED STATES AND CANADA

Family History Library and Family History Centers

Family History Library and Family History Centers
The Church of Jesus Christ of Latter-day Saints (LDS)
Salt Lake City, Utah

Beginning genealogists are often confused about the LDS and what it does. LDS is the abbreviation many genealogists use when they refer to the Family History Library operated by the Church of Jesus Christ of Latter-day Saints. The main library is located in Salt Lake City, Utah; there are branch libraries, called family history centers, throughout the United States and in many foreign countries.

Many people refer to the members of this church as Mormons. Mormons collect genealogical records because they believe in baptizing their ancestors and so must be able to identify those ancestors.

The LDS is the largest repository of genealogical records in the world. "The Family History Library was founded in 1894 to gather records which help people trace their ancestry," according to the LDS publication *Library Services and Resources, Family History Library and Family History Centers* (Series FHL, No. 1).

The library began microfilming records in 1938. The collection now contains many records—including church and civil registers, census records, passenger lists, military records, and court records—from the United States and more than forty-five ~~foreign~~ *OTHER* countries.

The Family History Library has almost half a million rolls of microfilm from the United States (including records from county courthouses, archives, the National Archives, and church records), and about 28,000 rolls of Canadian records. There are more than 10,000 rolls of microfilm from Poland, and microfilming of Polish records is still in progress.

For a list of Family History Centers (branches) near your home, send a SASE to Family History Library, 35 North West Temple Street, Salt Lake City, Utah 84150.

Your local family history center has several services, discussed below, that are very useful to Polish genealogists.

Locality Index

The Locality Index is a microfiche catalog of library materials available at the LDS arranged by place of origin of the records; it is also available on computer at some family history centers. The Locality Index is filed by country, then by the larger administrative units within that country, and then by the smaller units from the locality where the records originated. It is convenient to use if you want to find out if the LDS has records from a specific town, county, state, province, or country.

For example, if you want to know whether there are any civil birth records from Cleveland, Ohio, you would look at the fiche under "Ohio—Cuyahoga County—Cleveland—Civil Registration." The entry, if found, would tell you the types of records and what years they cover, along with other information, such as where the original records were located and if these are originals, copies, or abstracts. The LDS does not have microfilm copies of *all* records ever recorded, only the ones that it has been given permission to copy.

After you have found the records that you would like to examine, you can order the film by the number(s) provided on that entry. A small fee is collected for postage, and when the film (or fiche) arrives at the family history center, you will have three weeks to look at it; if desired, you may extend the loan for a small additional fee.

International Genealogical Index (IGI)

The IGI is a surname index that contains over 148 million names of deceased persons. In addition to LDS church information, the IGI contains birth, christening, and marriage information about the people in the index, and sometimes includes names of parents or spouses. These names come from extracted church and civil records, forms submitted by members, and LDS membership records.

The IGI is on microfiche and computer, and can be found at family history centers and some genealogical societies and libraries. The IGI is divided into geographic areas, for example a country and then a smaller locality. Records for persons from Poland may also be found under Austria, Germany (Prussia), or Russia.

Two caveats should be mentioned, however. First, there are not very many records of Poles or Polish-Americans (as compared to other ethnic groups) in the IGI. Second, if you find a surname in the IGI that matches your ancestor's surname, do not assume they are related. You must have definite proof of a relationship before you can say that your ancestor was related to someone you found in the IGI.

Computers

An increasing amount of information is becoming available on computers at the LDS. The Social Security Death Index, as one example, contains some useful information about a person's death, such as the date and place of death, and where to write to obtain that person's death certificate. Only deceased persons who had a Social Security number are on file. Check out the other programs if you are "into" computers.

Ancestral File™

"You are invited to contribute your family information to Ancestral File, a computerized collection of genealogies. It links individuals into families and pedigrees, showing their ancestors and descendants." Ancestral File is part of FamilySearch™, which includes "programs designed to work on personal computers and computer files of family history information that are published on compact discs."

Any genealogist can submit family history data to Ancestral File on diskettes, using a GEDCOM file. This project is intended to share genealogical information with others via computer. Most family history centers have computers that can be used free of charge; however, there is a small fee for printouts. The Polish Genealogical Society of America encourages the contribution of information on Poles. For additional information, request the pamphlet *Contributing to Ancestral File* from: Ancestral File Unit 2WW, Family History Department, 50 East North Temple Street, Salt Lake City, Utah 84150.

(Some material about Ancestral File is reprinted by permission. Copyright © 1990 by the Church of Jesus Christ of Latter-day Saints.)

Patron Microfilming Program

If you wish to share your genealogical research in another way, the LDS will microfilm photocopies (you do not need to send originals) of your documents, pedigree charts, and family history, and then return the copies to you.

One microfilm copy is then kept at the Granite Mountain Record Vault, and another at the main library. Copies are made available if requested by patrons. Each donor receives a complimentary copy of his film. For more information about this program write to: Acquisitions—Patron Microfilming, Family History Library, 35 North West Temple Street, Salt Lake City, Utah 84150.

The LDS also accepts anniversary books, or any type of material that would be useful to genealogists, as a donation to their collection. For other services provided by the LDS, visit your local family history center or write for the brochure *Library Services and Resources, Family History Library and Family History Centers.*

Polish Museum of America Archives and Library

> Polish Museum of America Archives and Library
> 984 North Milwaukee Avenue
> Chicago, Illinois 60622

Polish artifacts, fine arts, and folk arts are housed in the Polish Museum, which is also the headquarters of the Polish Roman Catholic Union of America and the Polish Genealogical Society of America.

The library and archives contain 25,000 cataloged volumes, over 2,000 periodicals, 500 maps, 2,000 photographs, 6,000 manuscripts and documents, 50,000 clippings, and many more items not yet cataloged. Polish gazetteers, biographical dictionaries, parish jubilee books, and microfilmed copies of Polish-American newspapers from Chicago and many other cities are just a few of the items that may help your Polish and Polish-American research. All articles are reference materials and must be used inside the library, but a photocopier and microfilm reader/printer are available.

The library is open 10 A.M. to 4 P.M. Monday through Friday, but call ahead for the best service. The library is located just off the Kennedy Expressway, at Augusta and Milwaukee avenues.

Allen County Public Library

> Allen County Public Library
> 900 Webster Street
> Fort Wayne, Indiana 46802

This public library's genealogy department is one of the most outstanding in the United States and contains many items of interest to researchers of recent immigrant ancestry. The microfilm holdings include all U. S. census records from 1790 to 1920 for all states, and the Canadian census records from 1825 to 1891.

The library has passenger lists, on microfilm, for the following ports: New York (1820 to 1900, no indexes); Baltimore (1820 to 1891, indexes for 1820 to 1897); Philadelphia (indexes only, for 1800 to 1906); and Boston (1820 to 1891, indexes for 1848 to 1891); as well as some smaller ports. The Hamburg passenger lists (departures from Europe) are also in the library's microfilm collection (see page 153).

National Archives and Records Administration

> National Archives and Records Administration
> 8th and Pennsylvania Avenue, N. W.
> Washington, D. C. 20408

The National Archives is the repository of valuable records relating to our nation's history. It is also a research facility offering public access to its records. The records are kept at the National Archives building in Washington, the National Records Center in Suitland, Maryland, and at the twelve regional archives branches around the country.

Records available for public use that are of special interest to Polish-American research are federal censuses (1790 to 1920) and census enumeration district maps; passenger arrival lists; naturalization records; passport applications; homestead applications; military draft registration records; cartographic records (including maps); and records of U. S. District Courts (criminal, civil, and bankruptcy) from 1789 to the mid-1950s. District court records are in the custody of regional archives branches.

The National Archives keeps only federal records. Local records are found in local government repositories (city, county, and state).

The National Archives does not perform research for patrons; however, special services by mail include locating and copying passenger arrival records and census pages, if you provide specific identifying information. Ask for the necessary forms and fees. The *Guide to Genealogical Research in the National Archives* describes in detail the materials held by the National Archives.

Regional branches of the National Archives are located throughout the country, each serving several states. For example, the Chicago branch has records for the states of Illinois, Indiana, Ohio, Michigan, Minnesota, and Wisconsin. Records available at the Chicago branch include census records, district court records (naturalization, bankruptcy, criminal, and civil files), Internal Revenue Service records, Immigration and Naturalization Service records for some of these states, and Selective Service Board records from 1917 to 1919. Find out ahead of time what is available at the location you plan to visit.

The locations of National Archives regional archives and the areas they serve are listed below.

Regional Archives of the National Archives

National Archives–New England Region
380 Trapelo Road
Waltham, MA 02154
Serves Connecticut, Maine, Massachusetts, New Hampshire, Rhode Island, and Vermont

National Archives–Northeast Region
201 Varick Street
New York, NY 10014
Serves New Jersey, New York, Puerto Rico, and the Virgin Islands

National Archives–Mid-Atlantic Region
5000 Wissahickon Avenue
Philadelphia, PA 19144
Serves Delaware, Pennsylvania, Maryland, Virginia, and West Virginia

National Archives–Great Lakes Region
7358 South Pulaski Road
Chicago, IL 60629
Serves Illinois, Indiana, Michigan, Minnesota, Ohio, and Wisconsin

National Archives–Southeast Region
1557 Saint Joseph Avenue
East Point, GA 30344
Serves Alabama, Georgia, Florida, Kentucky, Mississippi, North Carolina, South Carolina, and Tennessee

National Archives–Central Plains Region
2306 East Bannister Road
Kansas City, MO 64131
Serves Iowa, Kansas, Missouri, and Nebraska

National Archives–Southwest Region
501 West Felix Street
PO Box 6216
Fort Worth, TX 76115
Serves Arkansas, Louisiana, New Mexico, Oklahoma, and Texas

National Archives–Rocky Mountain Region
Building 48, Denver Federal Center
Denver, CO 80225
Serves Colorado, Montana, North Dakota, South Dakota, Utah, and Wyoming

National Archives–Pacific Sierra Region
1000 Commodore Drive
San Bruno, CA 94066
Serves California (except southern California), Hawaii, Nevada (except Clark County), and the Pacific Ocean area

National Archives–Pacific Southwest Region
24000 Avila Road
PO Box 6719
Laguna Niguel, CA 92677
Serves Arizona, the southern California counties of Imperial, Inyo, Kern, Los Angeles, Orange, Riverside, San Bernadino, San Diego, San Luis Obispo, Santa Barbara and Ventura, and Clark County, Nevada

National Archives–Pacific-Northwest Region
6125 San Point Way, N. E.
Seattle, WA 98115
Serves Idaho, Oregon, and Washington + CALIF CENSUS + ALASKA

National Archives–Alaska Region
Federal Office Building
654 West Third Avenue, Room 012
Anchorage, AK 99501
Serves Alaska

University of Illinois Library

University of Illinois Library
University of Illinois—Urbana
Urbana, Illinois 61801

This library has over 6.5 million volumes, and one of the most extensive Slavic collections—over 510,000 volumes.

National Archives of Canada

Polish Archives Program, National Ethnic Archives
National Archives of Canada
395 Wellington Street
Ottawa, Ontario K1A 0N3
Canada

The Li-RA-MA collection includes the papers of the Russian consuls in Canada from 1900 to 1922. There are more than 10,000 files on immigrants from the former Russian Empire, including Polish lands.

The archives also has papers of the Canadian Polish Congress, the Association of Polish Engineers in Canada, the Polish Alliance Friendly Society of Canada, and copies of the *Czas* newspaper.

University of Pittsburgh Slavic Department

Slavic Department
University of Pittsburgh
Pittsburgh, Pennsylvania 15260

Forty-five thousand volumes from the library of Alliance College, a recently closed Polish college, have been transferred to the Slavic Department of the University of Pittsburgh. These books will be cataloged and made available through a computer system to scholars throughout the United States.

Polish American Archives

Polish American Archives
Alumni Memorial Library
St. Mary's College
The Orchard Lake Schools
Orchard Lake, Michigan 48033

Located north of Detroit, this library has material about Poland and Polonia, and is open to the public. The staff does not do research but can tell you whether a book or reference is in the library's collection. An appointment is recommended.

Immigration History Research Center

> University of Minnesota
> Immigration History Research Center
> 826 Berry Street
> St. Paul, Minnesota 55114-1076

The Immigration History Research Center has material about ethnic groups originating in eastern, central, and southern Europe. The collection consists of newspapers and serials, fraternal society material, church records and publications, manuscript collections, oral histories, memoirs, family histories, and a reference collection. Most items are non-circulating, but some material on microfilm is available through inter-library loan.

University of Wisconsin Library and Archives

> University of Wisconsin—Stevens Point
> University Library and Archives
> Stevens Point, Wisconsin 54481

The University Library has many references for Polish research, including the *Polish Encyclopaedia*. The archives has naturalization, tax, census, and vital records of counties in the area, as well as the Emil Kitowski collection of Polish genealogy related to Portage County.

SOURCES FOR REGIONAL RESEARCH

Some genealogists have spent many years compiling data that they are willing to share with others. A number of them will do a quick search for you without requiring a fee and will send you detailed and accurate information about your ancestors. Consider sending them a monetary gift after you have received your information. Other genealogists do require a fee for searching their records, and sometimes the results of their research have been published and are for sale.

The individuals mentioned in the following sections have agreed to be listed in this book and are willing to do research for you. There are also other people doing the same type of research who do not wish to be included or who do not have enough material to be of general interest.

The following sources are a combination of the above-mentioned individuals and reference collections open to the public. Libraries do not do research for you, so you must use the materials in person, hire someone in the area to search the material for you, or borrow the ones that are available through inter-library loan.

Baltimore, Maryland

The majority of Polish immigrants settled in Baltimore around 1868. The first settlements were in Fells Point, Canton, and Curtis Bay, and later in Highlandtown and Dundalk. The Polish population of Baltimore ranked seventh nationally just before World War I.

Thomas L. Hollowak has been researching the history of Baltimore's Polish community from its origin in 1868 until the outbreak of the First World War in 1914. He has written about the establishment of Polish parishes and plans to write a comprehensive history of the Baltimore Polonia. Among the number of genealogical books he has compiled, two concern Baltimore's Poles: *The Index to Obituaries and Death Notices in the Jedność-Polonia, 1926–1946*, published by the Polish Genealogical Society of America, which abstracts deaths appearing in Baltimore's only extant Polish-language newspaper; and the *Index to the Polish Heads of Households in the 1910 Census of Maryland*, published by Family Line Publications.

His research has generated a wealth of information on Maryland's Polish immigrants and their descendants who were centered in Baltimore. Among the items he has accumulated are: census, city directory, military, tax, and voting registration records; as well as information from parish sacramental records. In order to make his research more readily available he has begun his own publishing company, Historyk Press. For a catalog of available publications, write to Historyk Press, 2804 Florida Avenue, Baltimore, Maryland 21227.

Connecticut and the Connecticut River Valley

The Connecticut State Library's Hale Collection, located in Hartford, is a compilation of gravestone inscriptions, including those from several Polish cemeteries. Another potentially useful record group is "Passport and Birth

Certificates of Work Permit Applicants 1870–1930" (RG 10) of the Connecticut Education Department.

Many of the early settlers in Connecticut came from the Łomża and Grodno areas of Russian-occupied Poland, as well as a few locations in Austrian Galicia. "The principal Polish settlement in Connecticut is New Britain, but sizeable settlements can also be found in Bristol, Hartford, Norwich, Middletown, Stamford, Meriden, Union City, and Enfield. Polish-Americans constitute approximately 10 percent of Connecticut's population," according to Jonathan Shea in two of his articles in the *Polish Genealogical Society Newsletter*: "The Poles in Connecticut—Observations, Genealogical Research," III (January 1981), and "Poles in Connecticut Additional Genealogical Sources," IV (Fall 1982).

Detroit, Michigan

Kashubs and Pomeranians, along with some Silesians and Protestant Prussian Mazurians, were the first Poles to arrive in Detroit, shortly after the collapse of Napoleon's Grand Duchy of Warsaw early in the nineteenth century. Records of these early arrivals can be found in the baptismal registers of the oldest Catholic church in Detroit, St. Anne's, founded by the French in 1701.

Father Wacław Kruszka (in his *History of Poles in America*, 1937) and other historians have established the route taken by early Poles to Michigan as being down the St. Lawrence River through Canada. At the beginning of the great Polish emigration, 1850 to 1870, Poles from Poznania used this same Canadian route. Most of the emigrants embarked at Hamburg and arrived at Quebec, and later moved along the Great Lakes water route to Michigan, Wisconsin, Minnesota, and Manitoba; some went on to California for the Gold Rush.

Polish town quarters sprang up in Muskegon in the 1830s and in Detroit in the 1850s. From Detroit, Poles spread throughout Michigan, founding Paris (later called Parisville) in Michigan's thumb in the 1850s, and Posen in northern Michigan in the 1870s.

About 300 Polish families lived in Detroit in 1870, at which time they attended church services at St. Joseph's (German) Church on Gratiot Avenue, the nearest church to their homes. Antagonized by the insulting attitude of the German priest and parishioners, the Poles built their own church, St. Albertus, in 1872. Many more Polish Catholic churches followed.

A large Polish settlement grew up in Hamtramck, in the middle of Detroit. Polish immigrants are still flocking to Hamtramck today.

Three area research facilities for Polish studies are the Burton Historical Collection of the Detroit Public Library, the Hamtramck Public Library, and the Polish American Archives at Orchard Lake.

If you would like to read more about the Poles in Detroit and Michigan, see *Poles in Michigan*, vol. 1. (Detroit: The Poles in Michigan Associated, 1955).

Wisconsin

The earliest Polish immigrants came from Prussian Poland and settled in the Stevens Point area in the late 1850s. Poles did not begin residing in Milwaukee in large numbers until after 1870. Poles also settled in large numbers in Trempealeau, Shawano, Oconto, and Brown counties in the nineteenth century.

The University of Wisconsin–Milwaukee's Golda Meir Library has a collection of Polish books, an area research archives, Polish geographical dictionaries, and the American Geographical Society collection, which contains maps of Poland from the sixteenth century to World War II. The Golda Meir Library is located on campus between Hartford Avenue and Kenwood Boulevard.

New England and the Mid-Atlantic States

The Polish Genealogical Society of Connecticut has been copying over half a million cemetery inscriptions from ten states and Poland. These are on file in the society's archives. Over 58,000 names from seventeen Polish cemeteries in New Jersey are indexed and printed in a publication that is available from the society. Also available are the publications of inscriptions from the states of Vermont and New Hampshire; Connecticut and Massachusetts will soon be available. Contact the Polish Genealogical Society of Connecticut, Inc., 8 Lyle Road, New Britain, Connecticut 06053.

Pittsburgh, Pennsylvania

The Poles in Western Pennsylvania Collection, in the Hillman Library at the University of Pittsburgh, is largely the work of Joseph A. Borkowski, Chairman of the Polish Historical Commission. The collection includes information about Polish churches, organizations, societies, and institutions; birth, marriage, and death records for the period 1875 to 1905; voter registrations; and more. The Hillman Library collection itself contains additional information: tax records for 1875 to 1900, World War I draft records for Allegheny County, county naturalization records, and the Polish newspaper *Pittsburczanin* from 1924 to 1976. Write for an appointment so that a curator can be on hand to assist you. Contact Frank A. Zabrosky, Curator, Archives of Industrial Society, 363 Hillman Library, University of Pittsburgh, Pittsburgh, Pennsylvania 15260.

South Bend, Indiana

The earliest Polish settlers began to arrive in St. Joseph County en masse in 1868, and most chose to settle on the west side of the town of South Bend.

In 1967 Mrs. Gene Szymarek began the task of compiling all records of Poles in St. Joseph County from 1859 through 1920. She and her sister Lucky Ladewski are entering their information into a computer. In the near future they hope to give this computerized data to the South Bend Public Library and the Indiana Historical Society in Indianapolis.

They do not encourage visits to their homes but will answer all letter queries. Include a SASE and three-ounces worth of first class postage. After you receive a reply, send at least a thank-you note; a small donation for copying costs would be appreciated, as all their work has been voluntary.

Mrs. Szymarek and Mrs. Ladewski have approximately 3,000 surnames on file on more than 30,000 family group sheets (which they will photocopy for you). Extracts of the following records were taken: church and cemetery records, civil marriage records, declarations of intention, petitions for naturalization, and obituaries from the local newspapers.

Heritage Books, Inc. (Maryland) has published three of the sisters' books: *Cedar Grove Cemetery Inscriptions* (1,907 grave sites); *St. Joseph Polish Cemetery Inscriptions, "Old Section"* (2,962 grave sites); *Polish Marriage Applicants, St. Joseph County, Indiana, 1905–1915,* 1988.

When you write to Mrs. Szymarek or Mrs. Ladewski, include as much information as you can give about your South Bend ancestors. It will help them locate the proper records, as well as fill in the blanks in *their* records. Contact either Mrs. Gene Szymarek, 1720 W. Ewing Avenue, South Bend, Indiana 46613 or Mrs. Lucky Ladewski, 1717 W. Ewing Avenue, South Bend, Indiana 46613.

Toledo, Ohio

Poles began arriving in Toledo in large numbers about 1870 and settled first in two separate areas: *Lagrinka*, along Lagrange Street in North Toledo, and in the central-south area called *Kuhschwanz* (in German), or "cow's tail." According to federal census statistics, Poles were the largest foreign-born group in Toledo in 1920.

Dr. David G. Chełmiński wrote two detailed papers about the early Poles in Toledo. His 1978 master's thesis was "The Ethnicity of the Poles in Toledo, 1830–1886." "Toledo's Nineteenth-Century Polonia: Ziomki i Rodacy (Countryfolk and Compatriots)" was the title of his 1989 doctoral dissertation. Both papers give the names and accomplishments of many of Toledo's earliest Polish settlers. Both can be found in the Toledo–Lucas County Public Library and the University of Toledo Library.

Dr. Chełmiński, I, and five young men wrote *The First Hundred Years, 1875–1975, A History of St. Hedwig Parish, Toledo, Ohio*, a comprehensive publication of Polish history, and Toledo and parish history, with over 400 photographs and information about the early Polish pioneers in Toledo. It is available at both of the above libraries and the Polish Museum of America Archives.

For further information on the Poles in Toledo, write to: Dr. David G. Chełmiński, 4148 Bowen Rd., Toledo, Ohio 43613-3847.

Cleveland, Ohio

The first Polish settlement in the Cleveland area was at the nearby community of Berea in the late 1860s. Poles originally settled in the city of Cleveland in the Czech neighborhood around Broadway and East 55th Street, and later formed their own settlement, Warszawa, in the Tod (E. 65th Street)–Forman Avenue area, which is currently known as the Slavic Village. Another Polish settlement, Poznan, was established in the East 79th Street–Superior Avenue area. Other smaller Polish neighborhoods were formed later: Josephatowa, Barbarowa, Kantowa, and an area along Madison Avenue near West 117th Street settled by Poles and Slovaks. Poles have been one of the largest ethnic groups in Cleveland in the twentieth century.

The Western Reserve Historical Society Library (which has local naturalization records and other genealogical materials) and the Cleveland Public Library system are two local research facilities.

Source: Grabowski, John J., Western Reserve Historical Society

SOURCES AND ADDITIONAL READING

National Historical Publications and Records Commission. *Directory of Archives and Manuscript Repositories in the United States.* 2nd ed. Phoenix: Oryx Press, 1988. A listing by state of libraries and other research facilities, and the materials they contain. Good reference for finding the addresses and hours of libraries in the locality in which you wish to do research.

Chapter Three:

POLISH
GENEALOGICAL SOCIETIES

If you are a beginning genealogist, the first thing you should do is join a Polish genealogical society. Even if you have been doing research for some time, you can also reap benefits from these organizations.

As far as Polish genealogical research is concerned, no general society will be able to help you as much as these can. Most Polish genealogical societies hold monthly meetings at which an expert in a particular field speaks on topics directly or indirectly related to Polish genealogy, such as maps, church records, local Polish history, or local resources. Most societies offer annual workshops at which a number of experts, some coming from their homes in Poland or Salt Lake City, give lectures and suggestions for solving problems.

These societies publish informative newsletters at least twice a year. Some have published very useful books, maps, and other publications as well. One of the best reasons for joining is that you will meet other researchers and exchange tips on research techniques.

There is one national Polish genealogical society, based in Chicago, that has members throughout America. All other Polish genealogical societies in the United States are local groups, interested both in research in Poland and in their own localities. Following are addresses of Polish genealogical societies, as well as a genealogical-heraldic association in Poland. Addresses of several Slavic and Jewish genealogical societies are also provided.

All Polish genealogical societies and their members are invited to participate in the Polish genealogical conferences that are held in Salt Lake City biannually. The LDS Family History Library makes special arrangements for conference participants to do research at the library.

Polish Genealogical Society of America

Polish Genealogical Society of America, Inc.
984 North Milwaukee Avenue
Chicago, Illinois 60622

The Polish Genealogical Society, organized in 1978, is a national organization of approximately 800 members who are located ~~throughout the United States and the world.~~ *worldwide* The society was founded with the purpose of providing genealogical assistance in the form of newsletters, bulletins, publications, meetings, conferences, and special genealogical tours. The society changed its name to the Polish Genealogical Society of America in 1992 to reflect its focus on Polish-American research.

The P. G. S. A. publishes a semi-annual newsletter and bulletin. The award-winning newsletter contains a column that answers questions sent in by members, articles written by genealogists (some articles are translations of books and articles written in Polish), a heraldry column, book reviews, an information exchange, and genealogy-targeted ads.

Meetings featuring guest speakers are held several times a year. There are annual conferences with local, national, and international speakers covering a wide range of genealogical topics. All events are held in the Chicago area.

The P. G. S. A. has published more than fourteen publications (books and maps) and distributes information packets on genealogical subjects. Send a SASE for a list of books and/or packets.

An ancestor index card file holds more than 12,000 entries containing genealogical data on the earliest ancestors being researched by members. This is an exchange service that can be requested by mail from the P. G. S. A. or used in the Polish Museum Library at 984 North Milwaukee Avenue in Chicago. When requesting a search of the index by mail, please send a SASE and limit the request to five surnames.

Polish Genealogical Society of Connecticut

> Polish Genealogical Society of Connecticut, Inc.
> 8 Lyle Road
> New Britain, Connecticut 06053

Outside of Connecticut the society is known as the Polish Genealogical Society of the Northeast. Formed in 1984, the affiliated societies serve the New England area, New York, Pennsylvania, Delaware, New Jersey, and Maryland. The society is concerned with all aspects of Polish-American genealogy but maintains a special focus on the Białystok and Łomża areas in Poland, primarily Dąbrowa Białystocka and Myszyniec, and has established special collections and services related to this region. The Society of Connecticut has an Archive and Resource Center which houses their collection of personal papers, reference books, parish histories, oral histories, cemetery inscriptions, photographs, and Polish-American ancestry file.

Benefits of membership include *Pathways and Passages*, the semi-annual newsletter. The society has published cemetery inscriptions from Poland and the United States, as well as several other books, and has organized genealogical trips to Poland and Lithuania.

Polish Genealogical Society of Massachusetts

Polish Genealogical Society of Massachusetts
P. O. Box 381
Northampton, Massachusetts 01061

This society, formed in 1989, has meetings, outreach programs, and all-day seminars. The semi-annual newsletter is the *Biuletyn Korzenie*.

Polish Genealogical Society of Western New York

Polish Genealogical Society of Western New York
299 Barnard Street
Buffalo, New York 14206

The P. G. S. W. N. Y., organized in 1988, offers guest speakers at monthly meetings and tours of local libraries and archives. The society's library includes a microfilm/fiche viewer, Polish research reels, Polish maps, and reference books. The semi-annual newsletter is called *Searchers*.

Polish Genealogical Society of Michigan

Polish Genealogical Society of Michigan
Burton Historical Collection
Detroit Public Library
5201 Woodward Avenue
Detroit, Michigan 48202

The P. G. S. M. was organized in 1978. The tri-annual newsletter, *The Eaglet*, was first published in 1981.

The P. G. S. M. maintains a database of more than 5,000 names in their Polonian Registry. Members and non-members are invited to submit information about the families they are researching; request a form from the society. When a match occurs, the parties are notified. The society is undertaking a project to recreate the records of the oldest Polish cemetery on the east side of Detroit; the records will be computerized and published. Meetings are held on Saturdays from September through June, and a genealogical seminar is held annually.

Polish Genealogical Society of Texas

> Polish Genealogical Society of Texas
> Route 1, Box 475-S
> Navasota, Texas 77868
> or:
> 3915 Glenheather
> Houston, Texas 77068

In 1854 Poles from Silesia founded the first permanent Polish settlement in the United States at Panna Maria, Texas, south of San Antonio.

The P. G. S. T. was formed in 1984 in Houston, and meets at least four times a year. The *P. G. S. T. News* is published quarterly. The society maintains a surname index of families that members are researching and regularly publishes an updated surname index.

Polish Genealogical Society of California

> Polish Genealogical Society of California
> P. O. Box 713
> Midway City, California 92655-0713

This society, founded in 1989, has regular meetings with guest speakers and beginner's classes, and participates in jamborees. *The Bulletin* is published quarterly.

Polish Genealogical Society of Wisconsin

> Polish Genealogical Society of Wisconsin
> P. O. Box 37476
> Milwaukee, Wisconsin 53237

The Polish Research Group of Milwaukee was in existence for several years before the P. G. S. W. was founded in 1989. *Korzenie/Roots* and a bulletin are published semi-annually. Meetings are held six times a year in Milwaukee, and a surname file is kept.

The Polish Genealogical Society of Greater Cleveland

The Polish Genealogical Society of Greater Cleveland
906 College Avenue
Cleveland, Ohio 44113

The P. G. S. of Greater Cleveland was founded in 1991. Meetings are held monthly. The society publishes a newsletter and plans to begin a surname index.

Polish Genealogical Society of Minnesota

Polish Genealogical Society of Minnesota
Branch of the Minnesota Genealogical Society
P. O. Box 16069
St. Paul, Minnesota 55116

This society was founded in 1992. For information about meetings and publications write to the society, which has just been granted status as a branch of the Minnesota Genealogical Society.

Towarzystwo Genealogiczno-Heraldyczne

Towarzystwo Genealogiczno-Heraldyczne
Wodna 27 Pałac Górków
61-781 Poznań
Polska (Poland)

Genealogical and heraldic studies were considered improper by the communists. So it was not until 1987 that the Genealogical-Heraldic Society in Poznań was founded by a group of scholars and amateurs. The society holds monthly meetings and is beginning research projects such as compiling inventories of archival sources, bibliographies, and indexing vital records. They do not do research for the public.

Members voluntarily contribute administrative work, lectures, and articles. The society is not funded by the government, but is a private organization and is seeking publishing funds. They would appreciate donations of genealogical or heraldic books and periodicals from other countries for their library collection.

The society is now accepting members from outside Poland. Members receive information sheets about current events, new publications, etc., several times a year, and copies of "Genealogical Data Bank," which lists surnames being researched by members and is updated semi-annually. The society has promised that the publications and information sheets will soon be available in English.

Membership includes a subscription to *GENS*, a quarterly magazine. *GENS* is published in Polish with a summary of each article in English.

If you are interested in this society, write for a membership application and information flyer; request that they be printed in English.

Polish Interest Group

> Polish Interest Group
> Catholic Family History Society
> Mr. Antoni W. Szachnowski, Coordinator
> "Woodcote"
> Laurel Grove
> Penge, London SE20 8QJ
> England

The Polish Interest Group is a small special interest group within the Catholic Family History Society. Since 1989 the society has expanded its scope to include anyone researching Catholic ancestry. A Polish interest group within the society was formed in 1990 for the purpose of building an index from records of Poles in England and to make contact with similar groups in other countries for their mutual benefit. The group does not undertake research for others but will consult their index for specific names. The journal of the C. F. H. S. is the *Catholic Ancestor*, which is published three times a year and occasionally publishes articles of interest to Polish researchers.

LITHUANIAN GENEALOGY

Balzekas Museum of Lithuanian Culture

> Balzekas Museum of Lithuanian Culture
> Genealogy Department
> 6500 S. Pulaski Road
> Chicago, Illinois 60629

Genealogija, a quarterly publication, is the first Lithuanian-American newsletter. The primary aim is to keep people informed about the progress of the Lithuanian Pioneer Project, which involves gathering information about the Lithuanians who immigrated to the United States before World War I. The project will ultimately be published in book form.

The following is one reference you may wish to consult: Alilunas, Leo J., ed. *Lithuanians in the United States: Selected Studies* (San Francisco: R&E Research Associates, 1978).

UKRAINIAN GENEALOGY

Ukrainian Genealogical and Heraldic Society
573 N. E. 102nd Street
Miami Shores, Florida 33138

Ukrainian Genealogical and Historical Society of Canada
1530 23rd Avenue
Calgary, Alberta T2M 1V1
Canada

VOLHYNIAN GENEALOGY

Society for Ancestral Research of Germans from Poland and Volhynia
3492 West 39th Avenue
Vancouver, British Columbia V6N 3A2
Canada

The *Wandering Volhynians* newsletter is written for the Germans from Volhynia (east of the Bug River from the city of Brest south to Łuck, now in the republics of Ukraine and Byelorussia) and Poland, and hopes to fill in the gaps in Polish research where Lutheran records are concerned.

SLOVAK GENEALOGY

Matica Slovenska

Milan Šišmiš
Matica Slovenska
Cintolrínska 10
911 01 Trenčín
Ceskoslovenska (Czechoslovakia)

Milan Šišmiš of the Matica Slovenska, the Slovak National Cultural Institution, intends to create a genealogical workplace, or archives, for Slovak research.

JEWISH GENEALOGY

Jewish Genealogical Society, Inc.
P. O. Box 6398
New York, New York 10128
For additional resources, see "The Hebrew Religion" in chapter 9.)

Part Two:

RESEARCH IN POLAND

BALTIC SEA

Venta

Niem

Kaliningrad
Pregoła

Koszalin
Gdańsk

Lidzbark

Suwa

Szczecin

Wisła

Olsztyn

Odra

Notec

Warta

Berlin

Inowrocław

Narew

Biały

Poznań

Płock

Bug

Drohiczyn

Zielona
Góra

Nysa

Warszawa

Dresden

Łódź

Pilica

Wisła

Wiepz

Odra

Warta

Lublin

Kłodzko

Częstochowa

Opole

Sandomierz

Prague

Katowice

San

Opava

Wisła

Kraków

Rzeszów

Ostrava

Nowy Targ

Wisłoka

Brno

S

Vienna

Budapest

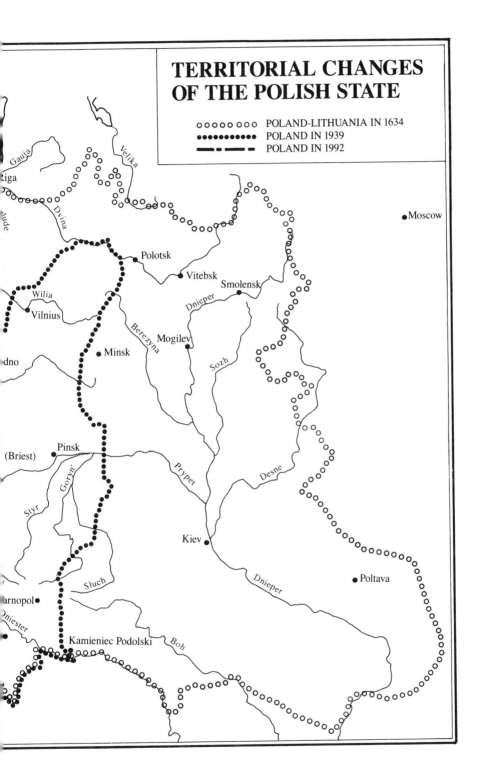

TERRITORIAL CHANGES
OF THE POLISH STATE

○○○○○○○○ POLAND-LITHUANIA IN 1634
●●●●●●●●●● POLAND IN 1939
▬ ▬ ▬ ▬ POLAND IN 1992

Gauja

Velika

Riga

Dvina

lude

•Moscow

Polotsk

Vitebsk

Smolensk

Wilia

Dnieper

•Vilnius

Berezyna

Mogilev

•Minsk

Sozh

dno

Pinsk

Prypet

Desne

(Briest)

Goryn

Styr

Kiev•

•Poltava

Sluch

Dnieper

arnopol•

Dniester

Kamieniec Podolski

Boh

Chapter Four:

LIFE
IN POLAND

HISTORY OF POLAND

There is a legend in Eastern Europe about three brothers who came from
✗ The East looking for land to colonize. They stopped in the area that was to
become Poland. One brother, *Czech*, went south and became the father of the
Southern Slavs. Another brother, *Rus*, went east and became the ancestor of
the Eastern Slavs.

The third brother, *Lech*, looked around and liked the vast plain he saw.
Pole (poh-leh) means "field" or "plain" in Polish, and *Polska* is the Polish
name for Poland.

Lech and his followers rested under a tree with a white eagle nesting in it,
and they considered this a good omen. Lech became the father of the Western Slavs. He built his own nest on the site in 550 A.D., establishing his capital, Gniezno, atop a hill called "Lech's Mountain." The name *Gniezno* is
derived from *gniazdo* (nest). The white eagle has been the symbol of the Polish state ever since. Poland is still known as *Lechistan* in many Eastern
countries.

Slavs and Balts settled in the lands between the Baltic and Black seas by
the sixth century. Germanic people pushed southward from Scandinavia by
the Roman times, and began moving eastward in the eighth century.

The foundation of Poland as a state is generally acknowledged to begin
with the rule of Mieszko I (the "Little Bear"), who was first recorded as the
King of Poland in 963 A.D. Poland joined Western civilization by Mieszko's
marriage to the Bohemian princess Dubrava. Mieszko and Poland adopted
Christianity in 966 A.D., which is historically considered the founding date
of the Polish state. Poland always identified itself with Western Europe,
adopting Roman Catholicism and the Latin alphabet, and not with the Eastern Slavs who adopted Greek Catholicism and the Cyrillic alphabet.

The Teutonic House of the Brothers Hospitallers of St. Mary of Jerusalem
(also known as the "Teutonic Order" and "Teutonic Knights") began to colo-

nize the Baltic states and northern Poland in 1201. Mongol Tatar ("Tartar") invasions reached Kraków and Legnica in 1241 and continued for about 500 years. Jews began to settle in Poland in the eighth century and were officially welcomed after 1264. Bohemian kings ruled Poland from at least 1296 to 1306 and took over Silesia in 1339.

Poland and Lithuania were united by the marriage of the young Polish Queen Hedwig to the Lithuanian Grand Duke Ladislaus Jogaila in 1385. The nation formed from this union, along with subsequent additions, eventually stretched from the Baltic Sea to the Black Sea. Poland-Lithuania was part of medieval (Renaissance to Baroque) culture via universities and royal intermarriages. Polish and Lithuanian forces defended Western civilization from Tatars and Turks for centuries.

In medieval Poland the average life expectancy was short—30 to 32 years for women and 33 to 36 years for men. Only 5 to 7 percent of the population lived to age fifty. The mortality rate for children was 30 to 50 percent, according to Jerzy Topolski in his *Outline History of Poland*.

During the sixteenth century Poland exported many goods to other parts of Europe: amber, silver, copper, lead, tin, timber, hemp, flax, furs, hides, salt, fish, wax, and honey. Polish wheat could be purchased in Europe for only 15 percent of the cost of Mediterranean wheat.

From 1600 to 1860 East Central Europe, including Poland, experienced a drop in the average temperature and frequent droughts, which had an adverse effect on Polish agriculture and economy. This was one of the principal reasons for emigration from Poland.

The following is a brief outline of Polish history from the time of the partitions, which is the period when most of our ancestors emigrated from Poland.

1772   First Partition of Poland: Joseph II Hapsburg of Austria takes 83,000 square kilometers of land and 2.5 million people. Frederick II ("the Great") Hohenzollern of Prussia takes 36,000 square kilometers and 1.5 million people. Catherine II ("the Great") of Russia takes 92,000 square kilometers and 1.3 million people.

1791   Constitution of May Third: first modern constitution in Europe tries to bring about the rebirth of Poland and regain the lost territories. Catherine of Russia thought such reforms were dangerous to her own autocracy and ordered a Russian invasion of Poland.

1793   Second Partition of Poland: Prussia takes 51,000 square kilometers of land and another 1 million people. Russia takes 250,000 square kilometers and another 3 million people. Austria does not participate, hoping to win Prussian and Russian support for Austria's plans to annex Bavaria.

1795   Third Partition of Poland: Austria takes 47,000 square kilometers of land and half a million people. Prussia takes 48,000 square kilometers and 1 million people. Russia takes 120,000 square kilometers and 1.2 million people. Many battles were fought against the aggressors before each partition.

1807   Napoleon Bonaparte creates Grand Duchy of Warsaw (under King of Saxony) from territory recovered from Prussia. Russia seizes Białystok district.

1809   Napoleon adds territory recovered from Austria to Grand Duchy of Warsaw.

1814–15 Following Napoleon's abdication and final defeat at Waterloo, the Congress of Vienna returns some territory to Prussian control, creates the Congress Kingdom of Poland (called *Kongresówka* in Polish) from most of the territory of the Grand Duchy of Warsaw (under the rule of the czar of Russia), but establishes the Free City of Kraków (a republic of 1,163 square kilometers and 95,000 people), which remained independent until 1846.

1830–31 The November Uprising (1830) in Russian-occupied areas, aided by Poles from the Austrian and Prussian territories. Emigration of upper classes and intelligentsia.

1831   First Asiatic cholera epidemic.

1836   Heavy flooding in Galicia (Austrian Poland).

1844   Beginning of peasant uprisings throughout Europe.

1844–48 Peasant uprisings in Silesia.

1846   The Revolution of Kraków: Austria takes over the Republic of Kraków. Peasant riots in Galicia.

1848   Uprising in Poznania.

1847–48 Typhus and cholera outbreaks.

1846–55	Poor crop yields cause starvation. Starvation and epidemic diseases claim the lives of 200,000 in sub-Carpathian region of Galicia.
1854	The Great Cholera Epidemic.
1854–56	Crimean War: Russia against Turkey, France, and the British Empire.
1863–64	The January Uprising (1863) in Russian-occupied areas led by the gentry with the assistance of the peasants. Heaviest fighting is in the area south of Kielce. Ten thousand emigrated, 38,000 were deported to Siberia, and several thousand killed.
1864	Russification program intensified as a result of the January Uprising.
1866	Small outbreaks of Asiatic cholera.
1867	Prussia incorporates West Prussia and Poznania: Prime Minister Otto von Bismarck begins *Kulturkampf* (Culture Struggle).
1870–71	Franco-Prussian War.
1873	The Little Cholera.
1871–75	Bismarck's *Kulturkampf* plan is implemented: anti-Catholic, anti-Polish campaign in Prussian territory. More intense pressure to Germanize the Poles. Land taken away from Polish farmers and sold to German immigrant farmers brought in by Bismarck.
1870–1914	More than 4 million people left ethnic Polish lands.
1884	Asiatic cholera epidemic.
1892	Asiatic cholera epidemic.
1900	Peasants comprise almost 80 percent of the population.
1905	Russia loses the Russo-Japanese War in which many Poles were forced to fight for the Russians.
1905–07	"The Revolution of 1905 to 1907": workers' strikes, demonstrations, strikes by farm laborers, and anti-czarist campaign.
1906	Largest U. S. reported annual total for arrivals of "Hebrew race or people" (153,748).

1907	Famine in Galicia.
1907	Largest U. S. reported annual total for arrivals of "Lithuanian race or people" (25,884).
1907	Largest U. S. reported annual total for arrivals from all countries (1,285,349).
1913	Largest U. S. reported annual total for arrivals of "Polish race or people" (174,365).
1914	Largest U. S. reported annual total for arrivals of "Ruthenian race or people" (36,727).
1914–18	First World War.
1918	Wielkopolska Uprising.
1918–39	Second Polish Republic.
1919	Versailles Treaty establishes Gdańsk/Danzig as a free city (until 1939).
1939–45	Second World War.
1945	Yalta Conference recognizes Soviet sphere of influence.
1956	Riots in Poznań.
1968	Riots in Warsaw.
1970	Riots in Gdańsk.
1976	Riots in Radom and elsewhere.
1981–83	Martial Law: "Solidarity" Free Trade Union outlawed, political refugees flee.
1989–90	First free elections in Soviet bloc bring about Third Polish Republic.

ADDITIONAL READING

Topolski, Jerzy. *An Outline History of Poland*. Translated by Olgierd Wojtasiewicz. Warsaw, Poland: Interpress Publishers, 1986. Includes not only history, but also economic development, culture, and society. Tells how people ate, lived, and worked in past centuries.

Zielenkiewicz, Andrzej. *Poland*. Orchard Lake, Michigan: Center for Polish Studies and Culture, The Orchard Lake Schools, 1971.

SOCIAL CLASSES IN POLAND

Magnates (*Magnacy*)

The feudal lords lived on large estates and owned castles, towns, and villages. The magnates became very powerful in the sixteenth century and had enormous political influence. Many had private armies. The magnates' primary income was rent from the lands their peasants farmed and money collected in other ways from the peasants. The magnates almost always managed to avoid paying taxes, which antagonized the lower nobility.

The gentry (magnates and nobility) dominated the social, political, and economic life of Poland, and tried to keep the burghers and peasants from participating in Polish culture.

Nobility (*Szlachta*)

The Polish nobility emerged as a clan system before 1000 A. D. Each clan had its own mark, a *taiga*, which eventually evolved into the symbols found on Polish coats of arms. The noble class became landowners.

At first, the nobility were known only by their first names and sometimes by the offices they held: Jan Sołtys, "John the Administrator." Most noble surnames were taken from the names of estates, called "family nests": Jan de Dębina, "John of the Oaks."

In the eastern territories Old Slavonic patronymic endings of *-ic* and *-icz* were preferred: Jan Piotric, "John Peter's son." In Lithuania *-owicz* was preferred: Jan Piotrowicz.

The names evolved into the format of *Title—Christian Name—de—Family Estate Name*: *Magnificus Jan de Dębina*, "The Wealthy John of the Oaks." *Magnificus* is a Latin term.

Sometimes the Polish *z* was used at the end of a name to mean "of" or "from." During the fifteenth century the *z* was changed to *-ski* or *-cki*, also meaning "of" or "from": Jan Dębinski or Jan Dębicki. People who were not nobles were forbidden to add *-ski* or *-cki* to their surnames.

While it is true that having a surname ending in *-ski* or *-cki* originally meant the bearer was of noble birth, eventually many peasants living on their lord's land took his surname. They were not related to him or of noble birth.

Beginning in the eighteenth century double names became popular, with the clan name followed by the surname: Jan Rawa-Dębiński, "John of the Bear Clan of the Oaks."

All nobility were equal in legal status, and all nobles were representatives in the *Sejm*, the Parliament. From 850 A. D. on, all nobles, rich or poor, voted to elect the rulers of Poland.

Lesser nobles soon came under the control of the powerful magnates. About 150,000 nobles had the power to cast votes in the Sejm; however, most nobles were controlled by about 300 magnate families. This began to undermine the power of the Sejm and led to the eventual downfall of the Commonwealth's powerful status.

Service to God and country were the duties of the nobility. They were given the duty of the military defense of Poland and had the right to hold public office and to own land. The only permissible occupations were soldier, gentleman-farmer, scholar, priest, public official, and administrator of an estate of a noble in a higher position than their own. This led to the immigration of many foreigners who filled business positions.

In Podlasie, Masovia, and the lands of Dobrzyn and Łomża, the nobility comprised up to 30 percent of the population. In most areas of Poland the nobility usually consisted of 10 percent of the population, the largest percentage of any European country.

Many members of the nobility owned a village and a manor house (*dwór*) and/or a full working farm (*folwark*) with many buildings.

Stanisław Wierciszewski, in a *Polish Genealogical Society Newsletter* article (June 1981), says "the Polish nobility was divided into several classes. Those of ancient lineage were the *Karmazynska Szlachta*, Crimson Nobility. The Magnacy were the wealthiest. The *Zamożna*, middle nobility, owned considerable land and possessed serfs. However, about 50 to 60 percent of the nobility were members of the *Drobna Szlachta*, minor or lesser nobility. They did not own serfs and worked the land themselves." Some of the more well-to-do peasants were wealthier than the poorest nobility.

One of the laws passed by the "Four-year Sejm" of 1792 allowed the nobility to work in commerce and business. During the partitions the nobility were substantially restricted, and their rights were eliminated in Prussia.

Peasants *(Chłopy)*

The peasants were always the largest class of people in Poland. Their status ranged from wealthy peasants, who could afford to hire laborers to work on their farms, down to paupers.

The peasants were obligated to work for the lord on whose land they farmed and lived. This obligation was called a *corvée* (in French) or *pan-szczyzna* (in Polish), and was the method of paying the rent for using the lord's land. Originally the peasant was to have worked one day a week on the lord's estate, but the corvée was increased over time and the amount depended on the peasant's status. The wealthier peasants were required to do the most work for their lords, but they could afford to pay others to do it. Since the nobles were representatives of the Sejm, they could create any laws they wished. The nobles increased their control over the peasants by passing a series of statutes in the sixteenth century that reduced the peasants to the same status as property. Serfs could be sold, and they needed their lord's permission to marry, move, and choose a trade. The peasants did not own the land on which they lived and worked.

There was a social order even among the peasants. A *kmieć* (*cemethonis* in Latin) was a farmer who worked enough land to support his family, usually a *łan*, 30 to 35 acres of land. The kmieć owned two or more of each of these animals: cows, horses, oxen, pigs, goats, and sheep.

He also owned several buildings on the farm: a house, barn, and other utility buildings. In some areas the kitchen/dining area was a separate building away from the main house. This arrangement kept the summer cooking heat away from the living quarters. It also was safer—in case of a fire, the only loss would be the kitchen house.

A *półrolnik* or *półkmieć*, literally a "half-kmieć," (*semicemethonis* in Latin) worked a half-size farm, about half a łan. A *zagrodnik* (*hortulanus* in Latin) owned a farmhouse, outbuildings, animals, and a vegetable garden. He worked a much smaller plot of land.

Many peasants held the status of *inquilinus* (Latin) and had no crop land. A *chałupnik* (*domesticus* in Latin) lived in a small cottage. A *komornik* was a tenant farmer or day laborer.

In many nineteenth-century church records the peasants with land were called *agricola* (Latin for farmer).

The Napoleonic Code abolished serfdom in the Grand Duchy of Warsaw (1807 to 1813). Serfdom ended in most of Prussian Poland in 1821 or 1823. The serfs in Austrian Poland were emancipated in 1848 but their farms were so small they were not able to thrive. Czar Alexander II abolished serfdom in all Russian lands in 1861, but delayed abolition in the Congress Kingdom ("Vistula Lands") until 1864, after the 1863 Uprising, and gave the land to the tenants who farmed it. Serfs could also be freed by their owners—or simply run away.

After the peasants gained their freedom in the nineteenth century they became more aware of their Polish national culture. Folk culture also gained popularity in the rural areas.

Peasants were more prosperous in some areas than in others, working more farmland in the German-occupied areas than in the Austrian-occupied lands (Galicia). Topolski, in his *Outline History of Poland*, says 70 percent of the peasants in Great Poland had brick houses in 1900. Only 5 percent of Galician peasants owned brick houses compared to 11 percent in the Western Kingdom of Poland and 1.5 percent in the Eastern Kingdom (Byelorussia and Lithuania).

Many Poles are still living in these old cottages, many of which are 200 years old. Some farmers have re-thatched their roofs, and sod has been used on some country roofs. Kitchen houses are still being used for cooking and serving meals. Horse-drawn carts are frequently seen in the country and even in the larger cities.

Burghers

The burghers were the free citizens of the town in which they lived. Most burghers were foreigners—Germans, Jews, Italians, Dutch, and Scots—who immigrated to Poland and worked as merchants, traders, bankers, and craftsmen—the occupations denied the nobles by law. Fifteen percent of the population in the seventeenth century were burghers.

Spectabilis was the title of the patricians, who were the highest-ranking burghers in the towns. The title *Honestus* was given to a craftsman or small business owner. The status or occupation of a burgher was often given as *civis*, "citizen," in vital records, and sometimes the name of his occupation was also given.

Intelligentsia

The emergence of professionals as a separate class came in the mid-eighteenth century. The intelligentsia came mostly from the gentry and burgher classes, and were physicians, scientists, clergy, scholars, teachers, architects, artists, writers, and lawyers.

Loose People

Three to five percent of the population were the "loose people," who came from all social classes and had no possessions. In vital records their status is listed as *luźny, wagabunda, hultaj, wałęsa* (all in Polish) or *vagantus, rusticus vagus*, and *liacus* (in Latin). Some were thieves, others were prostitutes or runaway serfs. Romanian Gypsies who lived in nomadic camps in Poland-Lithuania after 1501 were also called loose people.

By mid-nineteenth century the social structure of Poland had changed. While the gentry and peasants were still the two main groups of people, the burghers and working classes were growing larger. The workers represented less than 3 percent of the population but grew as industry spread. They put in long hours for low wages.

Remnants of the old feudal system can still be seen in Poland today. In rural areas you can still see the old manor houses and peasants' cottages being used as residences, some having been in the same family for many generations.

POLISH HERALDRY

A clan system began in Poland many centuries ago in which any number of unrelated families could belong to the same clan. Membership in a clan, and into the ranks of the nobility, was by birth, ennoblement by the king (this practice was eliminated in 1573), or adoption into a clan (until the practice was abandoned in 1633). However, the practice of buying titles was not eliminated until modern times.

Clan property marks, called taiga, were simple curved or straight-line designs. These were eventually adopted as devices on many Polish coats of arms when heraldry arrived in Poland. More traditional symbols appeared later: crosses, horseshoes, lances, castles, arrows, annulets, crescents, roses, fleurs-de-lis; and animals such as the eagle, bear, boar, bull, lion, and horse. Red fields were the most common, followed by blue.

Individual Polish families do not usually bear a distinct coat of arms, but each clan has a coat of arms shared by its member families. Each clan and its coat of arms has a name. A Polish coat of arms is called a *herb*.

You are not entitled to use a coat of arms just because your surname is the same as one that bears arms. If you want a coat of arms you can do one of two things: design your own or do genealogical research to prove that you are a direct descendant of a person who was entitled to a coat of arms. If you find that you are not a direct descendant of an arms-bearer, you will have to design your own coat of arms.

Be aware that there is no such thing as a "family crest." A crest is the symbol seen sitting atop the helmet in a coat of arms; the whole thing is called an "armorial achievement." A crest alone was never granted to a family or a person, but an entire coat of arms, along with the crest, was.

If you are interested in heraldry or designing your own coat of arms there are books on heraldry available at your public library.

SOURCES AND ADDITIONAL READING

Benet, Sula. *Song, Dance, and Customs of Peasant Poland*. New York: Roy Publishers, 1951, 1979.

Bystroń, Jan Stanisław. "Chłopi (The Peasants)." Translated by William F. Hoffman. *Polish Genealogical Society Newsletter* XIV (Spring 1991), 1, 7, 8, and 20.

Bystroń, Jan Stanisław. "Chłopi (The Peasants), Part II." Translated by William F. Hoffman. *Polish Genealogical Society Newsletter* XIV (Fall 1991), 32, 33, 36, and 40.

Chorzempa, Rosemary A. *Design Your Own Coat of Arms: An Introduction to Heraldry*. New York: Dover Publications, Inc., 1987.

Niesiecki, Kasper, S. J. *Herbarz Polski* (Polish Heraldry). Lipsk edition: Nakładem i Drukiem Breitkopfa i Haertela, 1842.

Ortell, Gerald A. *Polish Parish Records of the Roman Catholic Church*. Revised edition. Astoria, New York: Gerald A. Ortell, 1983.

Peckwas, Edward A. *Collection of Articles on Polish Heraldry*. Chicago: Polish Genealogical Society, 1978.

Prinke, Rafał T. "Beyond Names and Dates." *Polish Genealogical Society Newsletter* X (Fall 1987), 1 and 24.

Sokolicki, Count Juliusz Nowina. "The Noble Clans." *Polish Genealogical Society Newsletter* XII (Fall 1990), 1, 35, and 36.

Thomas, William I. and Florian Znaniecki. *The Polish Peasant in Europe and America*. 2 vols. New York: Dover Publications, Inc., 1958.

Topolski, Jerzy. *An Outline History of Poland*. Translated by Olgierd Wojtasiewicz. Warsaw, Poland: Interpress Publishers, 1986.

Chapter Five:

OTHER
ETHNIC GROUPS
IN POLAND

GERMANS

While the eastward thrust of Germanic colonization into historic Poland had been going on in previous centuries, the Germanic colonization of northern Poland and the Baltic states began in earnest in 1201 with the landing at Riga of the Teutonic House of the Brothers Hospitallers of St. Mary of Jerusalem (also known as the "Teutonic Order" and "Teutonic Knights"). The Prussians were originally a Slavic pagan tribe inhabiting the northern coast of Poland in the area later known as East Prussia. Professing a desire to convert the pagan tribes of the area, the Teutonic Knights invaded the area, exterminated the Prussians, and assumed their name. The Teutonic Knights then built an empire across northern Poland, Lithuania, and Courland.

The Germanic people also entered the ethnic Polish lands in two waves from the west and south: the Austrian wave, which went northward into lower Silesia, and the Saxon-Brandenburgers. The Brandenburgers pushed their borders eastward into Polish territory and then northward toward Pomerania and southward toward Silesia. These areas were mostly covered by forests and marshes and were sparsely populated.

Eventually the Germans filtered into Great and Little Poland. Some assimilated into the Polish population, although the German settlers on the Polish frontiers often kept their own nationality and their own religion, which after 1517 was usually Evangelical (Lutheran). By 1370 German immigrants formed the patriciate of many Polish towns. Medieval immigration consisted mostly of Saxons and Franconians, and a few Bavarians and Dutchmen.

Saxon immigration to Poland about 1700 was largely military. The Electors of Saxony—Friedrich-August of the House of Wettin, whose Polish name was August II Mocny ("the Strong"), and his son (Frederick) August III—were elected Kings of Poland-Lithuania from 1697 to 1763. Napoleon's

Grand Duchy of Warsaw (1807–13) was nominally under the rule of August III's grandson, Frederick Augustus III, King of Saxony.

After the First Partition, 200,000 Germans immigrated to the still-free areas of Poland, but those might have been mostly Poles who left the Prussian-controlled territories where they once lived. The Hohenzollerns, initiators of the partitions, brought German-Lutheran settlers into Prussian-occupied areas, forcing Polish farmers off their lands. These German immigrants came from all areas of Germany, but most were from Prussia or Saxony, or were Franconians from the Palatinate and Swabians from Württemberg.

Immigrants of all nationalities were called *colonus* (in Latin) and *kolonista* (in Polish). These terms can be found in vital records to describe a person or his occupation or status. Colonus can also mean a peasant or tenant farmer, or one who does not own the land that he farms.

The surnames of many Poles reflect German origins. My husband's grandmother's name was Szulc, the Polonized version of Schultz. Some other German names and their Polonized counterparts: Hoffman became Ofmanski, Baltzer became Balcerzak, Steinberg became Sztynberg, and Schneider became Sznajder. Surnames such as Niemiec, which means "German" in the Polish language, clearly show the ancestor's origin.

JEWS

Genealogy was just as important to ancient Jews as it is today to Mormons, but for a different reason. In ancient Hebrew society a person's ancestry dictated his or her social standing.

The two main groups of Jewish people are the Sephardim (Spanish-Portuguese Jews) and Ashkenazim (German-Polish Jews). The Sephardim emigrated from Palestine to North Africa, then to Spain and Portugal, and eventually to northern and eastern Europe, especially to Holland and England. The Ashkenazim emigrated from Babylonia to Mesopotamia to southern Russia, and then on to Germany, Poland, and the rest of Europe. Jews living in North Africa and the Middle East are called Oriental Jews.

The Ashkenazim began to settle in Poland at the time of the Crusades to escape persecution in German lands. The Sephardim began to settle in Poland-Lithuania around 1492, when they were expelled from Spain.

By the mid-eighteenth century, there were 750,000 Jews in Poland. Brandenburg-Prussia and Austria were deporting poor Jews (*betteljuden*) who were finding refuge in Poland. Jews from the Russian Ukraine also were fleeing to Poland. By the time of the partitions, 10 percent of the Polish population was Jewish. Poland contained the world's largest Jewish community until World War II and the Nazi Holocaust.

Many laws were enacted by the Polish kings and Sejms to protect the liberties of the Jews, beginning in 1264 with the General Charter of Jewish Liberties. The Jews were not compelled to defend Poland or speak Polish, and were allowed to keep their Judaeo-Germanic culture. Monetary penalties were levied on towns (which were run and populated mostly by Germans and other foreigners) in which anti-Jewish activities were allowed, and anti-Semitic literature was banned.

Most bankers and merchants were Jewish or other foreign nationals, as it was socially unacceptable for a Polish nobleman to engage in these occupations. Jews were eventually accepted into the Polish nobility, beginning in 1509 with Abraham Ezofowicz. Thus Poland became a Jewish sanctuary—and an autonomous Jewish nation based on Talmudic Law existed—until the Third Partition in 1795, when Polish laws ceased to exist.

After the partitions Polish Jews were persecuted by the governments of the partitioning powers, especially Russia. Russian laws of 1795 and 1835 limited Jewish people to the newly acquired areas of the former Polish commonwealth, which became known as the "Pale of Settlement" and encompassed the following districts: Vitebsk, Mogilev, Chernigov, Poltava, Ekaterinoslav, Taurida, Kherson, Kiev, Minsk, Podolia, Bessarabia, Volhynia, Vilna, Kovno, Suwałki, Grodno, Płock, Lublin, Siedlce, Łomża, Warszawa, Kalisz, Piotrków, and Kielce. The last ten districts are in modern Poland.

In 1880 the emigration of more than 2 million Jews began from the Pale to the United States, Britain, Europe, South America, and Palestine. By 1885 there were 4 million Jews living in the Pale, and more continually being forced into the Pale to live in *shtetls*.

CARAÏTES

A small number of Caraïtes, a Jewish sect that does not acknowledge the Talmud, still remained in Poland, even in the 1920s. The Caraïtes settled in the Crimea where they were subdued by the Tatars, and adopted the Tatar language. The Grand Duke of Lithuania called the Caraïtes and Tatars to Lithuania at the end of the fourteenth century, where they settled near Wilno, in Volhynia, and in Halicz (Galicia). The Caraïtes had their own prayer houses, did not marry other Jews, and taught their children the Hebrew language and their mother tongue, the Tatar.

SCOTS

Scottish immigration to Poland began at the end of the fourteenth century. The peak influx occurred from 1580 to 1610, due to crop failure and famine in Scotland in the 1570s and 1590s. Religious and political unrest also sent many Scots packing; both Catholic and Calvinist Scots emigrated. Most came from northeastern and eastern Scotland.

Poland always had a need for merchants, and the Scots helped to fill that void. Most Scottish immigrants were merchants, peddlers, traders, or craftsmen such as weavers, tailors, shoemakers, cutlers, smiths, and harnassmakers. Scottish foot soldiers were also a valuable asset to the Polish army.

Most Scots entered Poland through the Baltic ports of Gdańsk and Kaliningrad and moved southward, eventually reaching Kraków, Lwów, and Krosno. They preferred to settle in private or royal towns, and on country estates of the nobility.

Scots were assimilated into Polish society in two or three generations. Their names were Polonized, but the Scots often used their ancestral language in spoken and written forms. Records in Scotland occasionally state that the person emigrated to Poland, so eventually checking into Scottish records may be a possibility if your ancestors were Scottish.

It is difficult to estimate the number of Scottish immigrants to Poland. Some sources report between 15,000 and 40,000 Scots, or even 30,000 families. A contemporary source in 1620 suggests that there were 30,000 Scots in Poland by that time.

Many place names in Poland bear witness to the Scottish immigrants: Nowa Skocja, Skotniki, and Szkotowo, just to name a few.

DUTCH

Dutch people migrated to Poland in the early Middle Ages. Until the Dutch declared their independence of the Holy Roman Empire in 1579, they were probably called Germans or Frisians. Descendants of Franks, the Dutch and Flemish (Belgians) who settled along the Elbe River in the twelfth century, made up most of the "German" settlers in Silesia in the thirteenth and fourteenth centuries, and then proceeded to Great Poland, Little Poland, and the Śpiż (Spisz lands, in the Carpathian Mountains). A Frisian settlement established at Wilhamowice near Oświęcim in 1242 has preserved its own unique dialect and dress up to the present.

The sixteenth century saw many religious reforms in Europe, causing some people to leave their homelands and seek refuge in a more tolerant location. So it was that many Dutch, some of whom were Mennonites and Lutherans, came to Poland.

These Dutch first came to East Prussia and settled near Pasłek about 1526. It was the beginning of a mass immigration of *olęderski*, (Hollanders), from the Netherlands and northern Germany. Colonization spread southward and then westward into Great Poland.

After 1655 new Dutch immigrants almost always settled in western Poland. They preferred to live in areas near rivers, lakes, and swamps, and found an abundance of wetlands in Great Poland, especially in the Wolsztyn area.

Germans from northern Germany near the Dutch border began to replace the true Dutch people as "Dutch immigrants." By 1800 about 28,000 Hollanders were living in Great Poland.

A Dutch settler received about a half to one łan of land, with a contract to lease the land from the landowner for a period of thirty to sixty years. The settler did not have to pay the lease for the first seven years.

The Dutch brought their high-technology skills with them: cattle-breeding, reclamation of marshland, changing the course of waterways, and building canals and windmills.

While driving near Kościan, an area of marshes only twenty-five miles east of Wolsztyn, we saw many old wooden windmills in the fields. One of these was close to the highway and had a sign on it that read, "Wojciech r. 1805," meaning "Adalbert the year 1805" in English. Evidently each windmill was given a name and dated with the year of construction.

Hollanders often formed a complete village in a settlement. These Hollanders resisted military service, but they were hard-working, free peasants who became the wealthiest inhabitants of their settlements.

They were described as *olęder, olędry, olendrzy, Hollander,* and *Haullander* in parish records, and sometimes were also called *colonus*. Dutch immigrants of the eighteenth century were easily assimilated. Originally bearing non-Polish first names, they soon adopted Polish names and became Catholics. Their surnames were often altered to the point that it became difficult to determine the original spelling.

IRISH

There were many other nationalities present in Poland but not in as large numbers as the previously mentioned ethnic groups. Some Irish, such as the

Irland family, immigrated to Poland as early as the twelfth century. There is evidence of Irish names in Livonia and Podlasie in the fourteenth century. However, these Irish were members of the king's court and nobility, which makes it easier to locate them in records. Their surnames were also changed: O'Dolan became Odolanowski, O'Kelly became Okelli, and O'Connor became Okonnor.

ARMENIANS

Armenians first began to arrive in Poland, especially Ruthenia, during the eleventh century. Later, in the sixteenth and early seventeenth centuries, a small group of Armenians—peddlers, tradesmen, craftsmen, and translators of oriental languages—settled in the southeastern regions of the Commonwealth. They belonged to the Armenian Rite of the Greek Catholic Church, and had their own cathedral at Lwów. There were 100,000 Armenians in Poland-Lithuania in 1791, and soon after that they adopted Polish costume, language, customs, and even Polonized their names. Their descendants became landowners in Halicz, Bukovina, and Bessarabia, and had large communities in Lwów and Kuty in Halicz, and Suczawa in Bukovina.

RUSSIANS

A small number of Russians, also known as Great Russians, settled in the Russian-occupied territories of Poland, Lithuania, and Ruthenia. Most were soldiers and civil administrators sent to Polish lands during the time of the partitions. Some Russian tradesmen immigrated to Poland, as did colonists sent by the Russian government to farm land purchased by the government; the Russian government also rewarded some Russians with large estates confiscated from Poles after the uprisings of 1830 and 1863.

A number of "Old Believers" (*Burłak*, "barge haulers"), persecuted in Muscovy, settled in Lithuania and Byelorussia in the seventeenth century. However, most of the Russians inhabiting Polish lands were Orthodox.

BOHEMIANS

The Bohemian princess Dubrava (Dąbrówka in Polish) married Mieszko I about the year 966 A. D., making her the first historic queen of Poland. St.

Adalbert of Prague was her cousin. Wacław II and his son Wacław III ruled Poland from at least 1296 to 1306.

Members of the Bohemian Brotherhood (later reconstituted as the Moravian Church) were deported from Bohemia (now in Czechoslovakia) after riots in Prague. A large number fled to Poland around 1550 and settled in Great Poland.

TATARS

After 1400 Tatars from the Crimea flocked to Lithuania as immigrants, prisoners of war, or political refugees. There were about 100,000 Tatars in Lithuania in the seventeenth century, but their numbers have since been greatly reduced. Many of these Tatars received lands from the royal estates and founded the noble Tatar houses of Lithuania. Tatars soon intermarried with Christians and adopted the language of their new country, even though they still followed the teachings of the Koran.

TZIGANES

Gypsies (Cyganie in Polish, Tziganes in English) migrated to Polish lands in the fifteenth century from Romania, Transylvania, Bukovina, and Germany, and to Lithuania and Ruthenia in the sixteenth century. During the eighteenth century fixed residences were assigned to the Tziganes in certain villages in Lithuania, Byelorussia, and southeastern Halicz (Galicia) to subdue their nomadic tendencies, but this practice was not very successful. Tziganes did not mix with the local populations as they had done in other countries. Their occupations were suitable to their nomadic lifestyle: fortune-tellers, musicians, watermen, shoesmiths, horse dealers, beggars, and sometimes thieves.

ENGLISH

The English King Canute the Great was Mieszko's grandson; dynastic connections continued throughout English history. Fifty-five English merchants settled in Gdańsk in 1422. Captain John Smith travelled through

Turkey, Russia, and Poland before he came to America to establish the Jamestown colony; he brought several Polish craftsmen to Jamestown.

ITALIANS

Some 350 Italians accompanied Queen Bona Sforza, the Italian wife of the Polish King Sigismund the Old, to Poland in 1518. Most were connected with the royal court in some way, from servants to dignitaries, intellectuals, and skilled craftsmen. The Socinians brought Unitarianism to Poland in the sixteenth century.

SOURCES AND ADDITIONAL READING

Baxter, Angus. *In Search of Your German Roots*. United Germany edition. Baltimore: Genealogical Publishing Co., 1991.

Bieganski, Anna. "A Note on the Scots in Poland, 1550–1800." *Polish Genealogical Society Newsletter* XIII (Spring 1990), 1, 4, and 16.

Bolesta-Kozlowski, Robert A. "Of John O'Rourke & Several Other Polish Nobles." *Polish Genealogical Society Newsletter* XI (Spring 1988), 3–4.

Dobson, David. "Scottish Emigration to Poland: 1550–1650." *Polish Genealogical Society Newsletter* II (January 1980), 1 and 14.

Dubnow, S. M. *History of the Jews in Russia and Poland*. 3 vols. Philadelphia: Jewish Publication Society, 1916–1920.

Pentek, Zdzisław. "The Relationships of the So-called 'Dutch Populace' in Greater Poland . . . ." *Polish Genealogical Society Bulletin*. No. 19. (Summer 1991).

Pogonowski, Iwo Cyprian. *Poland, A Historical Atlas*. New York: Hippocrene Books, 1987.

Polish Encyclopaedia. Vol. II: Territory and Population of Poland. Geneva, Switzerland: Atar, Ltd., 1924. Reprint edition by Arno Press, Inc., 1972.

"Prussian Poland." *Polish Genealogical Society Newsletter* V (Spring 1983), 10–11.

Rottenberg, Dan. *Finding Our Fathers*. Baltimore: Genealogical Publishing Co., 1986 (reprint).

Stewart, Archibald. "Papers Relating to the Scots in Poland 1576–1793." Vol. XXXIX. Scottish Historical Society, 1915.

Thernstrom, Stephan, ed. *Harvard Encyclopedia of American Ethnic Groups*. Cambridge, Massachusetts: Belknap Press, 1980.

Tomaszewski, Wiktor. "The Scotch in Poland." Edinburgh: Edinburgh University, 1968.

Zarchin, M. M. *Jews in the Province of Posen, 18th–19th Centuries.* Philadelphia: Dropsie University Press, 1939.

Zborowski, Mark and Elizabeth Herzog. *Life is with People.* New York: Schocken Books, 1952. Customs and life in nineteenth-century Russian shtetls.

Inflanty

GULF OF
RIGA

Livo

Gauja

Riga

Venta

Lielude

Courland

Semigali

BALTIC

SEA

Samogitia

Niemen

Lithuania

Wilia

Vilniu

Gdańsk

Pregoła

Kaliningrad

Western
Pomerania

Koszalin

Pomerania

Kashubia

Warmia

Lidzbark

Mazuria

Suwałki

Kurpie

Szczecin

Odra

Wisła

Olsztyn

Grodno

Brandenburg

Noteć

Duchy of Prussia

Great

Kuyavia

Narew

Białystok

Warta

Poznań

Gniezno

Ostrołęka

Poland

Płock

Lusatia

Nysa

Warszawa

Bug

Podlasie

Mazovia

Polesie

Silesia

Pilica

Wisła

Wrocław

Odra

Warta

ŚWIĘTOKRZYSKIE
MOUNTAINS

Wieprz

Chełm

Styr

SUDETEN
MOUNTAINS

Sandomierz

Bełz

Little

San

Volhyn

Bohemia

Kraków

Wisła

Podhale

Poland

Wisłok

Moravia

Nowy Targ

Lvov

Halich Ruthen

BIESZCZADY
MOUNTAINS

BESKID MOUNTAINS

Dniester

CARPATHIAN MOUNTAINS

Transylvania

Choci

TATRAS MOUNTAINS

Bukovi

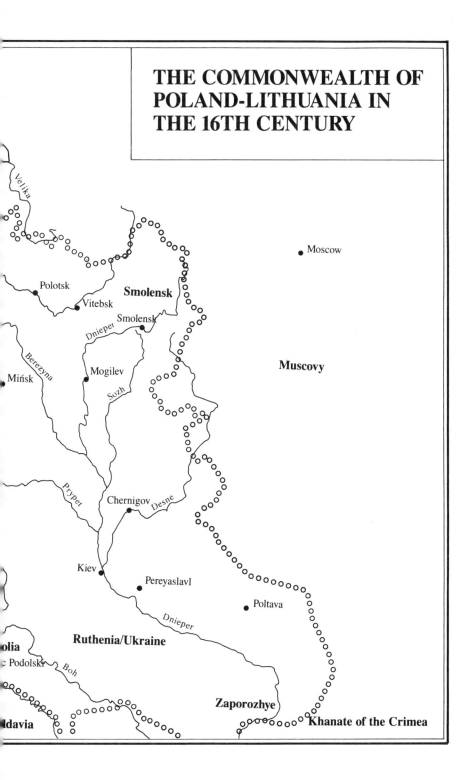

THE COMMONWEALTH OF POLAND-LITHUANIA IN THE 16TH CENTURY

Velika

Polotsk

Vitebsk

Smolensk

Smolensk

Dnieper

• Moscow

Muscovy

Berezyna

Mińsk

Mogilev

Sozh

Prypet

Chernigov

Desne

Kiev

Pereyaslavl

• Poltava

Dnieper

Ruthenia/Ukraine

olia

Podolsk

Boh

Zaporozhye

ldavia

Khanate of the Crimea

Chapter Six:

GEOGRAPHIC AND ETHNIC AREAS OF POLAND

GREAT POLAND (*WIELKOPOLSKA*)

The Warta River basin, the area from the Noteć River south to the Barycz River, is the area known as Great Poland. This was the home of the *Polanie*, an ancient Slavic tribe that lived in the heart of Poland. Great Poland is a vast plain, dotted with about 2500 small lakes.

Great Poland contains the oldest towns in Poland. Gniezno was an ancient castle town built in the eighth century, and the ancestral seat of the Polish people. (See the legend of Lech, Czech, and Rus on page 53.) It was also the first Polish capital. Poznań, the first diocesan see (968 A. D.) and the next capital, was founded before 900 A. D. Poland's first two Christian kings are buried in its cathedral.

This area was heavily influenced by Germanic culture brought by German colonizers. Great Poland was and is heavily populated, and led the country in industrialization.

In 1656 and again from 1700 to 1703, Great Poland was devastated by the Swedish invasions. At the First Partition in 1772, Prussia claimed Gdańsk and Chełmno, and both sides of the Noteć River including western Kuyavia. At the Second Partition in 1793, most of the rest of Great Poland and the cities of Toruń and Płock were taken by the Prussians.

The Grand Duchy of Warsaw, a French protectorate under Napoleon Bonaparte, was formed in 1807 and included the "departments" of Poznań, Bydgoszcz, Kalisz, Warszawa, Płock, and Łomża; in 1809 the "departments" of Kraków, Radom, Siedlce, and Lublin were added. In 1815 the Congress of Vienna gave control of most of the area to Russia, which renamed it the Congress Kingdom of Poland. Poznania, the area surrounding Poznań, and Toruń and Chełmno were returned to Prussia.

LITTLE POLAND (*MAŁOPOLSKA*)

Little Poland was the home of the Vistulans, another Slavic tribe, who lived along the upper Vistula River (Wisła) basin near Kraków. Little Poland also included the areas of the San and Wisłoka rivers.

Kraków was founded as a fortress about 700 A. D. It was the crossroads of two ancient trade routes: one from the Black Sea through Silesia to western Europe, and the second from southern Europe to the Baltic Sea. Kraków was the Polish capital (its third) from the twelfth century to 1596, when the capital was moved to its current location, Warsaw. Kraków has always been a center of Polish culture.

Mongol Tatar invaders, called Tartars by Europeans, came from Asia, pillaged Little Poland in the thirteenth and fourteenth centuries, and reached Kraków in 1241. Rzeszów and the surrounding area was devastated by successive Tatar invasions from 1502 to 1624. The Tatars took many slaves during their frequent invasions. Tatar characteristics can still be seen in some people from Little Poland and Ruthenia. The area was also invaded by Hungarians, Swedes, Saxons, and Russians.

The Świętokrzyskie (Holy Cross) Mountains area, near Kielce, was the major iron-smelting center in Europe for eleven centuries. Iron mines and stone quarries are found in Little Poland. Copper is mined around Kielce, and the Kraków-Wieluń area is mined for silver. The salt mines at Wieliczka have been operating since the eleventh century and are the oldest in Europe.

The Krosno area has been the center of the Polish petroleum industry since the mid-nineteenth century; it is the location of the first oil refinery in Europe. The area from Łańcut to Leżajsk is known for its folk pottery and weaving.

Most of the population was engaged in agriculture, with rye and wheat being major crops. Little Poland was the most economically underdeveloped area of the country and produced the greatest number of emigrants.

At the Third Partition of Poland in 1795, Austria took almost all of Little Poland including Kraków and renamed the area Galicia. Galicia is not a Polish name—the Poles always called the area Little Poland. Galicia is actually the Latinized version of the Polish *Halicz*. This renaming was just one way the Austrian government tried to subjugate the Poles.

Most inhabitants of the area west of the San River were Poles—this area was called West Galicia. Most inhabitants living east of the San River were Ukrainians—this was called East Galicia. The western section of Little Poland is now in present-day Poland.

MAZOVIA *(MAZOWSZE)*

Mazovia lies in the center of modern Poland. The heart of Mazovia is situated in the great central plain between the Warta and Vistula rivers. The land was originally inhabited by two Western Slavic tribes—the Kuyavians and the Mazovians, who occupied the land between the Bug and Vistula rivers.

The soil is mostly sandy and unproductive. Rye and wheat are the basic crops, with some corn. Red brick homes and buildings with red tile roofs are characteristic of the region.

Płock on the Vistula River is one of Poland's earliest towns, built around 900 A. D. The area of Łódź, Tomaszów, and Żyrardów has been known for its textile production since the fifteenth century. Łowicz is well known for *wycinanki* (paper cutouts) and wide-striped wool fabrics. Prince Konrad of Mazovia invited the Teutonic Knights to Poland in the thirteenth century. Remnants of their presence in the area can still be seen today in the castles, towns, culture, and the descendants of German colonists.

Beginning in 1420, and especially during the period 1540 to 1580, the Mazovians migrated to the forests of western Lithuania, especially to Podlasie. Some settled in the Duchy of Prussia (Mazury, the Mazurian Lakes district), which was located to the north of Mazovia.

The Duchy of Mazovia was incorporated into Poland in 1529. The main city has been Warszawa (Warsaw), the capital of Poland since 1596.

In the Second Partition in 1793 the western part of Mazovia was taken by Prussia, which also obtained the rest of Mazovia, Mazuria, Kurpie, and the city of Warsaw three years later.

The grand Duchy of Warsaw, encompassing Mazovia, Great Poland, Kuyavia, and western Ruthenia, was a French protectorate from 1807 until 1815. In 1815 much of this area became known as the Congress Kingdom of Poland under Russian rule.

Mazuria, Kurpie, and Warmia are areas within Mazovia.

MAZURIA

Mazuria was once populated by the Sudovians, a Balto-Slavic tribe exterminated by the Teutonic Knights. It was an area of ancient forests, some of which still exist. Mazuria is called the "Land of a Thousand Lakes," but there are in fact 3,000 in the area. Many rivers and canals are also found here.

Suwałki and Augustów, noted for their timber industry, are two large cities. Wheat and rye are the main crops. See more about the Suwałki region under "Lithuania."

KURPIE

Kurpie is another area of great virgin forests and is located in the region of the Narew River, where conditions are swampy and the soil is sandy. Farming, beekeeping, hunting, fishing, woodcarving, amber-crafting, and other folk arts are sources of income. Crops are rye, potatoes, cabbage, and other vegetables; pigs, horses, and cattle are raised.

The Catholic Church did not become established in Kurpie until the seventeenth century because of the influence of the East Prussian protestant pastors and the still-flourishing pagan cults.

People from all parts of Poland came to Kurpie, where they enjoyed almost complete freedom. The Kurpie people were hard-working and courageous, and enjoyed the freedom to hunt and develop apiculture. Poland is the world leader of apiarian (beekeeping) science.   *REALLY !*

There are two regions in Kurpie: Ostrołęka and Nowogrodzka. Towns in the area include Ostrołęka, Nowogród, Myszyniec, Chorzele, Kadzidło, and Łomża.

WARMIA (ERMLAND IN GERMAN)

The province of Warmia, along with northern Mazovia and Mazuria, was under Prussian rule until the final defeat of the Teutonic Knights in 1466. Warmia was almost completely surrounded by the Duchy of Prussia and was annexed again by the German-Prussians at the First Partition. Olsztyn and Lidzbark are major cities.

KUYAVIA (KUJAWY)

The Kuyavian tribe inhabited the area around the Noteć River southeastward toward Płock by the ninth century. The Teutonic Knights built a castle in 1231 at Toruń, which has become the cultural center of northern Poland. Bydgoszcz is known for its beer, minting, and handicrafts, especially basketry.

SILESIA (*SLĄSK* IN POLISH, *SCHLESIEN* IN GERMAN, *SLESZKO* IN CZECH)

A fortified Slavic settlement was built on Mount Ślęża twenty-five hundred years ago. This was the home of the Ślężanie tribe and the origin of the name Silesia.

Polish Slavs inhabited Silesia from the fifth century, and several other Slavic tribes—Bobrans, *Opolanie*, and Lusatians, as well as the Ślężanie (Silesians)—occupied the area before the tenth century. Silesia was settled by a mixture of these Polish and German people, along with some Czechs, during the Middle Ages.

The Sudeten Mountain range occupies the southern area of Silesia. Coniferous forests cover parts of the Sudeten foothills in Lower Silesia.

Wrocław on the Odra River was a major settlement before the tenth century and was made a bishopric in 1000 A. D. Silesia was a part of the Kingdom of Poland from the tenth century until the Polish King Casimir the Great recognized Bohemian control of Silesia in 1339. The area was ravaged by the Tatars in the thirteenth century.

The Austrian Holy Roman Empire took over Bohemia in 1526, along with Silesia and half of Hungary. The German Prussians took Silesia from Austria in 1740. Poland regained southeastern or Upper Silesia by plebiscite in 1920 to 1922, and the rest in 1945, when significant numbers of people from the lands Poland lost to the Soviet Union (particularly around Wilno) moved into northwestern or Lower Silesia.

Historically, Silesia also included northern Moravia (now in Czechoslovakia) and the German Cottbus and Dresden districts. The provinces of Katowice, Opole, Wałbrzych, Wrocław, Jelenia Góra, Legnica, and the southern part of Zielona Góra now make up Polish Silesia.

Silesia is considered the most Germanized area of Poland, but Polish Silesians retain their Polish culture, an example being the world-famous Śląsk dance troupe. Poles make up the majority of the population in the southeastern half of Silesia.

Silesia is not only the most heavily populated area of Poland, but also historically its most industrialized area. Silesia was well known as a woolen and linen textile-producing area by the sixteenth century. Textiles and coal mining were the area's leading industries in the nineteenth century. Ironworks are located north and east of Wrocław. Gold is mined in Lower Silesia. Coal, iron, lead, and zinc are mined in the Bytom, Katowice, and Starczynów areas. The world's largest lead-crystal ware works are located in Stronie. Corn is the major agricultural crop.

Many springs in Silesia have been known since medieval times for their healing properties. Numerous spas and health resorts extol the virtues of sulphur springs, iron, arsenic, radioactive gases, and other compounds, which are reputed to have therapeutic powers that alleviate rheumatism; skin disorders; anemia; gynecological diseases; and respiratory, circulatory, gastric, thyroid, and kidney disorders.

POMERANIA (*POMORZE*)

Pomorze means the land "along the sea." It was the home of the Western Slavic tribe known as the Pomeranians, who inhabited the coastal area near the Baltic Sea from the Odra to the Vistula rivers.

Southern Pomerania is an area of 4,000 small lakes and forested hills. Tuchola Forest (Bory Tucholskie) is a virgin forest. Northern Pomerania consists of sandy beaches, marshes, and peat bogs.

The soil is poor, though some farming takes place—rye and wheat crops are grown near Gdańsk, for example. Stockbreeding, mostly cows, is also an important economic activity. Many old Slavic fishing settlements are on the Baltic coast. Cottages are made of brick or timber.

Wolin is one of the oldest Slavic settlements and was frequently invaded by the Danes. Gdańsk was Poland's principal Baltic port from the sixteenth to the eighteenth centuries. Other large towns along the coast are Szczecin, Kołobrzeg, and Koszalin.

An old amber mine is located west of Gdańsk. Amber, which is used in jewelry, is a resin once exuded from ancient coniferous trees that has hardened into a yellow to yellowish-brown transparent lump. Amber has been mined since antiquity in this area, which is the largest source of amber in the world.

By the Treaty of Toruń in 1466, Eastern Pomerania (called Gdańsk-Pomerania by the Poles) was reunited with the rest of Poland after being lost to the Teutonic Knights in 1308, once again giving Poland access to the Baltic Sea. The new name given to this unified region was Royal Prussia.

Prussia annexed the area during the partitions and named it West Prussia. After World War I Eastern Pomerania, with the exception of Gdańsk (Danzig in German), was returned to Poland. Gdańsk was established as a free city in 1919, maintaining this status until the Nazi occupation in World War II.

KASHUBIA (*KASZUBY*)

The Kashubs, or Cassoubs (Kaszuby in Polish), are the descendants of Slavic Pomeranians who once lived in this area just west of Gdańsk, where the main town is Kartuzy.

The Kashubs speak a Slavic dialect similar to that of the extinct Polabians. The Kashubian dialect is the oldest of all Polish dialects, but is not as developed as the Polish language itself. Poles from other areas find it difficult to understand Kashubian.

Many small lakes dot the landscape in Kashubia, but the soil is not very fertile. However, some rye and wheat are grown, and farmers share hay crops. Most Kashubs work in the fishing trade; everyone in the village—man, widow, family, and priest—shares the profits.

WESTERN POMERANIA

The Polabians were ancient pagan Slavs who lived on the Elbe River. The Germans eventually converted them to Christianity but also destroyed their Polabian state and obliterated their Slavic identity.

The area was conquered by the Poles in 972 and held until 1025. The Danes invaded the area in the twelfth century, although most of Western Pomerania was under Swedish or Prussian rule.

Most of the area still lies in Mecklenburg district in eastern Germany, even though part of the area was returned to Poland after World War II. Szczecin is Poland's second largest city and the largest port.

PODHALE

The Carpathian Mountains form the southern border of modern Poland. The Carpathian range includes the Beskids (only the western portion is currently in Poland), a small part of the Bieszczady Mountains, and the Tatras. Podhale includes this high mountainous region as well as the fertile but small-in-area sub-Carpathian foothills, where agriculture is possible. Podhale ("pohd-hah'-leh") literally means "under the meadow."

Górale, the Polish mountaineers, live here. The górale were not a part of any state, but were independent and had little contact with the outside world.

Decorated with ornamental carving and much painting, their mountain homes are larger and have more amenities than peasant homes found in other regions.

Few crops are cultivated up in the highlands because of the poor soil, although some oats, barley, and potatoes are grown there.

Some mountain slopes are grassy, but most are covered by abundant fir and spruce forests. Grassy meadows (*hale*) are found high up in the mountains. These grassy areas provide pasture land for raising cattle and sheep, which is the major occupation of the area. The górale are also hunters and woodcutters. Lumber is a large industry, and mountain pottery is notable.

The capital is Nowy Targ, and Zakopane is a tourist center with health and winter sports resorts.

Podhale was a part of the Polish state for many centuries before parts of it were occupied by Austria in 1769–70; the rest of Podhale was annexed by Austria at the time of the First Partition.

LUSATIA (*ŁUŻYCE* IN POLISH, *LAUSITZ* IN GERMAN)

This land between the Elbe and Bobr rivers, between Meissen and Berlin, was the home of the Lusatian tribe. Lusatia (Łużyce) and Milzenland (Milsko), the southern portion of Lusatia, were held by Poland only in the eleventh century.

PODLASIE

Podlasie is the land "by the forest," and refers to the virgin Białowieża forest, remnants of which still exist. The Podlasie lowland is part of the vast central plain of Poland. Many rivers, including the Bug and the Narew, canals, and swamps cut through Podlasie.

The area was best known for its export of hides and furs, but an iron-smelting center near Węgrów is now a major industry. Białystok is one of the larger towns and the provincial capital.

In 1569 Podlasie was incorporated into the Kingdom of Poland. Many Mazovians from the region to the north migrated to Podlasie during the sixteenth century. The eastern part of Podlasie is now in the republic of Byelorussia.

PRUSSIA (*PRUSY* IN POLISH)

Two ancient Balto-Slavic tribes, the Sambians and the Prussians, who were related to the ethnic Lithuanians, lived in the Baltic coastal region called Prussia. The name was taken from the ancient Prussian tribe that lived in the Pregel (Pregoła in Polish) River basin and the surrounding area. These tribal people discovered amber in this area, and it has been mined ever since.

A major town is Królewiec (Polish), which was renamed Koenigsberg in German and Kaliningrad in Russian. St. Adalbert was martyred at Kaliningrad by the pagan Prussians in 997 A. D. while attempting to convert them to Christianity.

The Teutonic Knights exterminated the pagan Prussians in the name of Christianity during the thirteenth century. The Knights brought in German and Dutch settlers and assumed the name of the original pagan Slavs—the Prussians. Germans have been known as Prussians ever since.

With the final defeat of the Teutonic Knights by the Poles and Lithuanians, the Treaty of Toruń in 1466 decreed that Warmia be returned to Poland and the Duchy of Prussia become a Polish vassal state. GRIND THAT AXE LADY

In a 1657 treaty the Poles reluctantly gave the Duchy of Prussia to the Brandenburg government, but Warmia remained under Polish control. During the First Partition in 1772 the German-Prussian government took all of the old Prussian lands including Warmia.

Prussia, or Borussia (the Latin version), may be seen on a document as a place of origin. Both have the same meaning—that the person came from a place under Prussian (German) rule. It may have been any region under German domination during the time of partitioned Poland: Poznania, East Prussia, West Prussia, Pomerania, Warmia, or Silesia.

LIVONIA

The Gauja River and Baltic coast area (modern Latvia) was the home of the Livs (a Baltic tribe) and the Letts. This area was a low plain with many swamps, streams, and lakes, and some hills and forests.

The Teutonic Knights landed at Riga in 1201 and dominated the region for centuries, leaving behind a strong German influence on the language, law, and religion of the local population. The Danes invaded Livonia in the early thirteenth century, but the Danish king sold the territory to the Teutonic Knights in the mid-fourteenth century.

In 1561 northern Livonia was directly incorporated into the Polish Commonwealth and called Inflanty Polskie. Southern Livonia became the Duchy of Courland (an independent duchy under Polish rule) and Semigalia.

The Swedes conquered Livonia north of the West Dvina River in 1629, and then the Russian Empire took control of the area in 1721. Russia gave freedom to the serfs in Livonia in 1816 to 1819, but the serfs did not receive the right to own land.

Riga, on the Dvina River near the Gulf of Riga, and Tallinn, on the Gulf of Finland, are two principal cities.

COURLAND (*KURLANDIA* IN POLISH)

By the ninth century two tribes, the Kurs and Letts, occupied the area of the Venta and Lielude rivers and the mouth of the Dvina River. The area is a low-lying plain with many lakes, streams, marshes, and bogs.

Courland was part of Livonia from 1237 until 1561, when it became an independent duchy of Poland. The area was heavily influenced by the German language, law, and religion brought by the Teutonic Knights.

Courland was annexed by the Russian Empire at the Third Partition in 1795. The serfs in Courland were given their freedom in 1817, earlier than in the other regions of the Russian Empire.

LITHUANIA (*LITWA* IN POLISH, *LIETUVA* IN LITHUANIAN)

Pagan Lithuanians, a Baltic people, lived in the Niemen River basin. The area is a low-lying plain with numerous small lakes and rivers, but was originally a heavily wooded virgin forest area. Flax, hemp, and timber were exported.

The land northwest of Byelorussia, between Prussia and Kurlandia/ Inflanty, was called Samogitia (Żmudź in Polish). This was the cradle of the Lithuanian people, known as "ethnic Lithuania." So-called "historic Lithuania" eventually spread eastward and southward in the fourteenth century to the Dnepr (Dniepr in Polish) River, almost to the Black Sea.

During the thirteenth century the Teutonic Knights conquered the tribes living on the Baltic coast. The German nobility and merchants brought Western civilization and German law, language, and Christianity (later Lutheranism) to the Baltic states. The Knights returned Samogitia to Lithuania in 1411, but the German influence and settlers remained.

At the same time, the Poles forced the Lithuanians from Mazuria and Podlasie and advanced as far as Byelorussia. In southern historic Lithuania the Polish influence was not as great as in the northern region. Peasants in all parts of Lithuania continued to use the Lithuanian language.

The Teutonic Knights attempted to conquer all of Lithuania with the pretense of Christianizing the pagan Lithuanians and Byelorussians. Because of this, Poland and Lithuania formed a union that lasted until the partitions. In 1385 thirty-five-year-old Ladislaus Jogaila (Władysław Jagiełło in Polish), Grand Duke of Lithuania, married the eleven-year-old Polish queen Hedwig (who died in childbirth in 1399). Jogaila and Lithuania adopted Christianity, thwarting the Teutonic Knights' aggression and forming a strong alliance as a monarchical republic. Poland and Lithuania were formally united in 1569 as the *Rzeczpospolita*, the Commonwealth of Poland-Lithuania, or the First Polish Republic.

The Polonized Lithuanians made up the majority of the lesser nobility, but the wealthier Lithuanian nobility were even more Polonized. The nobility of the Kingdom of Poland welcomed the Lithuanian nobility into their clans, and some Jews also entered the ranks of the lesser nobility of Lithuania.

During the first two partitions, the Russian Empire annexed most of historic Lithuania. The Third Partition brought ethnic Lithuania—Samogitia—to Russia, except for Suwałki. Most of the inhabitants of northern Suwałki spoke Lithuanian, while the inhabitants of the southern part spoke Polish. Western Lithuania (the Suwałki region) from the Niemen to the Bug rivers was annexed by the Kingdom of Prussia in the Third Partition in 1795. Suwałki became a part of the Duchy of Warsaw, and in 1815 was acquired by Russia, originally as part of the Congress Kingdom of Poland. Russia secured the largest part—73 percent—of the Polish-Lithuanian Commonwealth during the partitions.

The Polish uprisings of 1830–31 and 1863–64 against the Russian government spread to Lithuania. In 1840 Lithuanian laws were replaced by Russian laws, and Lithuania was renamed the "Territory of the Northwest." After the Insurrection of 1863 the Czar tried to stamp out all traces of Polish culture in Lithuania. Many Poles and Lithuanians were deported to Siberia following each insurrection. The forced Russification of all aspects of life in Lithuania existed from 1864 until 1905.

SMOLEŃSK

The city of Smoleńsk on the Dniepr (Dnepr) River was a commercial center as early as 865 A. D. From the twelfth to the fourteenth centuries Smoleńsk was the seat of an independent principality. The city was taken by Lithuania in 1408, and then was under control of Moscow from 1514 until 1611. At that time Smoleńsk was incorporated into the Polish Commonwealth, but Russia reclaimed Smoleńsk in 1667. Smoleńsk was less than 200 miles from Moscow, and a very desirable possession to all governments in Eastern Europe.

BYELORUSSIA (*BIAŁORUŚ* IN POLISH)

Byelorussia, Bielorussia, and Belorussia are all names that describe White Ruthenia, which was one of the earliest areas to be settled by the Slavs, dating back to the sixth to eighth centuries. Byelorussia lies between Livonia, Lithuania, Poland, Ukraine, and Russia.

Byelorussia is a low-lying plain with some hills and many rivers. The major rivers are the Bug, Dniepr (Dnepr), Dwina (Dvina), Niemen, and Prypeć (Prypet). Major cities are Mińsk, Witebsk (Vitebsk), Mohylew (Mogilev), and Grodno.

The small princedoms of Mińsk, Pińsk, Połock (Polotsk), Słuck (Slutsk), and Turów (Turov) were formed by the year 800 A. D.; eventually all came under the suzerainty of Kijów (Kiev). Most Byelorussian towns were established by 1200 A. D. The Tatars overthrew the Kiev government in 1240; Kievan Ruś (see "Ruthenia and Ukraine") broke up, and many of the towns were destroyed.

The area then came under Lithuanian control. Most of the Byelorussian aristocracy were pagan Lithuanians, though some were Russian Orthodox. The Polish-Lithuanian union of 1386 made Roman Catholicism the official religion of historic Lithuania, and therefore of Byelorussia. A Polish-speaking Roman Catholic nobility developed, though the peasants remained Orthodox and spoke Byelorussian.

Almost all of the Byelorussian population were engaged in primitive agriculture. The land was fertile and yielded grain (chiefly barley), potatoes, and flax. The forests provided timber, pulp, and paper. Livestock and dairy farming were also prevalent, while textiles and paper were main manufactures.

Russia took eastern Byelorussia in the First Partition, the central region in the Second, and the rest in the Third. After the partitions the administrative divisions were Mińsk, Mohylew (Mogilev), Wilno (Vilnius), and Witebsk (Vitebsk). The serfs were emancipated in Byelorussia in 1861. Nineteenth-century industries were glassmaking, shipbuilding, and timber.

Almost 1.5 million people left Byelorussia from 1867 to 1917 and immigrated to the United States and Siberia. From 1896 to 1915 more than 600,000 of these 1.5 million went to Siberia.

POLESIE

The southern part of Byelorussia is called Polesie. Mostly swampland, the area is called the Polesie Marshes or Prypet Marshes for the Prypet (Prypeć in Polish) River, which runs through it. Because of the marshes, peat is abundant. Polesie was annexed by Russia in the partitions.

RUTHENIA AND UKRAINE

Ruthenia is Ruś and Ruś Zakarpacka ("Rus beyond the Carpathian Mountains") in Polish, and Rus in Ukrainian. Ruthenia is the old Latin term for Ukraine (Ukraina in Polish and Ukrajina in Ukrainian). The area is also known as Red Ruthenia. In Halicz the Ukrainians referred to themselves as *Rusyny* ("Ruthenian" in English), not to be confused with the English word "Russian." Ukrainian is written in the Cyrillic alphabet, and many letters do not directly translate into the Latin alphabet.

The area is a vast flat steppe through which flow the Dniepr (Dnepr) and the southern portion of the Bug rivers. Wax, honey, and timber were exported for many years.

The grain crops were predominantly rye and wheat. Some iron-smelting works and salt mines were in the Lwów (Lvov) and Przemyśl areas.

The state of Ruś, also called Kievan Ruś, included the areas of Kijów (Kiev), Czernihow (Chernigov), and Perejasław (Pereyaslavl). Kiev was the center of the principality in the eleventh and twelfth centuries, hence the name Kievan Ruś. It was called Mala Rossiya (Little Russia) by the Muscovites. Ruś expanded to the north and west during this time, but Tatar invaders destroyed the state in 1237 to 1241.

The Poles held Ruś for a short time before 981 A. D. and from 1018 to 1031. The town of Halicz was founded about that time, as was Przemyśl, which is now in southern Poland and boasts of having the oldest buildings in the area, dating from the tenth and eleventh centuries.

Lvov (Lwów in Polish, Lviv in Ukrainian, and Lemberg in German) was founded in 1256 and was an important commercial center. It was the seat of Roman Catholic, Ukrainian Orthodox, and Armenian Orthodox (later the Armenian Catholic Church) archbishoprics. Lvov was taken by the Poles in 1340 and continued under Polish rule for most of the time until the partitions, when it became the capital of the Austrian province of Galicia.

King Casimir the Great of Poland seized the Ruthenian principalities of Bełz, Chełm, Podolia, and Włodzimierz in 1366. The Tatars invaded Ruthenia many times in the thirteenth, fourteenth, and late fifteenth centuries, taking slaves and pillaging the area.

Kiev was conquered by the Lithuanians in their expansion toward the Black Sea in the fourteenth century. Ruthenia was separated from Lithuania and incorporated directly into Poland in 1569.

The Polish-Lithuanian nobles attempted to enslave the Cossacks and convert them to Greek Catholicism. The Cossacks rebelled in the uprising of 1648–51, but were defeated and lost their self-government. The native population of Ruthenia at this time was divided into three religions:

1. The Latin Rite Roman Catholicism, which spread from Poland and the West.

2. The Orthodox tradition, accepted at Kiev in 988 A. D., followed mostly by Cossacks and Russians.

3. The Greek Rite Catholicism, in which Orthodox Ukrainians were formally reunited under the Pope in Rome in 1596.

The Ukraine was partitioned by the Treaty of Andruszów in 1667. Poland received the region southwest of the Dniepr (Dnepr) River, Russia the lands to the northeast.

During the First Partition of Poland in 1772 Austria annexed Halicz Ruthenia with its mainly Ruthenian/Ukrainian rural population and made Lwów (Lvov) the provincial capital, renaming it Lemberg in German. The Austrians also renamed the entire region "Galicia," while the native Ukrainians called it Halychyna. The rest of the Ukraine was acquired by Russia at the Second and Third partitions.

The Russian Empire banned the use of the Ukrainian language in 1876. After major strikes against Russia in all parts of the empire, the Ukrainians were allowed to speak Ukrainian once again. A large number of Ruthenians/Ukrainians immigrated to the United States after 1880.

Zaporoże, Halicz Ruthenia, Podolia, and Volhynia are all part of Ruthenia/ Ukraine.

ZAPOROZHYE (*ZAPOROŻE* IN POLISH)

The peasants were forced to work for their lords. Many who were discontent with doing forced labor found it easy to escape to the southeast into a no-man's land. The fugitive was called a *kozak*, "outlaw." These Cossacks found refuge *zaporohy*, "beyond the cataracts (waterfalls or cascades)," of the lower Dniepr (Dnepr) River. This area was called Zaporozhye. More and more peasants from the Commonwealth fled to Zaporozhye in the sixteenth and seventeenth centuries.

HALICH RUTHENIA (*HALICZ* IN POLISH, *HALYCH* IN UKRAINIAN)

Halicz, a city on the Dniestr (Dnestr) River, also was a principality founded in the twelfth century. The principalities of Halicz and Volhynia were united in 1199. In 1349 they were incorporated into the Kingdom of Poland as the Principalities of Galicia and Lodomeria.

Galicia is the Latin form of the Polish *Halicz*. The Austrians used the most widely known name, Galicia, for the entire territory they annexed during the partitions.

East Galicia was the region east of the San River, populated mainly by Ukrainians. West Galicia was the area west of the San River, inhabited mostly by Poles, better known as Little Poland. Ethnically, however, Halicz (Galicia) was only the small principality near the city of that name.

VOLHYNIA (*WOŁYŃ* IN POLISH)

An ancient Slavic tribe, the Volhynians, occupied this territory in the ninth and tenth centuries. Włodzimierz (Vladimir), the capital of the province, was made a bishopric in 991 A. D. Włodzimierz and Horodło are two cities near the Bug River and on a major medieval east-west trade route. The region became the Duchy of Vladimir in 1366 when it was conquered by the Lithuanians and added to the Commonwealth.

PODOLIA (*PODOLE* IN POLISH)

Poland lost Podolia to the Turks in 1672 but regained it in a peace treaty in 1699. The Boh River lies to the north and the Dniestr to the south. Kamieniec Podolskie was the capital.

MOLDAVIA (*MOŁDAWIA* IN POLISH)

The Roman Catholic diocese of Moldavia was founded in 1369. The principality of Moldavia was a Polish fief from 1387 to 1478, and included Bukowina (Bukovina). Suczawa (Suceava) was the provincial capital. Moldavia lies between the Dniestr (Dnestr) and Dunaj (Danube) rivers. During this time the Polish Commonwealth was at its peak, ranging from the Baltic Sea in the north to the Black Sea in the south. After 1478 Moldavia became part of the Ottoman Empire. During the present century it was part of the USSR, but it is now an independent republic, lying between Ukraine and Romania.

BUKOVINA (*BUKOWINA* IN POLISH)

Bukovina lies in the northwest part of Moldavia and was part of the Polish Commonwealth from 1350 to 1500. Northern Bukovina is populated mostly by Ruthenians, with many Polish settlers and also a number of Germans, Jews, Romanians, Czechs, Magyars (Hungarians), Armenians, and Lipovanians (Old Orthodox Russians). Romanians predominate in southern Bukovina.

The Poles held much of the land in Bukovina and organized the local industry and commerce. Mining is one of the major industries in the area.

Two main towns are Chocim and Cernăuti (Czerniowce in Polish, Chernovtsy in Russian; it is now in Ukraine), where the Christian population was 26 percent Polish and 41 percent Roman Catholic in 1924.

Bukovina was the scene of frequent battles between Poland and the Turks and Tatars. Austria occupied Bukovina from 1774 until after World War I. However, from 1787 to 1849 and again from 1859 to 1861, Bukovina was a part of the Austrian Empire's province of Galicia.

The Polish influence was so strong in Bukovina that even after World War I, Polish schools and societies operated in Bukovina. Ukrainian, Romanian, and Polish were the languages of the people, even though German was the official language of the state.

SOURCES AND ADDITIONAL READING

"Bukovina." *Polish Genealogical Society Newsletter* XIV (Spring 1991), 10–11.

Magocsi, Paul Robert. *Galicia: A Historical Survey and Bibliographic Guide.* Toronto: University of Toronto Press, 1983. Very good resource for information about Ukraine, including minorities.

The New Encyclopaedia Britannica Macropaedia—Knowledge in Depth. Chicago: Encyclopaedia Britannica, Inc., 1987.

"Poles in Lithuania." *Polish Genealogical Society Newsletter* IV (Spring 1984), 10–11.

Polish Encyclopaedia. Vol. II: Territory and Population of Poland. Geneva, Switzerland: Atar, Ltd., 1924. Reprint edition by Arno Press, Inc., 1972. Used as the source for several articles in the *Polish Genealogical Society Newsletter*.

Chapter Seven:

MAPS AND GAZETTEERS

LOCATING YOUR ANCESTOR'S VILLAGE OR TOWN

Many people tell me their ancestor was from Poznań (or another large town), but they are unable to find any record of him or her in Poznań. My husband's grandfather Pokrywka said he was from Poznań, which wasn't exactly true. He was from Poznania, the region surrounding Poznań, but not from the town itself.

Further searching in American records revealed that he was from "Daszewice, kraj. Śrem," the village of Daszewice near the town of Śrem, just five miles south of the city of Poznań. The Polish road atlas I have is very detailed and has an index, but Daszewice was not in it—neither were many other small villages.

I knew I needed a map that showed more detail, so I went to the map department at the University of Toledo library. There I found the 1944 Army Map Service series of 1:100,000-scale maps of Poland. The village and town names are not indexed, but there is a grid map on which you can locate the general area, then select an area map. I found Śrem and looked for Daszewice in the same vicinity until I found it. I then made a photocopy of the map showing the Daszewice area.

There were many symbols on the map, and a key explaining the symbols was printed on each individual map. By checking the symbols I found there was a church in Głuszyna, which turned out to be the one that grandfather Pokrywka attended. Checking the rest of the symbols, I found out that the area was near the Warta River and that the landscape was hilly and marshy with some forests. I gambled on Głuszyna being grandfather's parish, and wrote to the parish priest requesting a copy of the 1865 baptismal certificate. It worked!

We also used photocopies of these maps to find churches and villages when my husband and I visited Poland in 1985. As my husband drove south out of Poznań I told him where to go and what to expect to see ahead. Was he surprised when all my predictions came true and we drove right up to grand-father Pokrywka's church!

VILLAGE NAMES

Villages and towns were named in many ways. The endings *-ek*, *-ka*, *-nki*, and *-ówko* denote a small version of the root word—a later and smaller settlement (for example, Orzechówko) near the original (Orzechowo) may bear the same name (*orzech*, meaning "nut") but with a different ending.

The suffixes *-ów* and *-owo* indicate a derivation. A place name with one of these endings means it was named after someone or something. For example, Kraków was named after the legendary King Krak. Dąbrowo was named for *dąb* or *dęby* (oak or oaks) and means "place of the oak(s)." Orzechowo was probably named for the abundance of nuts found there.

Many villages were named after the lords who founded or owned them. Sometimes the place name changed with the ownership of the village.

Some settlements were named after the inhabitants—Żydowo (Place of the Jews), Olędry (Place of the Dutch), and Niemica (Place of the Germans). Obvious geographical features dictated the naming of some places—Zielona Góra (Green Mountain) and Żelazno (Iron Place or Iron Town).

In the early period of Polish history service settlements were established in Great and Little Poland. Craftsmen who made items such as shields, arrows, and casks, or provided a specialized service such as horsekeepers, lived and had their workshops in a village whose name reflected the service performed.

These peasants performed the services for the state, which in turn granted the peasants land. Some village names of this type survive: Szczytniki "Shieldmakers," Złotniki "Goldsmiths," and Sokolniki "Falconkeepers." The suffix *-nik* refers to a worker.

People were encouraged to settle in the vast unpopulated forest regions, and on lands owned by the Church. Farming villages were created with the intention of making the wilderness territories more productive. The people who settled in these villages were given their freedom and did not need to pay taxes for several years on the land given to them. These villages use *Wola* or *Wolka* as part of their names, and usually are found in Mazovia, Little Poland, and Red Ruthenia (Ukraine). The term *Ligota* means the same and was used in Silesia.

A lord who wished to form a new town (sometimes called *Nowa Wieś*) would issue a Charter of Location to a man who would recruit settlers, often foreigners and usually Germans, to practice their trades and crafts in the new town. This agent (*scultetus* in Latin, *schultheiss* in German, and *sołtys* or *wójt* in Polish) would oversee the layout and planning of the new town, was granted land outside the town, and took charge of the administrative duties once the town was established. The office of scultetus was hereditary thereafter, and can even be seen in nineteenth-century vital records as an occupation or status.

A Polish village or town may have been divided into more than one part: *Górne*, abbreviated as *grn*, (Upper); *Średnie*, abbreviated as *śrd*, (Middle); or *Dolne*, abbreviated as *dln*, (Lower). You may also find the following words and abbreviations on a Polish map:

bagno (*bg*), *błoto*: swamp, marsh
bór (plural: *bory*): impenetrable (pine) forest
duża: big, large
dwór (*d*): manor house
folwark (*fw*): full working farm
góra (plural: *góry*): mountain
jezioro (*j* or *jez*): lake
kanał : canal
las (plural: *lasy*): forest
ligota: free (village residents)
mała, małe, mały (*mł*): little
miasto/miasteczko: city/little town
mokre: wet
nowa, nowe, nowy (*nw*): new
nowa wieś: new village
nad (*n*): on the, upon; as in *Dobrzyn nad Wisłą* (Dobrzyn on the Vistula)
puszcza: primeval or virgin forest
rzeka: river
stara, stare, stary (*st*): old
sucha, suchy: dry
wielka, wielki (*wlk*): large, great
wieś (*ws*) (plural: *wsie*): village
wola, wolka: free (village residents)

LAND MEASUREMENTS

Polish land measurements may seem strange at first, but learning the terminology may help you in your research. One *mórg* (called a *morg* or *morga* in olden times) is the "Polish acre" and is equivalent to 1.38 acres. The *łan* (also called *laneus, mansus,* and *włóka*) has been used for centuries and varies in size from 7.5 to 32 acres, depending on the region of Poland to which you are referring. The *Polish Encyclopaedia* (written in the 1920s) gives the size of a łan as "about 39.5 to 42 acres." One Prussian acre is equivalent to 0.63 acre.

MAP SYMBOLS

Map symbols can give you a good impression of the area in which your ancestor lived. Check the map legend to find out what the symbols mean. You will find symbols for churches, synagogues, cemeteries, windmills, wells, mines, quarries, clay pits, gravel pits, sand pits, marshes, orchards, vineyards, woodlands, and more.

MAP COORDINATES

You can find map coordinates for some localities in atlases and gazetteers. Two sets of numbers are given—the latitude and longitude. The latitude is the distance north of the equator; that does not present a problem.

The longitude, however, is the distance east or west of a certain point. But what point? Many countries chose a prime meridian in their own territory. That obviously presents problems when trying to locate places in another country.

Early European cartographers often chose Ferro, the western-most island in the Canary Islands in the Atlantic Ocean, as the prime meridian. If Ferro is used as the prime meridian, subtract 17 degrees 40 minutes (Ferro's own modern longitude) from the longitude given to yield the modern version.

Paris was also used as a prime meridian in the *Słownik Geograficzny*. If this is the case for your locality, add 2 degrees 20 minutes to the longitude.

Kraków was also used by Polish cartographers as the prime meridian in the past, probably because it was the capital for several centuries.

It was not until 1884 that an international standard of longitude was adopted, proclaiming Greenwich, England, as 0 degrees longitude, the prime meridian.

For more information about map coordinates, read: "Prime Problems,"

Polish Genealogical Society Newsletter VIII (Spring 1986). Mr. William Radlinski provided information about the same topics in his "Maps" lecture to the Polish Genealogical Society of Western New York on August 8, 1991, and graciously provided me with additional information about Polish map sources.

BOUNDARIES

The boundaries of Poland have been constantly changing. A map and information about the territories that at one time were part of the Polish State are found in chapter 6.

There were seventeen województw (provinces) in modern Poland after World War II. These are the administrative units used by the LDS in their Locality Index and Catalog.

These województwa were broken up into smaller administrative units in 1975; now there are forty-nine.

An administrative unit smaller than a *województwo* (province, abbreviated *woj.*) was called a *powiat* (county, abbreviated *pow.*) in Polish, and a *kreis* (county or circle, abbreviated *kr.*) in German. In the Russian-occupied region of Poland the term *gubernia* (abbreviated *gub.*) was used to denote a province or district, and *gmina* (abbreviated *gm.*) a smaller unit called a community.

Our ancestors often made written references to the villages in which they were born and resided—and to the parish to which their particular village belonged. Since you are seeking the parish records you will need to know the name of the village in which the parish is located.

My grandfather Dembinski came from the village of "Mliwiec, county of Toruń," according to his written statement. The parish church is located in Orzechowo. The LDS Locality Index (see page 109) lists parish records first by country, then by province and village, for example, *Poland—Bydgoszcz—Orzechowo*. Bydgoszcz was the correct province at the time the LDS Catalog was made (before 1975), and Toruń was the correct administrative unit when my grandfather was a young man in 1892. Since the redrawing of provincial boundaries in 1975, Orzechowo is now once again in the province of Toruń.

I wrote to the University Library of the Catholic University of Lublin for the correct address of the Roman Catholic parish in Orzechowo, and this is what they sent: Rzymsko-Katolicka Parafia, Orzechowo, 82–213 Ryńsk,

Polska. Ryńsk is the post office for the village of Orzechowo, while 87–213 is the Polish version of a zip code. A letter addressed to "Rzymsko-Katolicka Parafia, Orzechowo, woj. Toruń, Polska" *may* eventually reach its destination, as I have successfully sent letters addressed in this manner.

The National Library can help you locate villages. Give them as much information as possible. Include the name of the parish, województwo, powiat, kreis, gubernia, or gmina if available. Write to: Biblioteka Narodowa, ul. Hankiewicza 1, 00–973 Warszawa, Polska (Poland).

Common names (such as Nowa Wieś and Dąbrowa) were repeatedly used to name villages throughout Polish territory. You will have to know the województwo and powiat, and even the parish, in which your ancestor's village was located. Only then can you begin the search for records.

MAPS OF POLAND

Many major college libraries and some public libraries in the United States are repositories for federal documents and may have large-scale (detailed) maps of Poland and other European countries. In 1944 the U.S. Army Map Service made very detailed 1:100,000-scale maps of Poland; about eighty individual maps make up the whole country. There is no index—you must locate the approximate area on a grid map and then refer to the individual area map.

The Germans also made various maps of the area, in differing scales, so be sure to check out several different map series. There are also maps of Lithuania and Russia, although not as detailed as the maps of Poland and Germany. Check federal document repositories and the LDS Family History Library.

The U. S. National Archives has over 2 million maps, described in their "Guide to Cartographic Records in the National Archives" publication. Reproductions of the 1:250,000-scale maps of Poland and adjoining areas made by the U. S. Defense Mapping Agency are available.

The National Archives also has the German Luftwaffe aerial photographs of Poland taken in 1939 to 1945, at extremely detailed scales (1:15,840 to 1:31,380-scale). Eight-by-ten-inch copies are available.

Send the map coordinates and/or place name (along with names of nearby towns) so that they can identify the site and, if possible, include a photocopy of an area map with your desired location marked on it. Inquire about the costs and request NATF Form 72 from:

National Archives and Records Administration
Cartographic and Architectural Branch
841 South Pickett Street
Alexandria, Virginia 22302

The American Geographic Society Collection at the University of Wisconsin has an excellent collection of maps and gazetteers of Poland. It is best to make a trip to do your own research in the library. The staff does only the most basic of searches by mail, so be specific when you write to them. They do make photocopies of the maps, so ask what the charge might be.

The American Geographic Society Collection of
The University of Wisconsin–Milwaukee Library
P. O. Box 399
Milwaukee, Wisconsin 53201

ADDITIONAL READING AND MAPS

The Historical Atlas of Poland. Warsaw-Wrocław, Poland: Państwowe Przedsiębiorstwo Wydawnictw Kartograficznych, 1986. (written in English)

Pogonowski, Iwo Cyprian. *Poland, A Historical Atlas.* New York: Hippocrene Books, 1987.

Mapa Topograficzna Polski (Topographical Map of Poland). Wojskowe Zakłady Kartograficzne (Military Cartographic Institute), 1991. Large, folding sectional maps of Poland made in a detailed scale of 1:100,000. This series is currently being updated, since 1991, therefore not all sections of the country are completed. Write to the Military Cartographic Institute—Wojskowe Zakłady Kartograficzne, 00-909 Warszawa, Aleje Jerozolimskie 97, Polska (Poland)—to find out if your area has been completed yet, and what the cost of a map will be.

Samochodowy Atlas Polski (Road Atlas of Poland). Warsaw, Poland: 1975. A series of thirty-four, nine-by-ten-inch maps of modern Poland with indexes; very useful, but does not contain the smallest villages. Available in Polish book stores and gift shops in the United States.

Tactical Maps of the Old Polish Republic (1926–1938). Wojskowy Instytut Geograficzny (Military Geographic Institute). Contains detailed 1:100,000-scale maps of the areas that were in Poland between the two world wars, including the eastern territories that Poland lost to the USSR in 1945. (LDS microfiche 6,312,622.) The Library of Congress also has these maps, and a few at 1:25,000-scale, which are available at the following address: Library of Congress Geography and Map Division, James Madison Memorial Building (Capitol Hill), Washington, D. C. 20540.

Administrative maps of Poland can be purchased at Polish gift shops and book stores.

GAZETTEERS (GEOGRAPHICAL DICTIONARIES)

There are a variety of supplementary materials to maps that can enable you to locate a village or find out more about your ancestor's village.

Słownik Geograficzny Królestwa Polskiego i Innych Krajów Słowiańskich (Geographical Dictionary of the Kingdom of Poland and Other Slavonic Countries). Edited by F. Sulimierski, B. Chlebowski, and W. Walewski. Vols. 1–15 (in 16 vols.). Warsaw, Poland: Wiek, 1880–1902; reprinted 1983 by Państwowe Wydawnictwo Naukowe, Warsaw.

This dictionary includes all cities, towns, and even the tiniest villages in the Kingdom of Poland, and includes Prussia, Poznania, Galicia (Little Poland), Silesia, Bukovina, and Moravia. All place names are in alphabetical order. The description of a village may include: the number of inhabitants, number of homes, location (the distance from a large town, or the latitude and longitude), churches and synagogues in the area, history of the village (including when founded and by whom), important events, local industries; and the number of inhabitants who are Catholic, Evangelical (Lutheran), Jewish, and illiterate.

The content of each entry varies because several individuals wrote different parts of the work. All entries are in Polish and there is much abbreviation. However, with a little knowledge of Polish and time spent studying the entries, you (or a friend who knows Polish) should be able to pick out important information. The time period of the volumes is 1880 to 1902, so you can get a good picture of your ancestor's area about the time of emigration.

The Library of Congress has a copy of the *Słownik Geograficzny*. It is also found in The New York Public Library, the Burton Collection of the Detroit Public Library, and the Polish Museum of America Library, and no doubt in other major libraries.

Gazetteer of Poland. 2nd ed. 2 vols. U.S. Board on Geographic Names, Defense Mapping Agency, 1988. Contains about 57,000 entries, including alternate names, coordinates, and administrative divisions.

Kowallis, Otto K. and Vera N. Kowallis. *A Genealogical Guide and Atlas of Silesia.* Logan, Utah: Everton Publishers, 1976.

Mokotoff, Gary and Sallyann Amdur Sack. *Where Once We Walked: A Guide to the Jewish Communities Destroyed in the Holocaust.* Teaneck, New Jersey: Avotaynu, P. O. Box 1134, Teaneck, New Jersey 07666, 1991. This book lists over 21,000 villages and towns in Central and Eastern Europe that had Jewish communities before World War II. Alphabetical and Soundex System (phonetic) listings are used. The listing for each community includes alternate names of the locality, latitude and longitude, information about the Jewish population, and other items of information. This gazetteer should be useful to anyone, Jewish or not, trying to locate a village that is seemingly difficult to find.

Mueler's Verzeichnis der Jenseits der Oder-Neisse gelegenen, unter fremder Verwaltung stehhenden Ortschaftern, 1958. Alphabetical index of villages and towns east of the Odra-Nysa rivers, i.e., villages now in Poland, including their exact locations and present names. Indexed in German and Polish.

Peckwas, Edward A. *A Historical Bibliography of the Histories of Polish Towns, Villages, and Regions.* Chicago: Polish Genealogical Society, 1990. Listings for almost 1,000 books in Polish, German, and Russian languages, with index.

Rospond, Stanisław. *Słownik nazw geograficznych Polski Zachodniej i Pół - nocnej* (Dictionary of Geographic Place Names of the Western and Northern Territories of Poland). Wrocław, Poland: Polskie Towarzystwo Geograficzne, 1952.

Spis miejscowości Polskiej Rzeczypospolitej Ludowej (Place Names in the Polish Peoples' Republic). Warsaw, Poland: Wydawn. Komunikacji i Łączności, 1967. List includes provinces, counties, civil records offices, etc., for each village.

Chapter Eight:

RESEARCH USING RECORDS FROM POLAND

The most enjoyable time of your genealogical research may be when you have at last found your ancestor's village and can begin searching records from Poland. But what if you can't read a word of Polish?

Fortunately, it is not necessary to be fluent in Polish. You will learn many Polish terms integral to your family research as you begin to work with Polish records. You will learn to spot an ancestor's name in a paragraph of sometimes almost indecipherable Polish script. You may even copy a request in perfect Polish asking a civil records office or parish archives to find a document. Your Polish pedigree chart will grow.

How can these miracles happen?: By planning your research strategy carefully, using the resources in this book and others, sharing tips with fellow researchers of Polish genealogy, putting your detective cap on, and practice, practice, practice.

THE BIG THREE

There are three ways to obtain information from Polish records: using the LDS microfilmed records, writing to Poland yourself for the records, and hiring someone to do the research for you.

The LDS Family History Library has sent its representatives to Poland to microfilm church and civil records, which you can view at one of their many branch libraries throughout the United States. More information about the services available through the LDS can be found later in this chapter and in chapter 2.

If you would like to write to Poland for records, use the *Polish Genealogical Letter-Writing Guide* in chapter 14 to compose a letter in Polish. For English translations of Polish, Latin, and German terms that might be found in records or a certificate from Poland, see chapter 13.

It is also possible to hire someone else—such as a genealogist living here or a genealogist or research service in Poland—to do the research for you. Hiring someone else to do research will be costly, so be selective in what you want the researcher to do for you. Do as much of the research yourself as you can, then provide the genealogist with *all* the information you have collected on your ancestor, so you can avoid having to pay for something you already knew. Ask whether the fees include postage, photocopying, driving to the library, etc.?

The LDS provides a list of American genealogists for hire. Send a SASE to the Family History Library in Salt Lake City, Utah (see address in chapter 2). Polish genealogical societies and some libraries also may have lists of genealogists available. Sometimes it is necessary to hire a specialist when you come up against a problem that you can't solve by yourself.

RESEARCH SERVICES IN POLAND

The Chief Directorate of the State Archives in Warsaw provides a genealogical research service which has produced satisfactory results for many years. Correspondence must be in Polish and the following specific information must be provided: Christian or first names, surnames, and date and place of the event (birth, marriage, or death). They will search the available records and send you copies of the documents found. Once they locate the records, the researchers can work backward into the past and research the ancestors who are the subject of your inquiry.

Send the initial payment of $20.00 with your request. A fee of $10.00 is charged for each document, and $10.00 per hour of search time is also charged (and remember that prices are subject to change). Set a limit on your research costs, as your bill can easily reach $200.00 quickly. For example, tell them you wish to authorize only $50.00 (or whatever amount) at this time. Ask how payment should be made. Your research will be assigned a number (*Nasz znak _ _ _*); use it on all correspondence. Write to:

Naczelna Dyrekcja Archiwów Państwowych
ul. Długa 6
skrytka pocztowa Nr 1005
00-950 Warszawa
Polska (Poland)

The Piast Genealogical Research Center, which specializes in nobility research, carries out genealogical investigations for Americans. They handle archival research, travelling to the appropriate archives, and library research. The report will be in Polish, or English at an extra charge. Write for a brochure, available in Polish or English, which explains various services and fees:

> Dr. Leszek Pudłowski, Dyrektor
> Ośrodek Badań Genealogicznych "Piast"
> skr. poczt. 9
> ul. Podchorążych 89 m. 9
> 00-957 Warszawa 36
> Polska (Poland)

The College of Heraldry also does research for people with Polish ancestry. Write to:

> Kolegium Heraldyczne
> ul. Narutowicza 4
> 20-950 Lublin
> Polska (Poland)

WARNING! Recent reports indicate that these research services have a backlog of work and it may take quite a while to obtain your results.

STRATEGY FOR RESEARCHING POLISH RECORDS

Your "battle plan" for finding your ancestors in Polish records is much the same as searching American records. Once you have found the name of your ancestor's village, you will need to find its location. Then you must find the types of records available and the location of those records. Order the microfilms from the LDS, if they are available, and begin your letter-writing campaign.

Find your ancestor's birth record and note occupations, ages of parents, and godparents' names, if given. Search for the birth records of siblings also.

Now look for the marriage records of the parents, which may have been approximately twenty-five years before the birth right up to the birth. The marriage may even have occurred after the birth of the first child.

Are the ages of the marriage partners given? Check back to the years they were probably born, but keep in mind that stated ages are not always accurate. Match the bride's and groom's parents' names to those on the birth records of the bride and groom. Sometimes they are not the same! Make notes of unusual findings.

Some problems with names of parents not matching up with the names anticipated can be solved by searching the records of siblings. A mother who died was often quickly replaced to take care of the widower's young children. A widow with children often remarried soon after her husband's death to support her family.

Searching death records may seem pointless at first. But again it may help explain sudden changes in status, residence, or marriage partners. Sometimes children assumed the surname of their stepfather, and this fact does not become apparent until a search of death records has been made.

Keep working backward in this manner. Never pick out a person who was born 200 years ago and "see if you are related."

Many record books are indexed; many are not. If you are having trouble finding records, avoid the index and search through the records themselves. Even if you are not having problems, it's better to search through the records. Indexes contain many mistakes and omissions. Don't depend on indexes; use them only for a quick scan. It takes time to be accurate.

MISSING RECORDS

During the occupation of Poland by hostile forces, records were sometimes destroyed or carried off. Especially during the two world wars, many records were removed from parishes or civil records offices and taken to Berlin. Many microfilmed records at the LDS were filmed in Berlin, even though they originated in a Polish parish. When reviewing the LDS Locality Index, check to see where your records were microfilmed.

If your ancestor's parish does not have the registers you are seeking, check civil records offices and the LDS Locality Index. There have been several instances where a researcher wrote to the parish and was told the records no longer exist, then found these same records at the LDS. The researcher reported the discovery to the LDS, which then sent microfilmed copies of the registers to the parish in Poland to which the records originally belonged.

RESOURCES AT THE LDS FAMILY HISTORY LIBRARY

There are more than 10,000 rolls of microfilm pertaining to Poland at the LDS, and microfilming of Polish records is still in progress. The Locality Index will help you locate and order the films of the Polish records that you want to search.

The Locality Index is on microfiche and computer, and every branch (family history center) has the complete collection. The index is alphabetical and divided into countries. Those of interest to Polish research are Byelorussia, Czechoslovakia, Estonia, Germany, Latvia, Lithuania, Moldavia, Poland, Russia, and Ukraine.

Once you locate the packet of fiche for Poland, you will find further subdivisions: the pre-1975 województwo (province), then the village or town name.

What if you don't know what województwo your village was in or the present location of the village because you have a village with a German name? There are several gazetteers and maps on film or fiche that can help you. And at the very beginning of the Locality Index for Poland there is a section containing place names and changes for the localities included in the index. Another source for locating your ancestor's village is *Where Once We Walked* (see page 103).

My grandfather Franciszek (Frank) Boczkowski was born in the village of Wołowa near Płock, and baptized in the parish of Blichowo. There is no entry for Wołowa, but sometimes individual villages within a parish have separate entries. In this case, to see if there are any parish records available on microfilm, look for the entry *Poland—Warszawa—Blichowo (Płock)— Church Records.* Several microfilm reels are available.

Because my grandfather was born in 1878, I ordered the film containing birth, marriage, and death records for 1866 to 1879. The Locality Index tells me a lot more about these parish registers: what has been filmed is a copy of the Roman Catholic registers on file at the Archiwum Państwowym (civil records offices) in Płock and Warsaw. This *"copy"* is the civil transcript of the parish records, not a copy of the original records. Wołowa and seven other villages in the parish are listed. There is an index, and after 1868 the text is in Russian. These records were microfilmed in 1969 and 1981.

In 1984 the LDS microfilmed the same parish's records at the Diocesan Archives in Płock. These records are the original parish registers, not the transcripts used for civil purposes. In addition, the birth, marriage, and death records are much older, dating from 1662 to 1825, and a large part of the film consists of indexes.

The microfilm of the actual records can be ordered from the LDS. A small fee covers the cost of shipping the film from Salt Lake City to your local family history center. The film will remain at the center for three weeks, but you may extend the loan for either six months or indefinitely ("permanently").

The film must be viewed at the center, but microfilm/fiche copiers can give you a copy of your records to take home.

ADDITIONAL READING

"Records of Genealogical Value for Poland." The Genealogical Department of the Church of Jesus Christ of Latter-day Saints, Series C, No. 31, 1983; also on microfiche no. 6053503 at the LDS.

Chapter Nine:

CHURCH RECORDS

RELIGIONS IN POLAND

Many religions were practiced in pre-partition Poland due to the religious tolerance of the national government. However, the majority of Poles were Roman Catholic. The Latin Rite Roman Catholic faith was most widely practiced throughout the Commonwealth, and accounted for 53 percent of the population after the First Partition.

Established in 1596, the Greek Rite of the Catholic Church also had a large following, mostly in the eastern areas of the Commonwealth and in Ruthenia. The Ruthenian Greek Rite claimed 30 percent of the population after the First Partition, according to information from *The Latin Church in the Polish Commonwealth in 1772*. Armenians living in the southeastern regions belonged to the Armenian Rite of the Greek Catholic Church.

Various sects of Orthodox Christianity existed in the eastern regions of the Commonwealth. The gentry in Little Poland and Lithuania tended to adopt Calvinism more than the gentry in other areas. Rich families in Great Poland, Pomerania, and Silesia adopted Lutheranism, as did the burghers. The large German minority were the primary followers of Lutheranism, which was professed mainly in Great Poland, the Kingdom of Prussia, and Courland, and to a lesser extent in Lithuania. The Jews accounted for 10 percent of the population before the partitions, and 750,000 of them practiced the Hebrew faith.

In 1573 the Sejm passed the Toleration Act of Warsaw, which granted freedom of religion to all people living in the Commonwealth. In the early eighteenth century, however, laws were passed that limited the religious and civil rights of non-Catholics, but these laws were repealed in 1767. This occurred at a time in Poland's history when the power of the Sejm was being eroded and foreign influence in Polish politics was in the ascendant.

In Prussian Poland in 1816, there were 65.7 percent Catholics, 28 percent Protestants, and 6.3 percent Jews. By 1900 the proportion changed to 67.8

percent Catholics, 30.2 percent Protestants, and 1.9 percent Jews, according to the *Polish Encyclopaedia,* Vol. II (1924).

ROMAN CATHOLIC CHURCH

Catholicism has always played an important role in the history of Poland, beginning with Mieszko I, who was responsible for the emergence of the Polish State. Mieszko and his court were converted to Latin Christianity in 966 A.D., the date Poles celebrate as the founding of Poland.

The bishopric of Poznań was founded in 963 A.D., and those of Kraków and Gniezno in 1000 A.D. By the time of the partitions there were more than 6,400 parishes and branches.

Roman Catholic Church Registers

Parishes in Poland began to record births, marriages, and deaths in the late 1500s and early 1600s, following directives of the Council of Trent in 1563. The Council required parishes to keep baptismal registers, which were needed to prove couples were baptized Catholics before they could be wed. A formal mandate in 1614 directed the recording of baptisms and marriages as well as deaths.

Polish parishes were quick to comply with the mandate, although very few of these early registers, called *metryki*, still exist. However, it is not unusual to find parish registers still in existence that pre-date the partitions, or occasionally to find ones that reach back into the seventeenth century. Some registers also contain communion and confirmation lists and marriage banns.

Perhaps the pastors who recorded the major events in their parishioners' lives would have penned the words more carefully if they had known future generations would find them so important. But it was a tedious job for a busy priest, especially at the end of each year when he was required to copy all entries and send them to the local bishop or to the local civil records office for safekeeping.

There was often more than the one original copy of the register. If a copy is not available at the parish, there may be one at the diocesan or archdiocesan archives, or even at the state provincial archives for civil records. While it is true that many records were destroyed by fire, flood, and invaders, some may exist in unexpected places.

The parish priest in Orzechowo, north of Toruń, could not locate my grandfather's baptismal record in the register because that volume was missing. It was carried off to Gdańsk by the German army in World War II. Some registers were taken to Germany and are still there. Germans were meticulous recordkeepers, and it is doubtful that they would have destroyed all the records. They also needed records to prove who was Jewish and who was not.

During the partition period, 1772 to 1918, the baptismal registers were used at times by Russia, Prussia, and Austria to locate conscripts for their armies. Sometimes notations can be found in the margins of the registers' pages attesting to this fact. The handwriting is a different style than that of the main body of the registers' text, and these notations were probably made by a representative of the civil registrar or the military. The following are examples of notations that were found in the margins of a baptismal register from a Roman Catholic parish just south of Poznań in the village of Głuszyna.

Taufschein zum Militair d 3/11 40 ("Baptismal certificate sent to the military on the third of November [18]40." This was found in the 1808 baptismal entry of Mathias Daierling, and written in German script.)

Milit. Taufsch. d 13/3 35 ("Military baptismal certificate" or "Baptismal Certificate sent to the Military on the 13th of March [18]35." This was found in the 1816 baptismal entry of Stanisław Dłubala, also written in German script.)

Other notations can also be found in the margins of baptismal registers. The civil courts must have required identification and used the baptismal registers to provide baptismal certificates for use by the court. The following examples were found in the same parish register as those military notations above, and also were written in German script.

Taufschein dem Gericht d 13/7 37 ("Baptismal certificate [sent] to the Court on the 13th of July [18]37." From the 1789 baptismal entry of Andreas Kryszak.)

Taufs. dem Gericht beförd(ert) d 28/3 39 ("Baptismal certificate forwarded to the court on the 28th of March [18]39." From the 1817 baptism of Marianna Chodziak.)

Sometimes notations can be found in the funeral/death registers. The following entry was written in German script in the margin of Laurentius Chudziak's 1822 death record.

Tauf(schein) u(nd) Todsch(ein) d 10/2 36 dem Gericht ("Birth and Death Certificate(s) on the 10th of February [sent] to the Court.")

Metrykę do sądu in Polish is the same as *Taufschein dem Gericht* in German—"Certificate (sent) to the Court." *Sądowi* also means "to the court" in Polish. If there is such a notation in your ancestor's record, perhaps further research into court records would be profitable, or you might check other family records to see what happened around the same date as the certificate was sent to the court—perhaps one or both of the parents of a child died and the child was assigned a legal guardian.

(Some Polish court records are available for research, although many were destroyed or lost. The easiest court records to search are those few filmed by the LDS, so check the Locality Index. Hiring a genealogist, a lawyer, or a research organization in Poland is another alternative, but would be fairly expensive.)

Records of non-Catholic births can also be found in some of these Catholic registers because the partitioning powers ruled that the parish registers were also to be used as the civil registers for the villages in that parish. In rural areas one parish may have served up to ten villages. The baptismal registers did note whether the infant and his parents were *Catholica* (Catholic) or *Accatholica* (non-Catholic).

Registers were usually written in Latin until the time of the partitions, although in many areas they were kept continuously in Latin. In some areas the registers were recorded in Polish, German, or Russian, as required by the rulers of the partitioned areas.

There apparently was a difference in format for church records between the northern and southern parts of Poland, according to Stanley Schmidt, President of the Polish Genealogical Society of America. In the West Prussian and Pomeranian areas and in Poznania, handwritten narratives in paragraph form prevailed in the late eighteenth and early nineteenth centuries. Printed Latin forms with columnar headings became prevalent in the early to mid-nineteenth century in these areas. Some parishes had printed German headings with the fill-in-the-blank entries handwritten in Latin. House numbers were not often recorded in the registers in these areas. In the Russian-occupied areas handwritten narratives were used throughout the nineteenth century.

In Austrian Galicia in the late eighteenth and nineteenth centuries the forms were printed with Latin headings. There was always a place to record house numbers, which were assigned as the houses were built all around the village, not in numerical order down each street. House numbers may help you trace your ancestors back through the generations.

Mr. Schmidt has found that "records in several parishes in Galicia were kept in loose-leaf form. Each village or small group of closely-related villages were kept on one sheet. A typical sheet for a small village might have but one entry for the entire year. When a new church is built in that area, the records are removed from the old book and a new book started for the new parish." Keep this in mind if you cannot locate the records in the parish in which you think they should be.

It is also possible to visit the centuries-old churches of your ancestors. What a wonderful feeling it is to attend Mass in the same church in which your grandfather served Mass or was baptized. Most of our grandparents' churches are still in existence—we found two buildings over 700 years old! We stood in silence as we imagined the parade of our ancestors through the heavy wooden doors and wondered how many of them were baptized in the carved stone baptismal font.

Although the following information concerns the Roman Catholic Church specifically, records of other Churches in Poland may contain similar information. If your ancestors were not Catholic, you may still find valuable information in the following sections because many Catholic registers were used as civil registers and many non-Catholic births and marriages were recorded in them.

Birth/Baptismal Registers

These records are the most important of all vital records. From the birth records alone you can build a pedigree chart of many generations. A wealth of genealogical information and other interesting facts can be found in parish birth registers: names, date and place of birth and baptism, parents' names and sometimes their ages and occupations, and grandparents' names. Occupations of all the men named in the register, birth order (that is, "first child of"), legitimacy or illegitimacy, time of day the birth occurred, and the midwife's name are often recorded. Godparents' names frequently are accompanied by an occupation for the men, marital status, and place of residence, and occasionally show relationship to the parents. Such information is sometimes provided for the husband or father of the godmother. Sometimes the birth of a child occurred shortly after the parents' marriage and is so noted in the baptismal register. Sometimes the father died before the birth of his child and this is also noted.

The content of the entries often varies by locality and time period. In Russian-occupied Poland two male witnesses were required to accompany the father to report the birth of his child. Their names, ages, occupations, and places of residence are recorded. Sometimes these witnesses were relatives, sometimes friends and neighbors.

Notations were made in the margins of the pages or in the annotations column. This is where you can find clues to make your research more complete and interesting. The symbols ⚰ or ✝ in the margin of a birth or baptismal record indicate the person is deceased. The child may have died at birth or shortly afterward, or the pastor may have gone back to the baptismal register to note the date of death of an older child or adult. The spouse's name and date and place of marriage may have been added when the pastor checked the baptismal register to confirm the baptisms of the engaged couple. Military conscription may also be noted.

Children were usually given only one name, almost always that of a saint. Occasionally children were given two names, both of which were recorded in the register. The Latin word *binominis (-nus, -na)*, meaning "two names," or its abbreviation *bin.* or *binom.*, precede the child's name: *binom. Agata Karolina*. Children of nobility were often given more than one name. Some saints have a double name themselves, such as Jan Chrzciciel (John the Baptist) and Franciszek Ksawery (Francis Xavier).

Do not confuse the child given two names with twins. Multiple births are about twice as common in Poland than in the general population, a fact I discovered in researching my article "Results of the Genetic Survey of Americans of Polish Descent," published in *Polish Genealogical Society Newsletter,* XIII (Fall 1990). Twins occur about once in every forty-five births in Poland.

Twin births are recorded with the words *gemelli* or *gemini* (Latin) or *bliźniaczy* (Polish). Triplets are recorded as *trigeminus* or *tergeminus* (Latin) or *trojaczek* or *trojakiów* (Polish). Many times a boy/girl set of twins were named Adam and Ewa (Eve).

Legitimate and illegitimate births are always noted. In a case where a mother was not married to the child's father, the father's name was almost never recorded. Instead, the space reserved for the father's name was filled by *pater ignoti*, "father unknown," or a line was drawn through the space.

Not only were children who survived the birth process baptized, but sometimes so were those who died shortly after birth, were stillborn, or were miscarried. These babies were frequently baptized by the midwife, *bapt. ab obstetrix* or *ex aqua baptis ab obstetrix*, "of the waters of baptism by the midwife." A more lengthy explanation is sometimes seen: *ante susceptu*

Baptisma mortuus est . . . per obst . . . male, "before receiving Baptism . . . he died . . . (baptized) by means of the midwife . . . unsuccessful."

There is usually a pattern of births in a family; for instance, a child is born every twenty months. A gap in this pattern may indicate a miscarriage, still-birth, or the death of one wife and the start of a second family by the remarriage of the father. Another explanation might be the absence of the father for a period of time while he was in the army, at sea, or looking for employment in a distant city or country.

Marriage Registers

Most people were married in the winter months between October (after the harvest) and February (before Lent). Exceptions were usually widows and widowers with small children, who needed someone to look after them and their children. It was not uncommon for a single man in his twenties to marry a widow in her forties with small children.

The names of the couple, ages, birth places, whether previously married, and sometimes occupations, are recorded. Additional genealogical information can often be found. A widow's previous marriage partners and her maiden name or the names of the parents of the bride and groom are often recorded.

Death/Funeral Records

Some genealogists build their pedigree charts only on birth and marriage records and do not bother to search death records because they think birth and marriage records yield the most information. This may be true; however, searching the death records may provide a clue when you are stuck or may even save you a lot of time, and sometimes embarrassment.

My great-grandmother Marianna Modrzynska was born in 1847. I was searching for her parents' records and found a baptismal record for Marcianna Rygielska, born 2 November 1820. This was the correct name, and these records were from the parish nearest to my great-grandmother's birth place. From that reel of baptismal records I constructed what I thought was a pedigree chart for *four full generations* beyond my great-grandmother. What luck!

Then I ordered the death records and recorded all the Rygielskis I found. But I found one that I wish I hadn't—Marcianna Rygielska, the one born on 2 November 1820, died 1 January 1821. She couldn't be my great-great-grandmother! Now I will have to continue searching the surrounding parishes for Marcianna's birth record.

Baptismal register from Św. Jakuba Większego (St. James the Greater) Church in Głuszyna, from the year 1843. The translation of the Latin text of entry #71 is "Julianna and Marianna Marciniak . . . of Marlewo (village). On the 25th of June I baptized an infant of the name Julianna and Marianna born on the 19th of June at the hour of 1 at night the daughter of Vincent Marciniak, village administrator, and Anastasia Ryszka his legitimate wife. Godparents of the child are Andreas Wojkiewicz, administrator, and Francesca Marciniak." Such an entry may cause confusion, giving the impression that it records the baptism of twins. However, the word "bino," meaning "two (names)," was added above the word "noñe," an abbreviation of "nomine" or name, some time after the original entry was made to help clarify the situation. (LDS microfilm #191623)

Marriage register from Głuszyna parish from the year 1883. The translation of the Latin text of entry #5 is "(The month of May) 24 (th day, married by the Reverend Eduardus _____), Josephus Hirsch, widower, and Marianna Pokrywka, widow, from the first vows (i.e., first marriage, to) Kaźmierczak, the second vows Kowalska, from home (i.e., the maiden name of) Tomczak—both of Czapury (village). (He is 62 years old, she is 48, both are Catholic, the three banns were announced on the Sundays indicated.) Petrus Plenzler and Andrzej Hirsch (witnesses) both of Czapury." This is the bride's fourth marriage. (LDS microfilm #1191625)

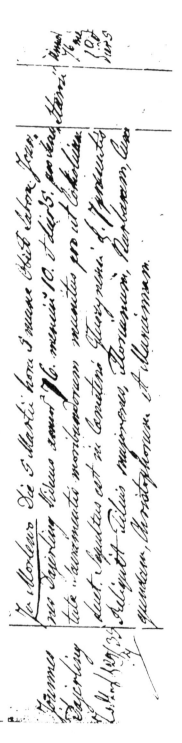

Funeral register from Głuszyna parish, written in Latin, for the month of March 1822. The second entry reads "Joannes Dajerling . . . of Marlewo. On the 5th of March at the hour of 5 in the morning died the industrious [a title for a hard-working peasant] Joannes Dajerling, widower, [aged] years 76, months 10, and days 5. The sacrament of Last Rites was administered. He was buried in the Cemetery of Głuszyna on the 7th. He leaves behind adult children, Florian, Barbara, Cunegunda, Christopher, and Marianna. [Cause of death column:] old age. [Age column:] years 76, months 10, days 5." The notation under the name in the first column indicates a death certificate was issued on 29 April 1835. (LDS microfilm #1191622)

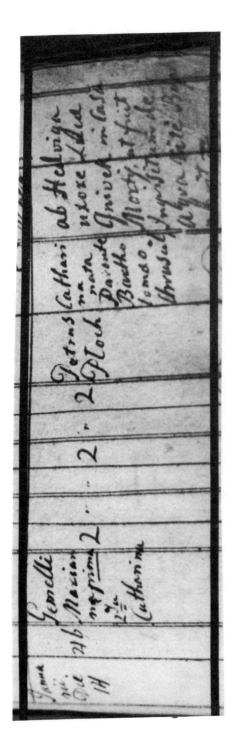

1791 baptismal entry from Widełka parish, Rzeszów province, Latin text. "January 14. House number 46. Twins, Marianna the first, the second Catharina. [The "2"s indicate both were Catholic, female, and legitimate births.] Father: Petrus Płoch, Mother: Catharina, born of the parent Bartholomeus Chrusciel. Godparents: At the hands of Hedviga wife of Lucas Gniwek. . . ." Evidently the twins were baptized by Hedwig Gniwek, who was probably a midwife (though that fact was usually noted) or a friend of the family, and present at the births. Midwives often baptized infants who were in frail health at birth and might not have lived long enough to have been baptized by the priest at a later date. (Photo furnished by Stanley Schmidt)

Polish Roots

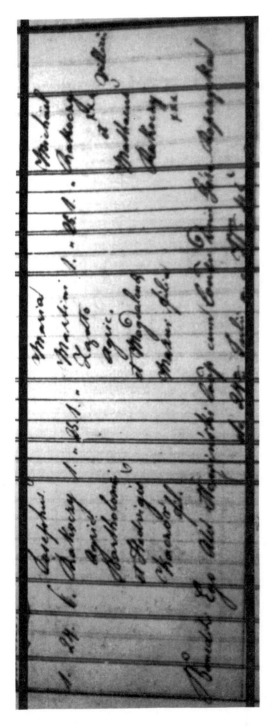

Marriage record from Kolbuszowa parish, Rzeszów province, for the year 1844, Latin text. "Number 1. July, 24. House number 6. Josephus Rakoczy, farmer, son of Bartholomeus and Hedwig Kaczor. Catholic, age 25, (previously) unmarried. Maria, daughter of Martin Ządło and Magdalena Mazur. Catholic, age 25, (previously) unmarried. Witnesses: Michael Rakoczy and Mathaeus Rakoczy, steward(s) (of an estate)." In Małopolska many parish registers were kept in loose-leaf format. Events were recorded with a separate page being used for each village in the parish (which might have served up to about ten villages). This page records the marriages of the residents of the village of Wola Starościńska for the year 1844—there is only this one page. (Photo furnished by Stanley Schmidt, from LDS microfilm #939973)

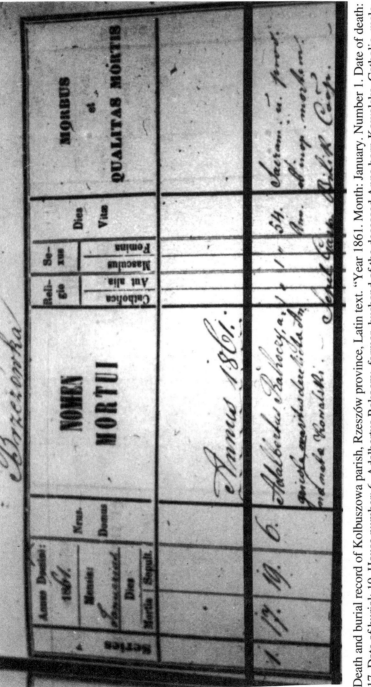

Death and burial record of Kolbuszowa parish, Rzeszów province, Latin text. "Year 1861. Month: January. Number 1. Date of death: 17. Date of burial: 19. House number: 6. Adalbertus Rakoczy, farmer, husband of the deceased Anna born Kowalska. Catholic, male. Age: 54 years." (Photo furnished by Stanley Schmidt, from LDS microfilm #939976)

In addition to the date of death and age of the deceased, many other items may be recorded in funeral or death registers: family relationships such as surviving children and spouses, names of parents and siblings, maiden names, birth order, occupations, social class, and the cause of death. Be aware that the ages given for elderly people are often inaccurate.

Looking over a page in the death register, you will immediately notice that most deaths are those of children. It was not unusual for a family with ten children to lose half of them before they became adults.

Depending on the parish, you may find death records for stillborn and miscarried babies. The age or cause of death in these cases may read *in viva* (female) or *in vivus* (male), "in/at life," meaning "died at birth." *Non viva* (female) or *non vivus* (male) means "not alive" at birth.

The Roman Catholic sacrament of extreme unction, or last rites, is given to dying people, or as soon as a priest reaches those already deceased. *Munitus* (male) and *munita* (female), meaning "fortified," and *extremum munitus (-a)* or *sacrementis totii munitiis*, "fortified by all the last rites," may also be found in eighteenth-century records. If a person died without receiving the last rites, you will find *non munitus* or *non munita*, "not fortified."

Availability of Roman Catholic Church Records

If you write to Poland for a church record, you should receive a certificate, (*świadectwo*) of the baptism, marriage, or death. The information will have been extracted from the original register (*metryka*). This certificate is an official certified record if it has the parish seal and is signed.

You may also want to see if the LDS has a microfilmed copy of the parish register. There may be more information of genealogical value in the original register than that written on the świadectwo.

Civil records, obtained from the local civil records office in the nearest town with such an office or in the state provincial archives, may also contain useful information. Some of these records may have been microfilmed by the LDS.

Recent records of baptisms, marriages, and deaths are found in local parishes. Most older records may be found in diocesan archives, state provincial archives, or in the parishes. If you write to the parish, your letter may be sent to the diocesan archives, or you may receive a reply telling you where to write to find the item that you are seeking.

You may also write to the Primate of Poland's office. You must provide the person's full name, correct name of the village and at least an approximate date of the event. This office will send your request to the proper parish or archives. Write to: Sekretariat Prymasa Polski, ul. Miodowa 17, 00-246 Warszawa, Polska (Poland).

Once you know the parish where your ancestor was baptized, you may be able to find additional information about your family from the Catholic University of Lublin's Institute of Polonian Migration and Religious Services at the following address: Biblioteka Uniwersytecka, Katolickiego Uniwersytetu Lubelskiego, ul. Chopina 27, 20-950 Lublin 1, Polska (Poland).

Roman Catholic Church Archives

If records cannot be found at your ancestor's parish, it might be best to try the diocesan or archdiocesan archives. If you are searching for older records a pastor will sometimes recommend that you correspond directly with the archives, or you may be directed to do so when you request the address of your ancestor's parish from the Catholic University of Lublin. In the list of archives that follows, the name of each diocese and archdiocese is in capital letters.

Archiwum Archidiecezjalne w Białymstoku
ul. Kościelna 1
15-087 BIAŁYSTOK
Polska (Poland)

Archiwum Diecezjalne w Częstochowie
al. Najś. Maryi Panny 54
42-200 CZĘSTOCHOWA
Polska (Poland)

Archiwum Diecezjalne w Gdańsku
ul. Opacka 5
80-330 GDAŃSK
Polska (Poland)

Archiwum Archidiecezjalne w Gnieźnie
katedra
62-200 GNIEŹNO
Polska (Poland)

Archiwum Diecezjalne w Katowicach
ul. Jordana 39
40-053 KATOWICE
Polska (Poland)

Archiwum Diecezjalne w Kielcach
ul. Świerczewskiego 23
25-013 KIELCE
Polska (Poland)

Archiwum Kurii Metropolitalnej w Krakowie
ul. Franciszkańska 3
31-004 KRAKÓW
Polska (Poland)

Archiwum Archidiecezjalne w Lubaczowie
ul. Adama Mickiewicza 77
37-600 LUBACZÓW
Polska (Poland)

Archiwum Diecezjalne w Lublinie
ul. Mariana Buczka 2
20-105 LUBLIN
Polska (Poland)

Archiwum Diecezjalne w Łomży
ul. Sadowa 3
18-400 ŁOMŻA
Polska (Poland)

Archiwum Diecezjalne w Łodzi
ul. Worcella 1
90-458 ŁÓDŹ
Polska (Poland)

Archiwum Diecezjalne w Olsztynie
ul. Staszica 2
10-020 OLSZTYN
Polska (Poland)

Archiwum Diecezjalne w Pelplinie
Ogród Biskupi 1
83-130 PELPLIN
Polska (Poland)

Archiwum Diecezjalne w Płocku
ul. Wolnej Afryki 2
09-900 PŁOCK
Polska (Poland)

Archiwum Archidiecezjalne w Poznaniu
ul. Lubrańskiego 1
61-108 POZNAŃ
Polska (Poland)

Archiwum Diecezjalne w Przemyślu
ul. Sanocka 20a
37-700 PRZEMYŚL
Polska (Poland)

Archiwum Diecezjalne w Sandomierzu
ul. Ściegiennego 2
27-600 SANDOMIERZ
Polska (Poland)

Archiwum Diecezjalne w Siedlcach
ul. Świerczewskiego 60
08-110 SIEDLCE
Polska (Poland)

Archiwum Diecezjalne w Tarnowie
pl. Św. Kazimierza 3
33-100 TARNÓW
Polska (Poland)

Archiwum Archidiecezjalne w Warszawie
ul. Świętojańska 8
00-288 WARSZAWA
Polska (Poland)

Archiwum Diecezjalne we Włocławku
ul. Mariana Buczka 9
87-800 WŁOCŁAWEK
Polska (Poland)

Archiwum Archidiecezjalne we Wrocławiu
ul. Kanonia 12
50-328 WROCŁAW
Polska (Poland)

(List provided by courtesy of the Polish Genealogical Society of Connecticut.)

ADDITIONAL READING

Chorzempa, Rosemary A. "Results of the Genetic Survey of Americans of Polish Descent." *Polish Genealogical Society Newsletter* XIII (Fall 1990), 29, 32, 34, and 40.

Litak, Stanisław. *The Latin Church in the Polish Commonwealth in 1772, a Map and Index of Localities.* Chicago: Polish Genealogical Society, 1990. A series of maps showing the Roman Catholic parishes in Poland in 1772; includes an index of all the parishes with map coordinates.

Ortell, Gerald A. *Polish Parish Records of the Roman Catholic Church, Their Use and Understanding in Genealogical Research.* Orem, Utah: Genun Publishers, P.O. Box 537. Includes much background information on the lives of our Polish ancestors.

Peckwas, Edward A. *Register of Vital Records of Roman Catholic Parishes from the Region Beyond the Bug River.* Chicago: Polish Genealogical Society, reprinted 1984. List of 522 parishes east of the Bug River, with the years available for each type of record—birth, marriage, and death—in each parish, mostly from the provinces of Lwów, Tarnopol, and Stanisławów. These records are available at the Presidium of the National Workers Council in Warsaw, whose address is given in the book.

Some from Volhynia

Polish Parish Maps. Chicago: Polish Genealogical Society, 1972. A set of four, 11-by-14-inch maps showing the Roman Catholic parishes, diocesan and decanate boundaries, as of 1972. Village and town names are not indexed. These maps can help you determine which church your ancestor may have attended, but you must know the map location of your village first.

GREEK CATHOLIC CHURCH

Most Orthodox Ukrainians were formally united with the Roman Catholic Church in 1596, but kept their Orthodox doctrines and liturgy. One such tradition is the baptism and confirmation of a member on the same day.

Greek Rite Catholicism was widely embraced in Ruthenia (Ukraine) and in the eastern regions of the Commonwealth. The Church was once referred to as the "Uniate" Church, a derogatory term, and is properly called the Greek Catholic Church.

Record-keeping began in the early 1600s, shortly after the union with Rome. Registers were written in Old Church Slavonic, Ukrainian, Polish, or Latin, and contained about the same information as the Roman Catholic registers.

Beginning in 1772, Czarina Catherine the Great began to persecute the Greek Catholics in the territories that Russia took over and forced the Greek Catholics to adopt the Russian Orthodox religion; thus more than two million people were "converted" to the Orthodox Church. Of the 5,000 Greek Catholic churches once in Volhynia and Podolia, only 200 remained in 1796. By 1839 the Czar and his representatives officially banned the Greek Catholic Church, but it existed in the Congress Kingdom of Poland until 1875, and in Galicia until World War II.

Most Eastern Churches in Europe, both Catholic and Orthodox, still use the Julian (old style) calendar, which is now thirteen days behind the Gregorian (new style) calendar. The Greek Rite uses the Byzantine Calendar of

Greek Catholic baptismal register from Gładyszów parish from the year 1776, for the village of Wierchni. The first entry reads "Month of September. Day: 9. Priest: Reverend B(azyli) Sembratowicz. Child: Maria. Parents: Grzegorz Drip-czak, laborer, from Wierzchni, (and his wife) Ahaphia. Godparents: Demitri Dziubina the industrious peasant, Theodossa the industrious wife of Theodore Skrypak, Maria the industrious wife of Mikolai Pawłow, from Gładyszów. Religion: Greek Catholic. House number: 7." (Photo furnished by Daniel Schlyter, from LDS microfilm #0766009)

Saints, which begins on September first, and contains many different feast days and saints than that of the Roman (Latin Rite) Calendar, which begins on January first.

For example, the Roman Catholic Church celebrates the Immaculate Conception of Mary on December 8, while the Greek Catholic Church celebrates the Conception of St. Ann (i.e., Mary's conception) on December 9. However, Greek Catholic churches in the United States have adopted many Roman Catholic practices, including the use of celibate priests, the Gregorian calendar, and the same major feast days, so now they also celebrate Mary's conception on December 8.

Availability of Greek Catholic Church Records

Recent records, those less than about 100 years old, can be found at the parish or local civil records offices. The state provincial archives and the Main Archives of Ancient Documents (see chapter 10) also keep Greek Catholic church records, and some have been microfilmed by the LDS. The archival collection of the Przemyśl diocese of the Eastern Rite is currently found in the state archives of Rzeszów province.

RUSSIAN ORTHODOX CHURCH

The Byzantine Catholic Church split with the Roman Catholic Church in 1054 A.D. and became known as the Orthodox Church. In 1448 the Orthodox Church in Russia proclaimed its independence from the patriarch in Constantinople and, in 1489, established a patriarchate in Moscow. The Russian Orthodox Church was continuously under the control of the Russian czars until the Russian Revolution. Orthodox Church members in Poland were mostly Byelorussians and Russians.

Registers were written in Old Church Slavonic or Russian, and began in the seventeenth century. Information found in these registers is about the same as that found in Roman Catholic Church records.

Availability of Russian Orthodox Church Records

Recent records are kept at parishes or local civil records offices. Orthodox records can also be found at the Main Archives of Ancient Documents and state provincial archives. Some have been microfilmed by the LDS.

EVANGELICAL (LUTHERAN) CHURCH

The Evangelical Church of the Augsburg Confession began as a movement by Martin Luther in the sixteenth century. Two sacraments are acknowledged: infant baptism and the Lord's Supper (communion).

The Evangelical Church began to keep registers in the early 1600s, recording births, marriages, deaths, and sometimes confirmations. Some registers were indexed. Registers were kept in the language of the people; thus they were recorded in German for the German-speaking inhabitants and colonists of Poland. The contents are the same as those of Roman Catholic origin.

Many parishes were started in the 1790s after the Third Partition, when large numbers of German immigrants were brought into the Prussian-occupied areas of Poland: Silesia, Pomerania, East and West Prussia, and Poznania. The Evangelical Church also was strong in Latvia and Estonia.

Availability of Evangelical Church Records

Recent Evangelical records are usually kept in the local civil records offices, or the parish itself if it is still active. They also may be found at state provincial archives or in Protestant or Catholic archives in Poland and Germany. Many Evangelical records have been microfilmed by the LDS.

A church-book information center founded by the Society of Eastern German Family Researchers may be able to help you find the present location of the church for which you are searching. Write to: Arbeitsgemeinschaft Ostdeutscher Familienforscher e. V., Kirchenbuchauskunftstelle, Sperlingstrasse 11a, 4236 Hamminkeln 4, Deutschland (Germany).

If your ancestors were from Pomerania, address your correspondence to the Pomeranian Evangelical Church in Greifswald, Germany: Pommersche Evangelische Kirche, Bahnhofstrasse 35, O-2200 Greifswald, Deutschland (Germany).

The Evangelical records in East Prussia were sent to the Central Archives of the Evangelical Church in Berlin: Evangelisches Zentralarchiv in Berlin, Jebenstrasse 3, W-1000 Berlin 12, Deutschland (Germany).

MENNONITE CHURCH

The Mennonite sect is a branch of the Anabaptist ("one who baptizes again") movement founded by Menno Simons in the early sixteenth century in Frisia (northern Netherlands near Germany). Adult baptism is the only recognized sacrament. Large numbers of Mennonites immigrated to Poland after 1642, most settling in the Gdańsk area.

Most Polish Mennonite congregations began keeping records of births and adult baptisms after 1772. Most are written in German; some of the early ones are in Dutch.

Availability of Mennonite Church Records

Mennonite records can be found in state and church archives in Poland and Germany. Some were brought to the United States and are in Mennonite archives or kept by the individual congregations.

REFORMED (PROTESTANT) CHURCH

The followers of Calvinism, like the other denominations being persecuted in Europe, found refuge in the Commonwealth. The Calvinist churches were called Reformed churches in Europe and Presbyterian [ARE CALLED] churches in America. There were about 140 Reformed churches in Lithuania in the seventeenth century.

Availability of Reformed Church Records

Some records are found in the parishes or in state or provincial archives, while those for Silesia may be found at the Central Archives of the Protestant Church, Jebenstrasse 3, West Berlin, Germany.

THE HEBREW RELIGION

[JEWISH]   *(HEBREW LANGUAGE)*

The Jewish immigrants were allowed to keep their language and culture as well as practice their faith until 1795 when Polish laws ceased to exist. The partitioning powers persecuted the Jews, severely limiting their civil rights.

The Hebrew calendar is different than the Gregorian calendar used by Christians. Our year 1 A.D., used by Christians as the birth of Christ, is equivalent to the Jewish year 3760. The year 1900 A.D. is equivalent to the Jewish year 5660. Christians use the initials A.D. ("Anno Domini," "the year of the Lord"). Jewish people prefer the initials C.E. ("Christian Era" or "Common Era") as the equivalent of A.D. The Jewish calendar counts the "Years of the World"—the time since creation. The Jewish New Year begins in late September or early October.

Eastern European Jews married early—the boys were often under eighteen years and the girls under sixteen. This tradition continued until about 1900. Consanguinity—marriage between first cousins or an uncle to a niece—was common. Jewish couples had very large families, and illegitimate births were rare.

Availability of Jewish Records

Births, marriages, and deaths were not consistently recorded. However, Jewish congregations kept marriage contracts, death memorial books, and circumcision records.

Many of these records were destroyed; however, many records from Europe are now in the United States. Check the books by Dan Rottenberg and Arthur Kurzweil (see Sources and Additional Reading at the end of the chapter), major public libraries, the Library of Congress, and the LDS. In addition to checking the village name in the LDS Locality Index, look under "Poland—Minorities" and "Poland—Military Records."

Several organizations throughout the world have been preserving Jewish records for many years. You may want to visit or correspond with the following:

Żydowski Instytut Historyczny
(Jewish Historical Institute)
al. Gen. Świerczewskiego 79
Warszawa
Polska (Poland)

YIVO Institute for Jewish Research
1948 Fifth Avenue
New York, New York 10028
YIVO was founded in 1925 in Wilno, Poland (now Vilnius, Lithuania), and is an acronym for *Yidisher Visnshaftlekher Institut*, Yiddish Scientific Institute. YIVO has one of the world's greatest archives on Eastern European Jewry.

Leo Baeck Institute
129 East 73rd Street
New York, New York 10021

The focus is on German-speaking Jews, including the parts of Poland occupied by Germany and Austria.

Jewish National University Library
Hebrew University
Givat Ram Campus
Jerusalem, Israel
The library has some birth and death registers, and some registers for a few dozen communities in the old Polish areas of Lithuania; some Russian records go back to at least the eighteenth century.

SOURCES AND ADDITIONAL READING

Kurzweil, Arthur. *From Generation to Generation: How to Trace Your Jewish and Personal History*. New York: William Morrow & Co., 1980.

Kurzweil, Arthur and Miriam Weiner, eds. *The Encyclopedia of Jewish Genealogy.* Vol. I. Sources in the United States and Canada. Northvale, New Jersey: Jason Aronson Inc., 1991.

Pogonowski, Iwo Cyprian. *Poland, A Historical Atlas*. New York: Hippocrene Books, 1987.

The Polish Encyclopaedia. Vol. II: Territory and Population of Poland. Geneva, Switzerland: Atar, Ltd., 1924. Reprint edition by Arno Press, Inc., 1972. See "The Jewish Population" on pages 638 to 667, and "The Jews in Poland" in the Appendix.

Rottenberg, Dan. *Finding Our Fathers*. Baltimore: Genealogical Publishing Company, 1986 (reprint).

Schlyter, Daniel M. "Sources for Genealogical Research in Poland." *Polish Genealogical Society Newsletter* IV (Fall 1982), 1, 31.

Tazbir, Janusz. *A State Without Stakes: Religious Toleration in Reformation Poland*. Translated by A. T. Jordan. New York: Kosciuszko Foundation.

Chapter Ten:

CIVIL RECORDS

RUSSIAN-OCCUPIED TERRITORY

Imperial Russia annexed 73 percent of the land in the Polish Commonwealth during the partitions of 1772, 1793, and 1795. Russia acquired the Grand Duchy of Lithuania, Courland, Livonia, Byelorussia, Ruthenia (Ukraine), Podlasie and Podolia, and in 1805 the Lublin area.

In 1807 the Grand Duchy of Warsaw was formed by Napoleon as a French protectorate. The Duchy was an irregular patch in central Poland that included Poznań, Warsaw, and (after 1809) Kraków. Most of the Duchy fell into Russian hands after 1815.

The former Polish-Lithuanian regions were divided into eight administrative units in 1801, and were largely controlled by Polish administrators until 1831. This area had the highest standard of living in all the Russian Empire.

Civil registration was introduced by Napoleon in 1808 in the Duchy of Warsaw and was continued by the Russian administration. The clergy were appointed civil registrars. Birth, marriage, and death registers were kept in Polish, and most have indexes for each year.

After the insurrection of 1863, an intense Russification program began: the Kingdom of Poland was renamed the "Vistulan Region," the Polish language was forbidden, and Catholic churches were persecuted, some being converted into Russian Orthodox churches. Peasants who resisted were tortured and deported to Siberia, and many villages were burned. Beginning in 1864, the Russian administration required that vital records be kept in the Russian language.

The Polish people could not tolerate the Russian administration any longer and began emigrating in large numbers in the late 1880s. At the same time, political activity increased, with the vision of an independent Poland on the horizon. One example of such activity was the assassination of Czar Alexander II in 1881 by a bomb thrown by a Polish engineering student, who was also killed.

GULF OF
RIGA

Livo

Gauja

Venta

Riga

Lielude

Dv

BALTIC

SEA

Klaipeda

Tilsit

Niemen

Królewiec (Königsberg)

Wilno (Vilnius

Gdańsk

Pregoła

Koszalin

Eastern Prussia

Wilia

Pomerania

Elbląg

Lidzbark

Suwałki

Szczecin

Western Prussia

Wisła

Olsztyn

Grodno

Brandenburg

Piła

Notec'

Bydgoszcz

Myszyniec

Białystok

Odra

Warta

Toruń

Narew

Poznań

Inowrocław

Płock

Poznania

Warszawa

Bug

Brest Litovsk

P

Saxony

Nysa

Silesia

Pilica

Wisła

Wieprz

Styr

Wrocław

Odra

Warta

Lublin

Chełm

Łuck

Częstochowa

Sandomierz

Bełz

Bohemia

Wisła

San

Bielsko

Biała

Kraków

Rzeszów

Galicia

Lvov

Tarnopol

Moravia

Wisłoka

Nowy Targ

Dniester

Spisz

Austria

Chocir

Bukovin

POLAND DURING THE PARTITIONS, 1772 TO 1795

TERRITORIAL CHANGES AFTER THE THIRD PARTITION

Russia took over the Lublin area in 1805. In 1807, the formerly Prussian-occupied areas of Poznań and Warsaw, and (after 1809) Kraków, became known as the Grand Duchy of Warsaw, a French Protectorate under Napoleon's rule. The Prussians retained parts of East and West Prussia and Silesia. Napoleon's legions defeated Austria in 1809, and liberated the Polish territory taken in the Third Partition and Zamość. In 1814–15, the Congress of Vienna gave the Duchy of Warsaw to Russia, and restored Zamość and the Austrian Third Partition territory to Austria, except the area around Kraków, which was established as a Free City (until the Austrian government again took control of this territory in 1846). The French Departments of Poznań (renamed the Grand Duchy of Posen) and Bydgoszcz (including Chełmno and Toruń; all being absorbed by West Prussia) were returned to Prussia.

Russia did not adopt the Gregorian calendar until 1918, although the Poles had been using it since 1582. You may find two dates, twelve days apart, on a vital record or in a register from the Russian area; the earlier date is the Russian date, the later date is the Polish/Gregorian date.

Availability of Russian Civil Records

Recent records, those less than 100 years old, are kept at the local civil records offices, while older ones may be found at the state provincial archives. Many records have been microfilmed by the LDS.

For areas not currently in Poland, see the latest information about genealogical research in Russia on page 228.

PRUSSIAN/GERMAN-OCCUPIED TERRITORY

The Germans expanded westward into Pomerania by the 1100s and colonized Prussia (extending their territory by the sword) from 1205 until their defeat in the 1400s. After breaking free of the Polish Crown in 1657 as the Kingdom of Prussia, the Germans continued to expand until they were able to seize Silesia from the Austrian Hapsburgs in 1740. Prussia gained 15 percent of the land of the Polish Commonwealth during the partitions of 1772, 1793, and 1795, including Great Poland, Poznania, Kuyavia, East Pomerania, Warmia, Mazovia, Mazuria, and Gdańsk Pomerania. About three-fourths of the 4 million people who lived in these areas were ethnic Poles.

In 1807 Napoleon's legions defeated Prussia, liberating most of the Polish territory taken in the partitions, from Poznania (which welcomed its liberators without a shot being fired in resistance), Bydgoszcz, and Toruń to the Niemen River. The Germans retained only part of what was called West Prussia, East Prussia, and Silesia.

In 1814–15 the Congress of Vienna gave most of the departments of Poznań and Bydgoszcz (which included Chełmno and Toruń) back to Prussia. West Prussia absorbed Chełmno and Toruń, while the rest was called the Grand Duchy of Posen (Wielkie Księstwo Poznanskie).

The Prussian administration required that the German language be used in church services in Silesia and seized the land of many Polish landowners in 1824. In 1834 an ordinance was passed to prohibit the use of the Polish language in schools in Pomerania. The ordinance was extended in 1887 to include Poznania, Warmia, and Mazuria. After 1900 more than 100,000 Polish school children participated in school strikes demanding education in the Polish language. Children were beaten in public for the protests, and their parents were jailed if they protested the beatings. Forced Germanization led to the Polish language and culture studies going underground; you may have heard stories of these events from your grandparents. Polish newspapers and associations were banned.

In 1858 the average peasant farm was 33 hectares (about 80 to 85 acres). As the hundredth anniversary of the partitions approached, the Prussians increased their anti-Polish policies. The German *Kulturkampf* (Culture Struggle) began as an anti-Catholic and anti-Polish policy of the Berlin government. The Prussian administration forced the Poles off their lands and sold the land to German settlers. This Germanization caused the mass emigration of Poles from the Prussian territories of Poland beginning about 1870. Over one million Poles emigrated from this area from 1870 to 1914, most coming to the United States.

In 1918 the Wielkopolska (Great Poland) Uprising established Poznania's independence, and the defeat of Germany in the First World War brought most of West Prussia ("The Polish Corridor" to the Baltic Sea) to the independent Second Republic of Poland. The Versailles Treaty established Gdańsk/Danzig as a free city from 1919, while Upper Silesia joined Poland by plebiscite in 1920–22. In 1939 Germany invaded and occupied Gdańsk and all Polish territory as far as the frontiers of Soviet-held territory.

In 1945 Poland regained its independence, including Pomerania (east of the Odra/Oder River), East Prussia, and Lower Silesia, which had been under foreign rule for some eight, seven, and six centuries, respectively.

Prussian laws required that church registers be kept. Civil registration was not introduced until 1874 and was administered by civil registrars; the records were almost always kept in German, occasionally in Polish. Persons of all religions were recorded in one register.

The LDS has microfilmed copies of these civil registers; however, all the ones that I have seen cover only the years 1874 to 1882 sporadically.

Availability of Prussian/German Civil Records

Most civil records from the Prussian-occupied areas are in local civil records offices in Poland. Some are in archives in Germany, and some have been microfilmed by the LDS.

AUSTRIAN-OCCUPIED TERRITORY

Austria took over Bohemia, its Polish territory of Silesia (under Bohemian control since 1339), and half of Hungary in 1526, but lost Silesia to Prussia in 1740. In 1769 Austria took the Spisz lands in the Carpathians from Poland.

Baptismal register entry in Russian text and Cyrillic alphabet from the Roman Catholic parish of St. Ann's in Blichowo, Warsaw province; at the time of recording it was in the Russian gubernia of Płock. For the year 1878, Wołowa (village), entry no. 66: "It happened in Blichowo on 9 October 1878 at the tenth hour that an appearance was made by Tomasz Boczkowski, laborer, resident of Wołowa, 44 years, in the presence of Mikołaj Stanisławski 44 years and Marcin Krzemiński 44 years, residents of Wołowa, and to present a child of the male sex born in Wołowa today at the fourth hour this morning, of his wife Katarzyna of Zaglewski (her maiden name) 40 years. Infant baptism on this day was performed by the Reverend Dobski who conferred the name Franciszek, and the godparents being Franciszek Boczkowski and Rozalia Pikała. This act stands and because of the inability of the witnesses to read over (the document) and write (their signatures) only my signature remains. I maintain the Civil Records Office of the Parish of Blichowo. Rev. Witalis Dobski." The parish priests acted as civil registrars in the Russian-occupied areas of Poland during the time the country was partitioned, and after 1864 the records were directed to be kept in Russian. In this area, records of all the villages in the parish were kept together. Baby Franciszek (Francis) may have been named for St. Francis of Assisi (feast day October 4) or St. Francis Borgia (feast day October 10) or after his godfather who had the same first and last names as the child; both traditions were practiced in Poland. (LDS microfilm #1201384)

A page from the death register from the Urząd Stanu Cywilnego in Kórnik, in the German-occupied area, from the year 1875, obtained from the Archiwum Państwowe in Poznań. Valentine, son of the deceased, reported his father's death to the civil records office in Kórnik, about eight miles from Daszewice, where the death occurred, on 10 February 1875, the day after the death. The deceased Peter Pokrywka was reported to be 90 years old. (His age in the church death register was given as 80, and his age was reported to be 25 at the time of his marriage in 1827.) His deceased wife's name was given—Maria(nna) born Adamczyk—but the most important piece of information found in this document is Peter's birthplace, "Jerzyce" (Jeżyce, in Poznań), which was unknown before this document was found. The records of Głuszyna parish, to which the village of Daszewice belonged, were very useful in tracing the Pokrywka family back to Peter Pokrywka. However, a problem appeared in the search for Peter's birth record, and was solved by checking *all* available resources, leading to the revelation that Peter's natural father Jacob Nawrot died when Peter was a child. His mother then married Antoni Pokrywka, and Peter assumed his stepfather's name, a common practice in the past.

The Austrian share of the Polish lands annexed during the partitions was 12 percent. In 1772 the Austrians acquired Little Poland and the western part of Ruthenia (Ukraine). The Third Partition in 1795 brought in the Lublin area.

The Austrian Empire renamed southern Poland, called Little Poland by the Poles (including the city of Kraków), Galicia and Lodomeria. Galicia and Lodomeria were names of Ruthenian/Ukrainian provinces. The policy of the Austrian government was to eliminate everything Polish, including place names. They imposed heavy taxes, censorship, a "police state" terrorizing the residents, and a German bureaucracy with its complex trivialities designed to antagonize the Poles. ᴸᴬᴺᴳᵁᴬᴳᴱ

In 1809 Napoleon's legions defeated Austria, liberating the Polish territory taken in the Third Partition, together with Zamość (held since the First Partition). In 1814–15 the Congress of Vienna restored this territory to Austria, except for the territory around Kraków, which it established as a free city. In 1846 Austria took over the Free City of Kraków. In 1918 all of Galicia, including Kraków, regained its independence as part of the Second Polish Republic.

Galicia had the highest birth and death rates in Europe, as well as the highest income tax rate. It was also the most underdeveloped area industrially; although agriculture was the basis of the economy, modern farming techniques were being implemented slowly. At mid-nineteenth century the average peasant farm was only 5 hectares (about 12 acres). Heavy floods devastated Galicia in 1836. The Great Famine occurred in 1853 to 1855, and another famine occurred in 1907.

Mass emigration began in Galicia in the late 1890s to 1900, later than in the other areas. By 1914 between one and two million Poles had left Galicia, most of them going to the United States.

The Austrian administration required that civil registration begin in Galicia in 1784. Catholic parish registers were used as the civil records. Duplicates were made for administration purposes (most likely for tax records, as a "census," and as a means of military conscription), but there may have been errors in the copying process. Non-Catholics were responsible for keeping their own vital records after 1869. If your ancestors were not Catholic, you may still find their pre-1869 records at the local Catholic parish or diocesan archives.

Availability of Austrian Civil Records

Recent records are kept at the local civil records office. Originals can be found at local parishes or church archives, and duplicates (watch for errors)

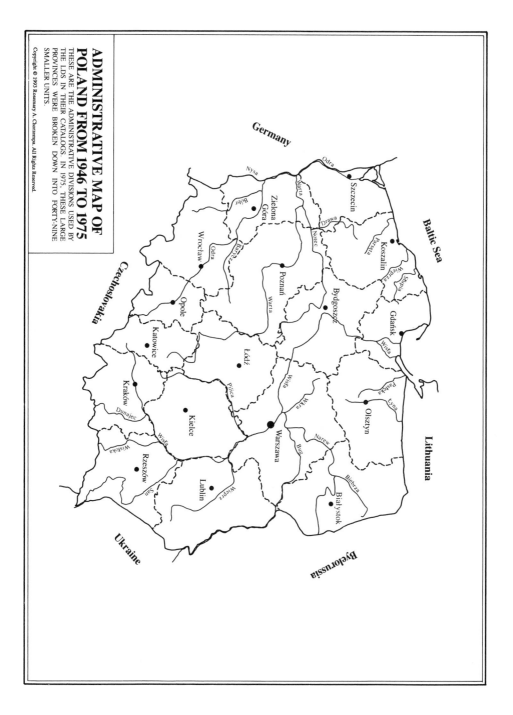

ADMINISTRATIVE MAP OF POLAND FROM 1946 TO 1975

THESE ARE THE ADMINISTRATIVE DIVISIONS USED BY THE LDS IN THEIR CATALOGS. IN 1975, THESE LARGE PROVINCES WERE BROKEN DOWN INTO FORTY-NINE SMALLER UNITS.

are at the state provincial archives. Many records have been microfilmed by the LDS.

ARCHIVES IN POLAND

National Archives

The Main Archives of Ancient Documents is the equivalent of a national records office. "Ancient documents" are those that originate before 1945. Among the records kept at this archives are judicial records, records of ennoblements, naturalizations, awards of coats of arms, and genealogical collections, including family histories.

The archives also houses the older records (more than 100 years old) of the Zabużański ("territory beyond the Bug River") collection of birth, marriage, and death records from 522 Roman Catholic parishes in Polish territories that were ceded to the Soviet Union after World War II. These parishes were in the East Galician districts of Lwów, Tarnopol, and Stanisławów; some records from Volhynia also are included. (See page 128 for Edward Peckwas' book about the Zabużański collection.) More recent records of the Zabużański collection are at the National Workers Council in Warsaw:

> Urząd Stanu Cywilnego
> Dzielnicowa Rada Narodowa
> Warszawa Śródmieście
> Archiwum Akt Zabużańskich
> ulica Jezuicka 1/3
> Polska (Poland)

The address of the Main Archives of Ancient Documents is:

> Archiwum Głowne Akt Dawnych
> ul. Długa 7
> 00-263 Warszawa
> Polska (Poland)

The Main Archives of New (Modern) Records houses records from 1945 to the present:

> Archiwum Akt Nowych
> aleja Niepodległości 162
> 02-554 Warszawa
> Polska (Poland)

State Provincial Archives/Regional Archives

Civil records older than 100 years are kept at the various state archives, while more recent registers and transcripts can be found at local civil records offices. In the former German territories, the records are divided at the year 1874.

Provincial administrations were divided into the following provinces (województwa) until 1975: Szczecin, Koszalin, Gdańsk, Olsztyn, Białystok, Warszawa, Bydgoszcz, Zielona Góra, Poznań, Łódź, Kielce, Lublin, Wrocław, Opole, Katowice, Kraków, and Rzeszów.

The LDS uses these seventeen provinces as the major subdivisions of Poland in their catalogs, but in 1975 these larger provinces were broken up into forty-nine smaller administrative units. When writing for civil records, use the following addresses of these smaller administrative units, always ending the address with the country name—Polska (Poland). The names of the administrative units are in capital letters. To find the correct archives, locate your village on a current Polish road atlas or administrative map (available in libraries or Polish-American bookstores or gift shops). If your village is closer to one of the branch archives, you may write to that branch.

Archiwum Państwowe w Białymstoku
Rynek T. Kościuszki 4
15-950 BIAŁYSTOK

Branch of Białystok Archives:
ul. Świerczewskiego 36
18-400 ŁOMŻA

Archiwum Państwowe w Bydgoszczy
ul. Dworcowa 65
85-009 BYDGOSZCZ

Branch of Bydgoszcz Archives:
ul. Narutowicza 58
88-100 INOWROCŁAW

Archiwum Państwowe w Częstochowie
ul. Warszawska 172
42-200 CZĘSTOCHOWA

Archiwum Państwowe w Elblągu (Archives for ELBLĄG)
Zamek
82-200 Malbork

Archiwum Państwowe w Gdańsku
ul. Wały Piastowskie 5
80-958 GDAŃSK

Archiwum Państwowe w Jeleniej Górze
ul. Podwale 27
58-500 JELENIA GÓRA

Archiwum Państwowe w Kaliszu
ul. Kolegialna 4
62-800 KALISZ

Archiwum Państwowe w Katowicach
ul. Jagiellońska 25
40-950 KATOWICE

Branch of Katowice Archives:
ul. Sienkiewicza 33
42-500 BĘDZIN

Branch of Katowice Archives:
ul. Słowackiego 80
43-300 BIELSKO-BIAŁA

Branch of Katowice Archives:
Pl. Thalmanna 2
41-902 BYTOM

Branch of Katowice Archives:
ul. Krakowska 21a
32-500 CHRZANÓW

Branch of Katowice Archives:
ul. Regera 6
43-400 CIESZYN

Branch of Katowice Archives:
ul. Zygmunta Starego 8
44-100 GLIWICE

Branch of Katowice Archives:
Muzeum Blok 1
32-603 OŚWIĘCIM

Branch of Katowice Archives:
ul. Brama Wybrańców 2
43-200 PSZCZYNA

Branch of Katowice Archives:
ul. Zamkowa 2
47-400 RACIBÓRZ

Branch of Katowice Archives:
ul. Rynek 18
44-200 RYBNIK

Branch of Katowice Archives:
ul. Gliwicka 5
42-600 TARNOWSKIE GÓRY

Branch of Katowice Archives:
ul. Marchlewskiego 2
34-300 ŻYWIEC

Archiwum Państwowe w Kielcach
ul. Rewolucji Październikowej 17
25-953 KIELCE

Branch of Kielce Archives:
ul. Wł. Rejmonta 21a
28-300 JĘDRZEJÓW

Branch of Kielce Archives:
ul. Batalionów Chłopskich 42
28-400 PINCZÓW

Branch of Kielce Archives:
ul. Basztowa 4
27-600 SANDOMIERZ

Branch of Kielce Archives:
ul. Spółdzielcza 2
27-210 STARACHOWICE

Archiwum Państwowe w Koszalinie
ul. Zywcięstwa 117
75-601 KOSZALIN

Branch of Koszalin Archives:
ul. Parkowa 3
78-400 SZCZECINEK

Archiwum Państwowe w Krakowie
ul. Sienna 16
31-041 KRAKÓW

Branch of Kraków Archives:
ul. Kazimierza Wielkiego 31
32-700 BOCHNIA

Branch of Kraków Archives:
ul. Szwedzka 2
33-300 NOWY SĄCZ

Branch of Kraków Archives:
ul. Królowej Jadwigi 10
34-400 NOWY TARG

Branch of Kraków Archives:
ul. Kniewskiego 24
33-100 TARNÓW

Archiwum Państwowe w Lesznie
ul. Bolesława Chrobrego 32
64-100 LESZNO

Archiwum Państwowe w Lublinie
ul. Trybunalska 13
20-950 LUBLIN

Branch of Lublin Archives:
Plac 1 Maja 1
22-300 KRASNYSTAW

Branch of Lublin Archives:
ul. Dzierżynskiego 2
23-210 KRAŚNIK

Branch of Lublin Archives:
ul. Międzyrzeczka 2
21-300 RADZYŃ PODLASKI

Archiwum Państwowe w Łodzi
Plac Wolności 1
91-415 ŁÓDŹ

Branch of Łódź Archives:
ul. Wandy Wasilewskiej 6
95-200 PABIANICE

Branch of Łódź Archives:
ul. 15 Grudnia 5
98-200 SIERADZ

Archiwum Państwowe w Olsztynie
ul. Zamkowa 3
10-074 OLSZTYN

Branch of Olsztyn Archives:
ul. Hanki Sawickiej 4
14-300 MORĄG

Branch of Olsztyn Archives:
ul. Armii Czerwonej 55
11-700 MRĄGOWO

Branch of Olsztyn Archives:
ul. Polska 35
12-100 SZCZYTNO

Archiwum Państwowe w Opolu
ul. Zamkowa 2
45-016 OPOLE

Branch of Opole Archives:
ul. Bolesława Chrobrego 17
49-300 BRZEG

Branch of Opole Archives:
ul. Kolejowa 15
48-300 NYSA

Archiwum Państwowe w Piotrkowie Trybunalskim
ul. Toruńska 4
97-300 PIOTRKÓW TRYBUNALSKI

Branch of Piotrków Trybunalski Archives:
ul. Tkacka 2
97-200 TOMASZÓW MAZOWIECKI

Archiwum Państwowe w Płocku
ul. 1 Maja 1
09-402 PŁOCK

Archiwum Państwowe w Poznaniu
ul. 23 Lutego 41/43
61-744 POZNAŃ

Branch of Poznań Archives:
ul. Wojska Polskiego 18
62-500 KONIN

Branch of Poznań Archives:
ul. Kilinskiego 12
64-920 PIŁA

Archiwum Państwowe w Przemyślu
ul. Polskiego Czerwonego Krzyża 4
37-700 PRZEMYŚL

Branch of Przemyśl Archives:
ul. Rynek 1
37-200 PRZEWORSK

Archiwum Państwowe w Radomiu
Rynek 1
26-600 RADOM

Archiwum Państwowe w Rzeszowie
ul. Bóżnicza 4
35-064 RZESZÓW

Branch of Rzeszów Archives:
ul. Lenartowicza 9
38-200 JASŁO

Archiwum Państwowe w Siedlcach
ul. 1 Maja 2
08-100 SIEDLCE

Archiwum Państwowe w Słupsku
ul. M. Buczka 17
76-200 SŁUPSK

Branch of Słupsk Archives:
ul. Grunwaldzka 1
77-200 MIASTKO

Branch of Słupsk Archives:
ul. M. Curie Skłodowskiej 1
76-100 SŁAWNO

Archiwum Państwowe w Starym Kisielinie
66-002 STARY KISIELIN 31

Branch of Stary Kisielin Archives:
Palac
66-200 WILKÓW ŚWIEBODZIN

Branch of Stary Kisielin Archives:
Plac Kardynała Wyszyńskiego 2
68-200 ŻARY

Archiwum Państwowe w Suwałkach
ul. Kościuszki 69
16-400 SUWAŁKI

Branch of Suwałki Archives:
ul. Kąpielowa 1
19-300 EŁK

Archiwum Państwowe w Szczecinie
ul. Św. Wojciecha 13
70-410 SZCZECIN

Branch of Szczecin Archives:
Bogdaniec
66-450 LUBCZYNO

Branch of Szczecin Archives:
ul. Zamkowa 2
73-310 PŁOTY

Branch of Szczecin Archives:
ul. Basztowa 2
73-110 STARGARD SZCZECIŃSKI

Archiwum Państwowe w Toruniu
Plac Rapackiego 4
87-100 TORUŃ

Branch of Toruń Archives:
ul. Mickiewicza 26
86-300 GRUDZIĄDZ

Branch of Toruń Archives:
ul. Kościuszki 13
87-800 WŁOCŁAWEK

Archiwum Państwowe Miasta Stołecznego Warszawy
(State.Archives of the Capital City of Warsaw)
ul. Krzywe Koło 7
00-270 WARSZAWA

Branch of Warszawa Archives:
ul. Wł. Jagiełły 31
13-200 DZIAŁDOWO

Branch of Warszawa Archives:
ul. Ks. Sajny 1
05-530 GÓRA KALWARIA

Branch of Warszawa Archives:
ul. Świerczewskiego 1
99-400 ŁOWICZ

Branch of Warszawa Archives:
ul. Nowotki 3
06-500 MŁAWA

Branch of Warszawa Archives:
ul. Kościuszki 1
05-100 NOWY DWÓR MAZOWIECKI

Branch of Warszawa Archives:
ul. Górna 7
05-400 OTWOCK

Branch of Warszawa Archives:
ul. Zaułek 2
06-100 PUŁTUSK

Branch of Warszawa Archives:
ul. Kościuszki 5
96-200 RAWA MAZOWIECKI

Branch of Warszawa Archives:
Plac Wolności 2
05-730 ŻYRARDÓW

Archiwum Państwowe w Wrocławiu
ul. Pomorska 2
50-215 WROCŁAW

Branch of Wrocław Archives:
ul. Poniatowskiego 57
58-370 BOGUSZÓW

Branch of Wrocław Archives:
ul. Piastowska 22
59-220 LEGNICA

Archiwum Państwowe w Zamościu
ul. Moranda 4
22-400 ZAMOŚĆ

(List of archives provided by courtesy of the Polish Genealogical Society of Connecticut.)

The five-digit numbers that appear before the name of each city are the Polish postal codes. Translations of some of the abbreviations used in addresses are provided here, in case you want to know what they represent:

al. (aleja)—avenue, boulevard, alley
pl. (plac)—square
ul. (ulica)—street
— (zamek)—castle

Local Records Offices

Most towns and large villages have or had an Office of Civil Records, similar to county courthouses in the United States. The National Library in

Poland can determine the correct local civil records office for your village (see address on pages 100 and 167), or a Polish gazetteer can give you the location of the nearest civil records office to your ancestor's village.

As already stated, civil registers and transcripts less than 100 years old are kept at local civil records offices, except those from the former German-occupied territories. In those areas, records from 1874 to the present are at local offices. Older civil records from all areas of Poland are found at state provincial archives.

If you wish to write to the local civil records office (Urząd stanu cywilnego), address your letter this way:

Urząd stanu cywilnego
(name of town)
Polska (Poland)

RECORDS OF DEPARTURE

More than four million people left ethnically Polish lands between the years 1870 and 1914. About 1,250,000 left the Russian-occupied territory, over 1,200,000 left the Prussian (German)-occupied territory, and two million left the poorest region, controlled by Austria.

Major ports of departure for the Poles were Hamburg and Bremen in Germany, Antwerp (Antwerpen) in Belgium, and Amsterdam in the Netherlands. Some families from Little Poland left Europe through Rotterdam in the Netherlands. Few records for Antwerp and Amsterdam exist. The Bremen passenger lists for 1832 to 1907 were destroyed by the German government due to a lack of storage space, and later lists were destroyed in World War II.

Wien-Konskriptionsemt (Vienna Passport Registers) are available at the LDS on microfilm with indexes for the years 1792 to 1901, for those emigrants who left via that route.

The Hamburg passenger lists were compiled from 1845 until 1934 for those emigrants who left Europe via Hamburg, Germany. Name, age, occupation, and place of residence were recorded for each person.

The Manuscript Division of the Library of Congress in Washington has some of these Hamburg lists and indexes on microfilm; so do the Burton Collection of the Detroit Public Library and the Allen County (Indiana) Public Library, and probably other research facilities as well. The LDS has microfilmed records and indexes for the years 1850 to 1934.

The Historic Emigration Office can provide you with a certificate containing your ancestor's personal data—age, occupation, marital status, number of children, city of origin, name of the ship, date of departure—if your ancestor sailed through Hamburg from 1845 to 1934. You must provide the exact year of emigration.

> Historic Emigration Office
> c/o Tourist Information am Hafen
> Bei den St.-Pauli-Landungsbrücken 3
> P.O. Box 102249
> D-2000 Hamburg 36
> Germany

There are other records from Hamburg that may contain your ancestor's name if he or she travelled through that city. *Reisepassprotokolle* (travel passport records) from 1852 to 1929 and *Allgemeine Fremden Meldeprotokolle* (general out-of-town arrivals) for male and female laborers and servants (1843 to 1890) and male and female transients (1868 to 1899) are all available at the LDS on microfilm.

To locate these records look in the Locality Index under "Germany—Hamburg—Emigration and Immigration," "Germany—Hamburg—Occupations," and "Germany—Hamburg—Population." Most are indexed, but not everyone passing through Hamburg was registered on these rolls.

POLISH MILITARY RECORDS

Poles were drafted into the military services of all three partitioning powers shortly after those new territories were acquired. See the references to military records under Poland, Russia, Austria, and Germany or Prussia in the Locality Index at the LDS.

Russian-occupied Territory

In 1874 a new law required that members of all classes be subject to military draft at age twenty-one. Information of genealogical value is found in the Draft Commission records, which are written in Russian and are available at the LDS.

Prussian-occupied Territory

Mandatory military service was introduced in 1816. Many Poles served in Prussian or German military units up to and including World War I.

Parish baptismal registers were used by the Prussian government to enlist conscripts. Notes were made in these registers that attest to the conscript's service: "Z. militair 26/5 (18)37," for example.

Austrian-occupied Territory

Clergy, nobility, government officials, and a few other occupations were exempt from military service. Obviously the Austrian government did not want intelligent, well-educated men to stir up trouble in their army, as it was just such men who led the wars of the partitions, and the uprisings of 1830–31, 1844–48, and 1863–64.

People with Jewish ancestors may find genealogical information in the Austrian military records, though of course many other Jewish records were destroyed. The government did not discriminate against the Jews, and they were conscripted along with the Catholics, Protestants, and Orthodox. Jews were also conscripted into the Russian military.

The LDS has microfilmed many Austrian military records. See the entry "Austria—Military History" in the Locality Index.

If you have a definite location and year of birth for your ancestor, check LDS film no. 1186632, item 1 (distribution location index of the Austro-Hungarian Empire army and navy troops, regiments, etc.), which lists the Austrian units that recruited in each area and when they were in each locality. Then you can check that unit's records for your ancestor.

SOURCES AND ADDITIONAL READING

Blodgett, Steven W. "Great Grandfather Was in the Imperial Cavalry: Using Austrian Military Records as an Aid to Writing Family History." *Polish Genealogical Society Newsletter* VI (Spring 1984), 3, 6, and 12.

Diestler, Martin A. A. "Tracing Emigration Through Hamburg Police Records." *Polish Genealogical Society Newsletter* XII (Fall 1989), 34.

Grimstead, Patricia Kennedy. *Archives and Manuscript Repositories in the U.S.S.R.: Estonia, Latvia, Lithuania, and Belorussia*. Princeton, New Jersey: Princeton University Press, 1981.

Himka, John-Paul and Frances A. Swyripa. *Sources for Researching Ukrainian Family History*. Research Report #6, 1984. Available from the publisher: Canadian Institute of Ukrainian Studies, 352 Athabasca Hall, University of Alberta, Edmonton, Alberta, Canada T6G 2E8

Chapter Eleven:

SURNAMES

People took surnames to distinguish their family from their neighbors. Then families altered these names or assumed new ones to distinguish *their* line from others with the same name. People adopted new names to reflect new homes or other accomplishments.

Your ancestor's surname may be a clue to the origin of your family in the old country. The following surname patterns are most frequently used by these ethnic groups, but exceptions do occur.

POLISH SURNAMES

Polish surnames are derived from the following origins, as are most other European surnames: place names; patronymics and matronymics; trades and occupations; and physical appearance, personality, or nicknames.

Criminals and outlaws might assume new names to hide their identity—likewise, during the 123 years of the partitions or during the six-year Nazi occupation or the attempted suppression of Solidarity in 1981–83, insurrectionists or other resistance members (freedom fighters) assumed new names not only to protect themselves but to avoid government retaliation against their families.

Finally, former serfs (officially emancipated in the early to mid-nineteenth century) assumed surnames, often taking the names of the lords for whom they had worked, or possibly the names of famous, widely admired men like Kościuszko or Pulaski (Puławski).

While it is true that centuries ago *-cki* and *-ski* were signs of noble birth, they no longer are. Names ending with *-cki* and *-ski* are found more frequently in Great Poland than in Little Poland. Women's surnames can end in *-ówna*; if the name ends in *-cki* or *-ski*, the feminine form ends in *-cka* or *-ska*, respectively.

There were ancient noble surnames that never ended in *-cki* or *-ski*: most importantly, Piast (the surname of all Polish kings from Mieszko I to Casimir III "the Great," the first and only true Polish national dynasty). Jagiełło (the second national dynasty), Radziwiłł, Rejtan, and Kościuszko are really of Lithuanian origin. Wasa and Batory are, respectively, Swedish and Hungarian.

Place Names

The earliest use of surnames was by the nobility; the surnames were taken from the names of their estates. Let's look at a fictitious nobleman and see how surnames evolved in Poland.

The nobleman John was known as *Sokół*, the "Falcon," because of his bravery. He began to call himself *Jan Sokół*, "John the Falcon." His estate was called *Sokołów*, "the Falcon's Place."

His son Jacob became known as *Jakub z Sokoła*, "Jacob (son) of the Falcon." He was also known as *Jakub z Sokołowa*, "Jacob of the Falcon's Place." During the fifteenth century the *z* was omitted and *-cki* or *-ski* added to the estate names, so that the surname became *Sokołowski*.

Jacob's son Peter built a village near his estate and called it *Sokół*, "the Falcon," in honor of his grandfather John. Soon there were so many residents in Sokół that it became necessary for the villagers, as well as the people living on the estate, to take surnames. Some servants who lived on the estate decided to use *Sokołowski*, and some of the villagers selected *Sokólski*. Even the parish priest became confused and sometimes referred to *Adam Sokołowski* as *Adam Sokólski* in the parish registers.

John the nobleman's great-grandson Martin became interested in falconry and sent for a man named Joseph to care for his falcons. Joseph's occupation was a falconkeeper (*sokolnik*) and he became known as *Józef Sokolnik*. Joseph's son Michael did not want to be a falconkeeper and was known as *Michał Sokolnikowicz*, "Michael, son of the falconkeeper." Michael's son wanted to be like everyone else in the area (most had surnames ending in *-ski*), so he changed his surname to *Sokolnikowski*. In the same area, nobles, free villagers, and serfs could have all been known by the same or similar surnames.

In addition to estate names, other place names, such as geographical features, towns, and countries, were also used as sources for surnames.

Patronymics and Matronymics

These surnames were derived from old Slavic first names and Christian first names of ancestors. A patronymic name is one that is taken from a father (or another male relative); a matronymic name is one that is taken from a mother (or another female relative). Most often, a patronymic was derived from a father's first name and was originally literally interpreted as "son of."

The surname endings *-icz*, *-wicz*, *-owicz*, and *-ewicz* are all Byelorussian or Ruthenian (Ukrainian) in origin. They were first used in eastern Poland, but their use soon spread throughout the entire nation. Having a surname with one of these endings does not mean that a person was an ethnic Ruthenian or Byelorussian; those are merely the areas where the *use* of these particular suffixes originated.

Michałowicz means the original owner of this surname was the "son of *Michał* (Michael)." *Adamicz* is the "son of Adam."

Surnames ending in *-czak*, *-czyk*, *-iak*, *-ak*, *-ik*, and *-yk* could denote a patronymic origin. *Pawelczak* is the "son of *Pawel* (Paul)." *Jakubiak* is the "son of *Jakub* (Jacob)."

The suffixes *-yc* (pronounced "its") and *-ic* (pronounced "eets") were more commonly used in the eastern Kingdom of Poland than in the western and central areas. *Jakubic* is the "son of Jakub." *Adamic* is the "son of Adam."

J.....czak, J.....czyk, and *J.....yniak* also denote the "son of." *Jendruś* is one nickname for *Andrzej* (Andrew). *Jendrzejczak* is the "son of Andrew." *Jaugustyniak* and *Augustyniak* both are the "son of August."

Matronymics were occasionally used in Poland when the female ancestor was more respected or wealthier than the male. She may have been a rich widow or a generous woman who did good works in the community. *Dorotiak* is the "son of Dorothy," and *Jewiarz* is the "son of Ewa (Eve)."

In some cases the patronymic ending has been dropped and only the original root word of the surname remains. *Sokołowski* became *Sokoł, Lisak* became *Lis,* and *Janowicz* became *Jan.*

Occupational Names

Many times surnames originated with a trade or occupation. The tailor (*krawiec*) became *Krawiec.* The farmer (*gospodarz*) or his son became *Gospodarek* (literally "little farmer"). The smith (*kowal*) became *Kowal, Kowalski,* or *Kowalewicz.* The baker (*piekarz*) became *Piekarz, Piekarski,* or *Kołacz* (from a "round cake"). The well-to-do peasant farmer (*kmieć*) became *Kmieć.* The peasant (*chłop,* literally "man" or "fellow") became *Chłop* or *Chłopecki.* The village administrator (*sołtys*) became *Sołtys* or *Sołtysiak.* The vagabond (*luźny*) became *Luźny.* The ending *-nik* means "worker" or "maker of." *Szczytnik* was a shieldmaker. *Złotnik* was a goldsmith (*złoto* is "gold").

Physical Appearance, Personality, and Nicknames

Occasionally these are used as sources for surnames. *Lisak* is the "son of the fox (*lis*)"; perhaps he was a sly or deceitful person. *Wysocki* (from *wysoki* meaning "tall" or "high") was probably a tall or important man. *Niemiec* and *Niemir* are descendants of German immigrants to Poland.

More About Polish Surnames

Sometimes it is difficult to determine a surname's origin at first glance. This is where a little detective work and a good Polish-English dictionary become necessary. If all else fails, try taking the surname apart syllable by syllable.

The name *Zawiślak* was given to a person who lived "beyond the Vistula River": *za + Wisła + ak* = beyond + Vistula + son of. This surname is an example of one derived from a place name.

If your Polish surname begins with an *H* it may have originally begun with a *Ch*. In the Polish language a *c* is silent when it is followed by an *h* at the beginning of a word. Therefore, *Chełmiński* could evolve into *Helminski*. *Chorzępa* has evolved in a few cases into *Chorzempa*, *Horzempa*, and even into *Orzempa*.

Ci- and *Cz-* in surnames sound the same as the English *ch-* and are found interchangeably both in Poland and America. *Cielusta* and *Czelusta* are both pronounced "Che-loos-tah."

In the Russian-influenced areas of Poland the *h* may have been replaced by a *g*, as there is no *h* in the Russian language.

While searching through Polish records, you may find several similar entries—for example, *Bór*, *Borowa*, and *Borówna*—and wonder whether they are the same name. Yes, they are—*Bór*, "forest," is the masculine and family name. *Borowa* refers to the married woman, and *Borówna* is the name of the unmarried woman or girl.

Borowczak, *Borowczyk*, and *Borowiak* are three surnames found in Sadki parish and were all used to denote the same family in different entries in the register. There is a thick pine forest (a *bór*) not more than thirty miles from this parish, and a few centuries ago the forest may have been much closer to the settlement. The original owner of this surname may have been a descendant of a forest dweller or one who worked in the forest.

Other name changes may have occurred as the immigrant entered his new homeland. Most names that had Polish diacritical marks unfamiliar to English eyes and sounds unfamiliar to English ears were Anglicized. Almost all diacritical marks were dropped and the surnames altered to compensate for the loss of the marks. Some *Chorzępas* became *Chorzepa* and some *Chorzempa*. *Gołąbowicz* turned into *Golombowitz*. People unfamiliar with the Polish *ł* often mistake it for an English *t*, and *Chałas* sometimes became *Chatas*. This error is a common one found in typeset and computer print.

Some surnames bear no apparent resemblance to their original Polish spelling and pronunciation until you study the situation. Why did *Jagodzinski* become Berry? Because *jagoda*, the root word, means berry in Polish. Look up the root word of your surname in a Polish-English dictionary to find out what it means in English.

LITHUANIAN SURNAMES

Lithuanian patronymic endings are *-vicius*, *-auskas*, *-unas*, *-ajtis*, and *-aitis*; the Germanized version of the last two endings is *-eit*. *Balciunas* is the "son of the fair-skinned man," as *baltas* means "white." *Urbajtis* is the "son of Urban."

LIVONIAN SURNAMES

Some Livonian (Latvian) surnames end in *-ins* or simply *-s*.

ESTONIAN SURNAMES

Estonia is called *Inflanty* in Polish. The surname suffix *-ste* is Estonian, equivalent to the Finnish *-isto*. The Estonian language is a branch of the Finno-Ugric language, not of the Slavic languages. Other common Finnish surname endings are *-nen* and *-la*. Many Finnish surnames are taken from the surrounding landscape.

BYELORUSSIAN SURNAMES

Patronymics are the main source of White Russian surnames. A Byelorussian *h* is seen as a *g* in Russian. The Byelorussian *Halicz* is seen as *Galich* in Russian.

Common surname suffixes are *-ov*, *-ovich*, *-ovych*, *-evych*, *-onok*, *-yonok*, and *-enock*. The Polish suffixes *-icz*, *-wicz*, *-owicz*, and *-ewicz* are Byelorussian or Ruthenian in origin.

RUSSIAN SURNAMES

Russian surnames are usually patronymics, and occasionally matronymics. Common surname suffixes are *-ev*, *-ov*, *-in*, *-un*, *-chuk*, *-chak*, *-ych*, *-ovych*, and *-evych*. Because the Russian language has no *h* and uses a *g* instead, *Herbnik* becomes *Gerbin* in Russian ("coat of arms maker").

The Russians use the Cyrillic alphabet, which cannot be translated directly into the Latin alphabet used by the Poles and English. Therefore, these are only approximations of the Russian suffixes.

UKRAINIAN (RUTHENIAN) SURNAMES

The first surnames appeared in the Ukraine in the thirteenth century but were most likely nicknames and usually not passed on to descendants. Surnames appeared in written records in the fourteenth and fifteenth centuries, but belonged to the upper classes. By the sixteenth and seventeenth centuries the middle classes were using surnames, but it was not until the seventeenth and eighteenth centuries that the peasants began using surnames.

The oldest Ukrainian surnames were taken from birds, animals, and occupations. There are four main types of Ukrainian surnames—those taken from first names, place names, occupations (and social status), and characteristics. The Ukrainians use the Cyrillic alphabet, which cannot be directly translated into Polish or English; therefore the names given below are only approximations.

More surnames were derived from first names than from any other source, and most are patronymic, with very few being matronymic. Patronymic and matronymic suffixes are: *-ak*, *-chak*, *-ets*, *-evych*, *-iuk*, *-iv*, *-ovych*, *-ych*, and *-yn*, with the most popular being *-enko*, *-chuk*, and *-uk* (all meaning "son of" and used with Christian names, surnames, and occupational names).

Petrenko is the "son of Petro (Peter)." Peter's wife would be known as *Petrykha*, and a matronymic surname would be *Petryshyn*, "son of Peter's wife."

Surnames deriving from place names are of two kinds: the place where an ancestor came from or was residing, and the ethnic, national, or tribal origin of an ancestor.

Zabolotnyj is "one who lived beyond the marsh." *Volyniak* probably came from the Volyn (Volhynia) region. *Tataryn* had a Tatar ancestor. *Boychuk* is one from the *Boyko*, an ancient Slavic tribe of Trans-Carpathia.

The Ukrainian nobility took their surnames from their estates or the localities they administered and added *-cky*, *-sky*, *-skij*, *-skyj*, and *-zky*, much like the Polish nobility who added *-cki* and *-ski*. Adjectival surnames use the suffixes *-ck-*, *-sk-*, and *-zk-*, and have the endings *-yj* or *-ij* for the masculine forms and *-a* or *-ia* for the feminine.

Occupations and the social status of people greatly influenced surnames, and therefore Ukrainian surnames may give a clue to the occupation of one of your early ancestors—*Tkach* (the weaver), *Kravets* (the tailor), *Pekar* (the baker), and *Spivak* (the singer).

Other surname endings are *-ar*, *-is*, *-iy*, *-ka*, *-kar*, *-man*, *-nik*, *-nyk*, *-sur*, *-un*, *-yk*, and *-ylo*. The most typical Ukrainian surname ending is *-enko*, which is not found in any other ethnic group, and is commonly found in central and eastern Ukraine. The surname endings most common to western Ukraine are *-chak*, *-chuk*, *-iuk*, *-uk*, *-ckyj*, *-skyj*, and *-zkyj*.

SLOVAK AND CARPATHO-UKRAINIAN SURNAMES

The ending *-ula*, a Latin diminutive, i.e., meaning "little," is seen in Polish, Slovak, and Carpatho-Ukrainian surnames, such as *Mikula*, "little Nicholas," and *Babula*, "little old lady." Some *-ula* endings, however, do not mean "little," for example *Cebula* (onion) and *Fabula* (from the Polish *fabuła* meaning "fable" or "story"). The surname ending *-ulka* is a Slovak diminutive ending. The suffix *-ek* is also seen in surnames of this area.

SERBIAN AND CROATIAN SURNAMES

Croats were living along the Dniestr River about the year 1000 A.D., in the area of Halicz Ruthenia and Podolia. The patronymic endings *-ic*, *-vic*, *-vici*, and *-ych* are common.

CZECH SURNAMES

Czech is spoken in Bohemia and Moravia. The Czech language has no *g* so the Polish *góra* (mountain) is *hora* in Czech. Most Czech surnames are patronymics and occupations, but physical appearance and nicknames are also used. Many surnames show the strong German influence present in the area. Some surname endings are *-l*, *-ek*, and *-cek*.

ARMENIAN SURNAMES

A number of Armenians immigrated to Poland. An Armenian patronymic ending is *-ian*, sometimes spelled *-yan*, and means "of the tribe of" or "descendant of." An example is *Sheroian*.

WESTERN SLAVONIC SURNAMES

Slavonic languages greatly influenced the Germanic languages in the area known as Lusatia (Łużyce in Polish, Lausitz in German). The Polabian language of Wendish was spoken in the Brandenburg area, and the Sorbian language of the Serb language group was spoken in Saxony. Many German surnames of these two areas are of Slavic origin. The people from these areas settled in the western areas of Poland, bringing their languages and surnames with them.

Occupations and nicknames were commonly used as surnames. *Von*, meaning "of" or "from," followed by a place name was often used by the nobility. Wendish surname endings are *-itz* and *-witz*. Also of Slavonic origin are *-isch*, *-ke*, and *-usch*.

GERMANIC SURNAMES

Patronymics, occupations, and nicknames were commonly used for surnames. German patronymic endings are *-sohn*, meaning "son," as in *Jakobsohn*, and the possessive *-s* added to the father's name, as in *Jakobs*. Two surname endings that denote occupations are *-er*, meaning "one who does something," like *Bauer* the farmer, and *-macher*, "the maker of," as in *Schuhmacher* the shoemaker.

Names that denote an ethnic background or place of origin are also found—*Schlesinger*, the Silesian and *Posner*, the "man from Posen (Poznań)." The nobility originally used *von*, meaning "of" or "from," followed by a place name to indicate ownership and residence. However, not all people with such surnames are descendants of nobility.

Swiss and Alsatian surname endings are *-lin*, *-li*, and *-i*. Swabian endings are *-len* and *-le*. Some Bavarians and Austrians use *-l*. In the Rhineland the suffixes *-gen* and *-ken* are found in surnames. Wesphalian endings are *-er* and *-ing*.

DUTCH SURNAMES

The Dutch immigrants brought their language and surnames to Poland. The surnames were usually Polonized, but you may find remnants of the old Dutch names.

Patronymics were often used, with *-sen* meaning "son of." This ending was altered to *-se*, *-sze*, *-sz*, *-s*, *-x*, and *-zen*. Place names were another source for many Dutch surnames, although they rarely denoted nobility. The prefixes *van*, "from" or "of," *van den*, "from the," and *van der*, "from the," are all used before a place name. *Van den Berg* or *Vandenberg* means "from the hill." *Ten* means "at the," as in *Ten Eyck*, "at the oak."

The prefix *de*, "the," is used before a nickname or occupation, so that *Pieter de Bakker* is "Peter the Baker."

Frisian is also spoken in the Netherlands. The name endings *-ma*, "man," and *-stra*, "-ster" (a person "who is ..." or "makes ...") are Frisian.

JEWISH SURNAMES

German and Eastern European Jews traditionally were known by their given name and their father's name. Of course, that meant that names changed with each generation. After Poland was partitioned the ruling powers decreed that all Jews take surnames—beginning in 1785 in Austrian territories, in 1808 in the Napoleonic Empire, 1812 to 1845 in Prussian territories, and in 1844 in the Russian Empire.

Sources for most surnames were patronymics, place names, occupations, and family symbols. On some occasions when Jewish people were forced to assume surnames, haggling went on between the Jew and the bureaucrat issuing the names. A large sum of money was needed to obtain a pleasant-sounding name. Wouldn't you pay more to be called "rose garden" rather than "cow's tail"?

Ben Elisha, "son of Elisha," is a patronymic that on occasion has been modified to the Sephardic *Benelisha* and then shortened to *Belish*. In some Slavic areas *-wicz*, *-vitch*, and *-witz*, all meaning "son of," were added to the parents' first names.

Matronymics were derived from the name of the mother or wife, such as *Edels*, *Perle(s)*, and *Rose*. *Perlmann* was the "husband of Perl."

In the past, Jewish surnames were not always inherited from the father. Sometimes a child was forced to adopt the mother's name because the civil government did not consider the child legitimate if his parents were married under Jewish law and not the local civil law.

Beginning in the thirteenth century, Jews in southern Europe sometimes had family names that were taken from the family's place of origin. This practice makes it easier to trace these families' origins.

Place names were often relied upon to produce surnames: *Deutsch* the German; *Leon* from the province of León in Spain; *Hess* and *Preuss*, both German states; and *Schlesinger* the Silesian. Occupational names can be found in many surnames: *Schneider* the tailor and *Kauffman* the merchant.

The Jewish culture draws upon many centuries of traditions not found in other cultures. A family of Levites may have had a jug carved on their door—the jug symbolizing Levites who poured water over the priest's hands before the priest blessed the congregation. If this family spoke a Germanic language (including the Yiddish dialect) they may have chosen *Kann*, "jug" in German, as a surname.

Some other sources for surnames were characteristics, animals, abbreviations, and acronyms. Ben Rabbi Israel in abbreviated form makes the surname *Bry*. A man named Judah (the Old Testament Judah was symbolized by a lion) might have taken a "lion" name: *Lyon*, *Loeb*, *Lowe*, or *Leibowitz*. A small man may have been known as *Klein*, one with dark skin and hair may have been called *Schwartz*, and *Gottlieb* was "God-loving."

Sometimes a Jewish surname was translated when the family arrived in America—*Pulvermacher* (powdermaker) became Powder. Moses Powder was a Polish Jew who became a police officer in Toledo in the 1880s, and served the local Polish community because he spoke both Polish and English.

SURNAME RESEARCH IN POLAND

The Institute for the Study of Polish Onomastics (listed below) can assist you in finding the origin of your surname. In writing to them include the time period and village or area in Poland where your ancestor lived.

I wrote a letter in Polish to this institute. Dr. Klimek's reply, however, was in English, explaining that the origin of the *Dajerling* surname was German. The Dajerlings first appeared in the Poznań area in the 1790s and came up in my personal research. Dr. Klimek said *Dajerling* was the "son of Deier," meaning a "man of worth." He added that although many Poles bear German surnames, thousands of them suffered at the hands of the German military during the occupation. He also stated that the institute does not have genealogical data on individuals in Poland; that information must be obtained from parish registers:

> Dr. Zygmunt Klimek
> Instytut Języka Polskiego
> Zakład Onomastyki Polskiej
> Pracownia Antroponimiczna
> 31-113 Kraków
> ul. Straszewskiego 25
> Polska (Poland)

The National Library may also be able to help with surname research:

> Biblioteka Narodowa
> ul. Hankiewicza 1
> 00-973 Warszawa
> Polska (Poland)

SOURCES AND ADDITIONAL READING

Bieder, Alexander. *A Dictionary of Jewish Surnames from the Russian Empire.* Teaneck, New Jersey: Avotaynu, Inc., 1992.

Fabula, Andrew G. "Eastern European '-ula' Names." *Polish Genealogical Society Newsletter* XI (Fall 1988), 29.

Hanks, Patrick and Flavia Hodges. *A Dictionary of Surnames.* New York: Oxford University Press, 1988.

Herzog, Marvin I. *The Yiddish Language in Northern Poland: Its Geography and History.* The Hague: Mouton, 1965.

Johnson, Arta F. *Origins, Development, and Meanings of German Names.* Columbus, Ohio: published by the author, 1984.

Kurzweil, Arthur. *From Generation to Generation: How to Trace Your Jewish Genealogy and Personal History.* New York: William Morrow & Co., 1980.

Obal, Thaddeus J. *Polish Family Tree Surnames.* Vols. II-VI. (Available from the author: Thaddeus J. Obal, 739 Hillsdale Avenue, Hillsdale, New Jersey 07642.) This is an on-going project to collect Polish surnames—ethnically Polish surnames as well as surnames of foreign origin borne by people who once resided in Polish territories. Genealogists send in the Polish surnames and the village locations of their ancestors they are researching, to be compiled into a list and index in each volume. There is no cost to have your surnames listed in the volumes, the only cost being the purchase of printed volumes. Additional research tips sent in by genealogists and short articles are included. Send a SASE to Mr. Obal for further information on how to submit names, and for a flyer and price list.

Rottenberg, Dan. *Finding Our Fathers*. Baltimore: Genealogical Publishing Company, 1986 (reprint).

Swietochowski, Robert. *Germaniacja Nazwisk Polskich na Terenie Gdańska w latach 1874–1944* (The Germanization of Polish Family Names in the Gdańsk Area 1874–1944). Wrocław, Poland: Wydawnictwo Polskej Akademie Nauk, 1969.

Chapter Twelve:

CHRISTIAN
OR FIRST NAMES

FEAST DAYS OF THE SAINTS

The Poles have long been staunch followers of the Roman Catholic religion, and have placed much importance on the saints and often called upon them in times of trouble. Many saints had particular duties—St. Isidore the Farmer was the patron of farmers, St. Cecilia was the patron of musicians and singers, and St. Anastasia aided weavers. You prayed to St. James the Greater if you were afflicted with rheumatism.

Since most farmers could neither read nor write, they followed the Church's calendar of feast days. The saints' feast days were used to predict the weather and to tell farmers when to plant, harvest, and do other work. Many rhyming Polish proverbs were made up for these purposes, such as this one from *Polish Proverbs* by Helen Stankiewicz Zand (Scranton, Pennsylvania: Polish American Journal, 1961): *Deszcz w Święty Marek, ziemia jak skwarek*, "Rain on St. Mark's, the soil will be parched." St. Mark's was celebrated on April 25.

POLISH CUSTOMS IN NAMING CHILDREN

Considering how important the saints and their feast days were to the Poles, it is not surprising that many Polish parents consulted their pastor or the Proper of the Saints (Roman calendar) to select a name for their child. They searched for an agreeable saint whose feast day was near their child's birth or baptismal date. The feast day was most often on or just after the child's birth or baptismal date, usually no more than three weeks after the event.

Poles did not celebrate their birthdays, but most often celebrated their namesake's feast day (*imieniny*), or even the anniversary of their baptismal day. Many families in Poland today still observe this tradition.

When asked to provide a birth date for American records, many Poles gave their baptismal date or feast day in place of their actual birth date. Many of them probably did not know their birth dates, but could easily remember the feast day or baptismal date.

Another custom was naming a child after one of his or her godparents. This custom varied by locality and was not as common as the feast day custom. Children were also occasionally named after a relative other than their godparents.

Even if they were not already related by blood or marriage, the godparents became the *kumy* of the child's parents. A godfather was called a *kmotr* or *kumoter*, and a godmother was called a *kumoszka*. This was a "relationship of gossip," or support.

Christian names were Polonized. John became Jan and Michael became Michał .

Many Polish (Slavic) names have no direct translation into English, for example Przemysław, Czesław (Ceslaus in Latin), Mieczysław (Miecislaus in Latin), Bolesław (Boleslaus in Latin), Stanisław (Stanislaus in Latin), Bronisław (Bronislaus in Latin), Kazimierz (Casimir(us) in Latin), Władysław (Vladislaus in Latin, Laszlo in Hungarian), Wojciech (Adalbert(us) in Latin), Wanda, and Bożena. As seen in the last two examples, names ending in *-a* (in the nominative case) are usually feminine.

Attempts were made to Anglicize most of these names by finding the closest-sounding English name—so Czesław became Chester. But some names, like Przemysław, have no similar English name.

As Przemysław entered the United States or began work in America, he may have been given or chosen a completely new name, perhaps Peter or John. He may have decided to keep his original name, no matter how the Americans spelled or pronounced it. He may have been known by more than one first name—Przemysław to his Polish friends and Pete at work—or have adopted an abbreviated Polish nickname like Sławek.

COMMON POLISH NAMES

The following list shows common Polish names based on saints and their feast days, using the old-style (pre-1969) Proper of the Saints of the Roman calendar. In 1969 changes were made in the dates of celebration for many saints. Therefore, in consulting modern sources (post-1969), you may find different dates for feast days than those used by our ancestors.

The Polish name of each saint is listed first, followed in parentheses by the

English name; the common Anglicized substitute is in quotation marks, as that name is not a direct translation. If there is more than one saint with the same name, the saints are then distinguished by their secondary names or titles.

Dates in italics are feast days that are found in the old-style Proper of the Saints, which would have been used by our ancestors to name their children. Many saints were not included in the Proper of the Saints; their feast days were not celebrated universally, but were celebrated in various localities. These saints are also included if they have a special significance to Poles or other Slavs, and are marked as such.

This list can be used to find out the English equivalent for the Polish name or to add interest to your family history by finding out for whom your ancestor was named. Because the feast day was more important to Poles than the actual birth date, the feast day may be noted on vital records in place of the birth date, therefore, if you are searching for your ancestor's birth date and birth record in a birth register on microfilm and have many years of records to look through, it may be possible to locate your ancestor faster by just searching the entries near the saint's feast day.

For example, if you know your ancestor Adalbert was born around 1850 but you don't know the exact birth date, you would most likely need to search only April entries for each year around 1850 instead of the whole year's birth entries because the list below shows you that April 23 is Adalbert's feast day. It is possible, however, that your ancestor may have been born at a different time than suspected, and he is named Adalbert for some other reason.

Note: To aid English readers, the Polish *Ł* is listed under *L*. Names spelled with *C* in Latin or English may appear in Polish under *K*. Names spelled with *PH* in Greek, Latin, or English will appear in Polish under *F*. The feminine equivalent of names is often formed by adding *-a*.

Adalbert (Adalbert, "George") Adalbert of Prague, patron of Prussia,
    Bohemian April 23
Adam (Adam) *December 24*
Agata (Agatha) *February 5*
Agnieszka (Agnes) Agnes *January 21*; Blessed Agnes *Bohemian* March 2
Albert (Albert) Albert the Great *November 15*
Aleksander (Alexander) *May 3*
Aleksandra, see Olga
Aleksy (Alexis) *July 17*
Alfons (Alphonsus) Alphonsus Liguori *August 2*

Alojzy (Aloysius) Aloysius Gonzaga *June 21*
Ambroży (Ambrose) *December 7*
Anastazia, Anastazja (Anastasia) *December 25*
Andrzej (Andrew) Andrew Corsini *February 4*; Andrew Avellino
    November 10; Andrew, patron of Russia *November 30*
Aniela (Angela) Angela Merici *January 27, May 31, June 1*
Anna (Anna) mother of Mary *July 26*
Antoni, Antonin (Anthony, Antonius) Anthony, abbot *January 17*; Anthony,
    bishop *May 10*; Anthony of Padua *June 13*; Anthony, d. c. 1342,
    Lithuanian June 14; Anthony Mary Zaccaria *July 5*; Anthony
    Pechersky *Ukrainian* July 10
Antonia, Antonina (Antoinette, Antonina) February 28, May 4, June 12
Apolonia (Pauline) *February 9*
Apolinarius (Apollinaris) *July 23*
Apolonius (Apollonius) *April 18*
August, Augustyn (Augustine) Augustine of Canterbury *May 28;*
    Augustine of Hippo, Doctor of the Church *August 28*
Baltazar (Balthasar) January 6, July 23
Barbara (Barbara) *December 4*
Barnabas (Barnabas) Barnabas the Apostle *June 11*
Bartłomiej (Bartholomew) Bartholomew the Apostle *August 24;*
    Bartholomew November 11
Bażyli (Basil) Basil the Great *June 14*
Bede (Bede) Bede the Venerable *May 27*
Benedykt (Benedict) Benedict, abbot *March 21;* Benedict *Polish* April 23;
    Benedict, Pope July 11
Bernard (Bernard) *August 20*
Bernardyn (Bernardine, male) *May 20*
Bibiana (Bibiana, Viviana) *December 2*
Błażej (Blaise) *February 3*
Bogumił (Bogimilus, Theophilus) *Polish* June 10; see *Teofil*
Bolesław (Boleslaus, "William")
Bolesława (Boleslava, "Wilhelmina," "Mina")
Bonifacy (Boniface) Boniface of Tarsus, d. 300 A.D. *May 14;* Boniface,
    Apostle of Germany *June 5;* Boniface, Second Apostle of the Prus-
    sians, (born Bruno of Querfurt) d. 1009 June 19
Bożena ("of God") see *Teodora* and *Teodozia*
Bronisław (Bronislaus, "Bruno")
Bronisława (Bronislava, "Bernice," "Bertha") *Polish September 3*
Brunon (Bruno) patron of Ruthenia (Ukraine) *October 6*

Brygida (Bridget, Birgitta) patron of Sweden *October 8*

Cecylia (Cecilia) *November 22*

Cyprian (Cyprian) Cyprian, bishop *September 16;* Cyprian, martyr *September 26*

Cyryl (Cyril) Cyril of Alexandria *February 9;* Cyril of Jerusalem *March 18;* Cyril (of Saints Cyril and Methodius) *Slavic July 7* (now February 14)

Czesław (Ceslaus, "Chester") *Polish* July 17 and 28

Czesława (Ceslava) feminine version of *Czesław;* also see *Teresa*

Dawid (David) Dewi of Wales, March 1; David *Russian* September 19; Biblical (Old Testament) King David, December 30

Doloreta (Dolores) Seven Sorrows (Dolores in Latin) of the Blessed Virgin Mary, September 15

Domicylla, Domitilla (Domitilla) May 7 and 12

Dominik (Dominic) *August 4*

Dorota (Dorothy) Dorothy of Montau, patroness of Prussia, October 30

Edmund (Edmund) November 20

Edward (Edward) March 18, October 13

Elżbieta (Elizabeth) Elizabeth, Queen of Portugal *July 8;* Elizabeth of Hungary *November 19*

Emilia, Emiliana (Emiliana, Emily) August 24, December 24

Ewa (Eve) the Eve of Christmas Day, December 24

Fabian (Fabian) *January 20*

Felicia (Felice, Felicity, "Phyllis") *March 6*

Feliks (Felix) Felix of Nola, priest/martyr, d. c. 260 A.D. *January 14;* Felix I, Pope *May 30;* Felix, martyr, d. 303 A.D. *July 12;* Felix II, Pope *July 29;* Felix, martyr *August 30;* Felix of Valois *November 20*

Filip (Philip) Philip, Apostle *May 1, May 11;* Philip Neri *May 26;* Philip Benizi *August 23*

Florentyna (Flora, Florence) June 20, November 24

Florjan (Florian) patron of Poland and Upper Austria, May 4

Franciszek (Francis, "Frank") Francis de Sales *January 29;* Francis of Paola *April 2;* Francis Caracciolo *June 4;* Francis Borgia *October 10;* Francis of Assisi *October 4*

Franciszek Ksawery (Francis Xavier) *December 3*

Franciszka (Frances) *March 9*

Fryderyk (Frederick) July 18

Gabriel (Gabriel) Archangel *March 24*

Genowefa (Genevieve) January 3

Giertruda (Gertrude) *November 16*

Grzegorz (Gregory) Gregory the Great, Pope *March 12;* Gregory
    Nazianzen *May 9;* Gregory VII, Pope *May 25;* Gregory the
    Wonder-worker *November 17*
Gustaw (Gustav, August, Augustine) see *August, Augustyn*
Gwidon (Guy) September 12
Halina, Helena (Helen) August 18
Henryk (Henry) Henry of Bavaria, Emperor of Germany *July 15*
Henryka (Henrietta, "Hattie") feminine version of *Henryk*
Hiacynt, Jacek (Hyacinth, male) Hyacinth, patron of Poland (Hyacinth
    Ronski) *August 17;* Hyacinth, d. 260 A.D. *September 11*
Hiacynta, Jacinta (Hyacintha, female) January 30
Hieronym (Jerome, "Henry") Jerome Emilian *July 20;* Jerome, Doctor of
    the Church *September 30*
Hipolit (Hippolytus) *August 13*
Honorata (Honorata) January 11
Honoratus (Honoratus) January 16
Ignacy (Ignace, Ignatius) Ignatius, bishop/martyr *February 1;* Ignatius of
    Rostov *Russian* May 28; Ignatius of Loyola *July 31*
Irena, Irina (Irene) April 3
Isabela (Isabelle) Elizabeth of Portugal (born Isabella) July 4 and 8
Izydor (Isidore) Isidore of Alexandria, January 15; Isidore the Farmer
    March 22, d. May 15; Isidore of Seville, bishop *April 4;* Isidore of
    Chios, May 15; Isidore, d. 250 A.D., December 14
Jacinta, see Hiacynta
Jacek, see Hiacynt
Jadwiga (Hedwig, "Hattie") Blessed Hedwig, Queen of Poland *February
    28;* Hedwig, patroness of Silesia *October 16*
Jakub (Jacob, James) James the Less, Apostle *May 1, May 11;* James the
    Greater, Apostle *July 25*
Jan (John; Joannes in Latin) John Chrysostom *January 27;* John of Matha
    February 8; John of God *March 8;* John Damascene *March 27;* John
    Capistran *March 28;* John the Apostle, Before the Latin Gate *May 6;*
    John *Lithuanian,* d. 1342, April 14; John of San Facundo *June 12;*
    John Gualbert *July 12;* John of Dukla, patron of Poland and Lithuania,
    July 10 and September 28; John of the Cross *November 24;* John,
    Apostle and Evangelist *December 27*
Jan Baptysta, Jan Chrzciciel (John the Baptist) Birth of *June 24;* Beheading
    of *August 29*
Jan Józef (John Joseph) March 5
Jan Kanty (John of Cantius) patron of Poland and Lithuania *October 20*

Jan Nepomucen (John Nepomucene) patron of Czechoslovakia, May 16

Januariusz (Januarius, January, "John") *September 19*

Jerzy (George) patron of England and Germany *April 23* (not the same saint as Adalbert, but they share the same feast day)

Joachim, Joakim (Joachim) *August 16*

Joanna (Joanne, Jane, Jean, Joan, "Jennie") Joan of Arc, May 30; Jane Frances de Chantal *August 21;* see also *Jan* entries

Jolanta, Jolenta (Yolanda) Blessed Jolenta *Polish/Hungarian* ("Helen of Poland"), June 12 and 14

Józef (Joseph) Joseph, foster father of Jesus *March 19;* Joseph the Workman *May 1;* Joseph of Cupertino *September 18*

Józefa, Józefina (Josephine) feminine version of *Józef*

Józefat (Josaphat) *Polish/Lithuanian November 14*

Julia (Julia, Julie) May 22

Julian (Julian) January 9

Juliana (Julianna, Julie) Juliana Falconieri *June 19*

Justin, Justyn (Justin) *April 14*

Justina, Justyna (Justina) *September 26*

Kajetan (Cajetan) *August 7*

Kamil (Camile, Camillus, male) Camile of Lellis *July 18*

Kamila (Camila, Camille, female) feminine version of *Kamil*

Karol (Karl, Charles) Blessed Charlemagne of-France, January 28; Charles Borromeo *November 4* ~~THE FRANKS~~

Karolina (Carolina, Charlotte) feminine version of *Karol*

Kasper (Caspar) Caspar, one of the Magi, January 6, July 23; Caspar del Bufalo, January 2

Katarzyna (Catherine) Catherine of Siena *April 30;* Catherine of Alexandria *November 25*

Kazimierz, Kaźmierz (Casimir) patron of Poland and Lithuania *March 4*

Klara (Clara, Clare) *August 12*

Klemens, Klement (Clemence, Clement) Clement, d. 308 A.D., January 23; Clement, d. c. 250 A.D., February 13; Clement Slovensky of Okhrida, Apostle of Bulgaria, July 17 and 27; Clement I, Pope *November 23*

Klementyna (Clementine) feminine version of *Klemens*

Konrad (Conrad) Blessed Conrad of Bavaria, February 14, March 15; Conrad of Piacenza, February 19; Conrad of Swabia, bishop of Trèves, June 1; Conrad of Constance, bishop, November 26

Konstanty (Constant, Constantine) Constantine, King of Cornwall, first martyr of Scotland, March 11; Constantine, d. 1321, *Russian,* September 19

Konstantyna (Constance) feminine version of *Konstanty*

Krystyna (Christine) Christine of Bolsena *July 24;* two other Christinas also on July 24; Christina (also called *Nino*) *Russian* Apostle of Georgia, December 15

Krzysztof (Christopher) *July 25*

Kunegunda (Cunegunda) Cunegunda of Luxembourg and Bavaria, March 3; Blessed Cunegunda (Polish and Magyar name is *Kinga*) *Polish/Hungarian,* patroness of Lithuania and Poland, July 21 and 23

Leokadia (Leocadia, "Laura") December 9

Leon (Leo) Leo I, the Great, Pope *April 11* (now November 10); Leo IX, Pope, April 19; Leo III, Pope, June 12; Leo II, Pope *July 3;* Leo IV, Pope, July 17

Leonard (Leonard, "Leon") November 6

Lidia (Lydia) August 3

Lorenz (Lawrence) Lawrence of Brindisi *July 21;* Lawrence (martyr of the hot gridiron) *August 10;* Lawrence Justinian *September 4 and 5*

Łucja (Lucy) Lucy, martyr *September 16;* Lucy of Sicily, martyr *December 13* (Her name is in the Canon of the Mass.)

Łucjan (Lucian) Lucian of Antioch, January 7; Lucian of Beauvais, January 8; Lucian, d. 250 A.D., October 26

Ludmila (Ludmila) *Bohemian* September 16

Ludwik (Louis) Louis IX, King of France *August 25*

Ludwika (Louise) *March 15*

Łukasz (Lucas, Luke) Luke the Evangelist *October 18*

Maciej (Matthew) Matthew, Apostle and Evangelist *September 21*

Magdalena (Mary Magdalene, Madeline) Mary Magdalen del Pazzi *May 29*; Mary Magdalene, sister of Martha and Lazarus *July 22*

Maksymilian (Maximilian) Maximilian, d. 295 A.D., March 12; Maximilian of Lorch, October 12; Maksymilian Kolbe *Polish* August 14

Małgorzata, Margarita (Margaret) Margaret of Hungary, d. 1270, January 18 and 26; Margaret (born in Hungary), Queen of Scotland, d. 1093 on November 16, *June 10;* Margaret, d. c. 255 A.D. *July 20*

Marcelian, (Marcellianus) twin of Mark *June 18*

Marcianna, Martyna (Marcyanna, Martina) Marciana, d. 303 A.D., January 9; Martina, d. 228 A.D. *January 30*

Marcin (Martin) Martin of Tours (born in Pannonia, now Hungary) *November 11;* Martin I, Pope *November 12*

Marek (Mark) Mark the Evangelist *April 25;* Mark, twin of Marcellianus *June 18;* Mark, Pope *October 7*

Maria, Marja, Marya (Mary) Feast Days of the Blessed Virgin Mary
(BVM): Solemnity of Mary, Mother of God *January 1;* Purification
of the BVM *February 2;* Annunciation of the BVM *March 25;*
Queenship of the BMV *May 31;* Visitation of the BVM to Elizabeth
July 2; Assumption of the BVM *August 15;* Immaculate Heart of
Mary *August 22;* Our Lady of Częstochowa, patroness of Poland
August 26; Nativity of the BVM *September 8;* Most Holy Name of
Mary *September 12 (*Pope Innocent XI extended this feast on the
occasion of the liberation of Vienna from the Turks, greatly aided by
the Poles, in 1683); BVM of the Rosary *October 7;* Immaculate Con-
ception *December 8 (Marianna* and *Marjanna* are often used interchangeably with *Mary* for the same person.)

Marta (Martha) Martha, martyr *January 19;* Martha, sister of Mary
Magdalene and Lazarus *July 29*

Martyna, see Marcianna

Mateusz *(*Mathias) Mathias, the Apostle who took the place of Judas *February 24 and 25;* Matthew, Apostle and Evangelist *September 21*

Melchior (Melchior) January 6, July 23

Metody (Methodius) *Slavic* Cyril and Methodius, Apostles of the Slavs
July 7 (now February 14)

Michał , "Mieczysław" (Michael) Michael the Archangel, Apparition of
May 8; Michael of Chernigov *Ukrainian/Russian* September 21;
Michael the Archangel *September 29*

Michalina (Michalina) June 20

Mieczysław (Miecislaus) *Mieczysław* (Mieszko) I, saintly King of Poland
who accepted Christianity for his nation on April 15, 966 A.D., feast
day January 1

Mikołaj (Nicholas) Nicholas of Tolentino *September 10;* Nicholas I, the
Great, Pope *November 13;* Nicholas, patron of Russia *December 6*

Monika (Monica, "Mona") mother of St. Augustine *May 4*

Nikodem (Nicodemus) Nicodemus of the Holy Mountain (Orthodox), July 14

Norbert (Norbert) Norbert of Germany *June 6*

Olenka, see Olga

Olga (Alexandra, Sandra, Olga) *Ukrainian/Russian* July 11

Onufrius, Onufry (Onuphrius) June 12

Otto (Otto) Otto, born in Swabia, worked in Poland, July 2 and 3,
September 30

Paulina (Pauline) January 26

Pawel (Paul) Paul the Hermit *January 15;* Conversion of Paul the Apostle *January 25;* Paul of the Cross *April 28;* Paul the Apostle *June 29 and 30;* Dedication of the Basilicas of Peter and Paul *November 18*

Pelagia (Pelagia, "Paula," "Pauline") Pelagia of Tarsus, May 4; Pelagia of Antioch, June 9; Pelagia the Penitent, October 8

Petronela (Petronilla) *May 31*

Piotr (Peter) Chair of St. Peter at Rome *January 18;* Peter Nolasco *January 28;* Chair of St. Peter at Antioch *February 22;* Peter Damian *February 23;* Peter Canisius, Second Great Apostle of Germany *April 27;* Peter of Verona *April 29;* Peter I Celestine, Pope *May 19;* Peter, martyr, d. 304 A.D., *June 2;* Peter the Apostle *June 29;* Peter's Chains, the Apostle *August 1;* Dedication of the Basilicas of Peter and Paul *November 18;* Peter Chrysologus *December 4*

Prakseda (Praxedes, Praxey) *July 21*

Rafał, Rafael (Raphael) Archangel *October 24*

Rajmund (Raymond) Raymond of Pennafort *January 23;* Raymond Nonnatus *August 31*

Regina (Regina) September 7

Roch (Roch, Rock) August 16

Roman (Roman) *August 9*

Romuald (Romuald, male) died on June 19, *February 7*

Romualda (Romualda, Roma) feminine version of *Romuald*

Róża (Rose) Rose of Lima *August 30*

Rozalia (Rosalie, Rose) Rose of Viterbo, September 4

Ryszard (Richard) February 7

Sabina (Sabina) *August 29*

Salomeja (Salome, "Sarah") Salome (also called "Mary Salome"), mother of James and John the Apostles, October 22; Blessed Salome *Polish* November 6 and 17 and 18

Sebastian (Sebastian) *January 20*

Seweryn (Severin) Severinus of Noricum (Austria) January 5

Simeon, Szymon (Simeon) Simeon the Stylite, January 5; Simeon, bishop/martyr *February 18;* Simeon, the old man in the Temple, October 8; see also *Szymon*

Sofia, Zofia (Sophie) September 30

Stanisław (Stanislaus, Stanley) Stanislaus, Bishop of Kraków *May 7* (now April 11); Stanislaus Kostka, patron of Poland, November 13

Stanisława (Stanislava, "Stella") female version of *Stanisław*

Stefan, Szczepan (Stephen) Stephen of Perm *Russian* April 26; Stephen
  Pechersky *Ukrainian* April 27; Stephen I, Pope *August 2;* Finding the
  Body of Stephen the First Martyr *August 3;* Stephen, King, patron of
  Hungary *September 2;* Stephen the First Martyr *December 26*
Stefania (Stephanie) feminine version of *Stefan*
Sylwester (Sylvester) Sylvester, abbot *November 26;* Sylvester, Pope
  December 31
Szczepan (Stephen) Stephen the First Martyr *December 26*
Szymon (Simon) Simon of Lipnica *Polish* July 15 and 30; Simon the
  Zealot, Apostle *October 28*
Tadeusz (Thaddeus, "Ted") Jude Thaddeus the Apostle *October 28*
Tekla (Thecla, "Tillie") *September 23*
Teodor (Theodore, "Ted") Theodore the Black *Russian* September 19;
  Theodore *Ukrainian/Russian* September 21; Theodore, soldier and
  martyr *November 9;* Theodore Graptoi, December 27
Teodora (Theodora, Dora, Dorie) April 28, September 17
Teodozja (Theodosia) April 2, May 29
Teodozjusz (Theodosius) Theodosius Pechersky (also known as Theodosius
  of the Caves of Kiev), abbot, *Ukrainian/Russian,* May 3 and July 10
Teofil (Theophilus) Theophilus the Penitent, February 4
Teofila (Theophila) feminine version of *Teofil*
Teresa, Tereza, "Czesława" (Theresa) Teresa of Ávila *October 15*
Timoteusz (Timothy) Timothy, bishop, d. 97 A.D. *January 24;* Timothy,
  martyr, d. c. 300 A.D. *August 22*
Tomasz (Thomas) Thomas Aquinas *March 7;* Thomas of Villanova
  September 22; Thomas Cantelupe of Hereford, *October 3;* Thomas
  the Apostle *December 21;* Thomas Becket *December 29*
Urban (Urban) Urban I, Pope *May 25*
Urszula (Ursula) *October 21*
Wacław (Wenceslaus, "Walter") *Bohemian* patron of Czechoslovakia
  September 28
Walburga (Walburga) February 25
Walenty (Valentine) Valentine, abbot, January 7; Valentine, bishop/martyr
  February 14
Walentyna (Valentina) July 25; also feminine version of *Walenty*
Walerian, Walery (Valerian, Valery) *April 14*
Wanda (Wanda) Wanda, Queen, daughter of King Krak of Kraków *Vislanian*
  (pre-Christian Polish); related to Lithuanian *wanduo,* "water" (A leg-
  end tells of Wanda jumping into a river rather than marrying a German.)

Wawrzyniec (Lawrence), see *Lorenz*

Weronika (Veronica) July 12

Wicenty, Wincenty (Vincent) Vincent of Saragossa, Spain, martyr
January 22; Blessed Wincenty Kadłubek, bishop of Kraków *Polish*
d. March 8, feast day October 11; Vincent Ferrer *April 5;* Vincent de
Paul *July 19*

Wiktor (Victor) Victor of Marseilles, martyr, July 21; Victor I, Pope *July 28*

Wiktoria (Victoria) Victoria, martyr, d. 304 A.D., February 11; Victoria, martyr, d. c. 250 A.D., December 20 and 23

Wilhelm (William, "Bill") *June 25*

Wilhelmina (Wilhelmina, Mina) feminine version of *Wilhelm*

Wincenty, see Wicenty

Wita, Witus (Vitus) *June 15*

Władimir (Vladimir) Vladimir of Kiev, patron of Russia, July 15

Władysław (Ladislaus, "Walter") Blessed Ladislaus of Gielnów, patron of
Poland, Galicia, and Lithuania, died on May 4, feast day on May 11
and September 20; Ladislaus (called *Laszlo* in Magyar), King of Hungary, died on July 29, feast day June 27

Władysława (Ladislava, "Charlotte," "Hattie") feminine version of
Władysław

Wojciech (Adalbert, "Albert," "George") *April 23*

Zachariasz (Zachary) Zachary, Pope, March 15 and 22; Zachary, father of
John the Baptist, November 5 and 15

Zenon (Zenon) December 22

Zofia, Sofia (Sophie) September 30

Zuzanna (Susanna, Susan) Susanna (also called "Anne"), martyr, d. 918
A.D., July 23; Susanna, martyr, d. 295 A.D. *August 11;* Susanna, martyr, d. c. 473 A.D., October 17

Zygmunt (Sigismund) Zygmunt III Wasa, saintly King of Poland, October 31;
Sigismund, King of the Burgundians, martyr, December 30

Zyta (Zita) April 27

UKRAINIAN CUSTOMS IN NAMING CHILDREN

Christianity was introduced in the Ukraine in 988 A.D., at which time the
Ukrainian people began to give their children Christian names. These Christian names were of Greek, Hebrew, and Roman origin and were modified by
the Ukrainian language: John became Ivan and Michael became Mykhailo.
Many children also were given the names of Slavic or Ukrainian saints,
many known only in Eastern Europe.

Ukrainian children were given names within eight days of their birth. The name was frequently selected by the priest, not the parents, but sometimes the parents suggested a name that was approved by the priest. The chosen name was the name of the patron saint on whose feast day the child was born or baptized, or a patron saint whose feast day fell within seven days after the baby's birth. Godparents took the child to the church, but the parents were usually not present at their child's baptism and often did not learn of the chosen name until the godparents brought the child back home.

Christian names are also called *kalendarni imena,* "calendar names," in Ukrainian, after the custom of choosing names for children based on the church calendar. However, the Ukrainians used the Byzantine Calendar, which begins with September and contains many different saints' names than the Roman Calendar. Some of the dates for feast days also differ between the two church calendars.

There were almost as many inhabitants of the Polish Commonwealth who spoke Ukrainian (30 percent) as there were who spoke Polish (40 percent). The following list of Ukrainian Christian names is therefore presented for those readers who may have had Ukrainian ancestors. As with the Polish names, this list may help you determine an approximate birth date (month and day) for your ancestor if the birth date is unknown.

(Information about Ukrainian naming customs was provided by the Reverend Peter Waslo, St. Michael's Ukrainian Greek Catholic Church, Rossford, Ohio.)

UKRAINIAN CALENDAR NAMES

Many girls were given names of male saints. By adding -*a* to the male name, a female name was created. The letters *M* and *F* following the Ukrainian names denote male and female names.

Ukrainian Name	Ukrainian Name or English Equivalent	Julian Calendar Date
Августи́н (M)	August	August 28
Августи́на (F)	Augusta, Augustina	November 23
Авре́лія (F)	Avrele, Avrelia	December 23
Ага́та (F)	Agatha	February 5
А́гнія (F)	Agnes	July 5
А́да (F)	Ada	October 21
Ада́м (M)	Adam	January 14

Ukrainian Name	Ukrainian Name or English Equivalent	Julian Calendar Date
Áлла (F)	Ella	March 26
Альвíна (F)	Alvina	May 4
Амврóсій (M)	Ambrose	December 7
Анастácія, Настáся, Нáстя, Настýня (F)	Anastasia, Stasia	December 22
Анатóль (M)	Anatole	July 3
Ангелúна (F)	Angeline	December 10
Андрíй, Андрíйко (M)	Andrew, Andriy	November 30
Андрiя́н (M)	Andrian	August 26
Андрiя́на (F)	Andriana	August 26
Анíна (F)	Anina	March 13
Антíн, Антóн (M)	Anthony	July 10
Антонíна, Антóнія (F)	Antonina, Antonia	June 10
Аполлінáрій (M)	Apollinary	July 23
Аполлінáрія (F)	Apollinaria	January 5
Аполлóнія (F)	Apollonia	December 14
Аркáдій (M)	Arkadiy, Arkad	January 26
Богдáн (M)	Bohdan	January 1
Богдáнна (F)	Bohdanna	July 4
Богуслáв, Слáвко (M)	Bohuslav, Slavko	August 25
Богуслáва, Слáвка (F)	Bohuslava, Slavka	August 25
Боніфáтій (M)	Boniface	December 19
Борúс (M)	Boris	June 24
Борислáв, Слáвко (M)	Boryslav, Slavko	June 24
Борислáва, Слáвка (F)	Boryslava, Slavka	June 24
Валентúн (M)	Valentine	October 24
Валентúна, Вáля (F)	Valentina, Valia	July 16
Валер'я́н, Валерiя́н (M)	Valerian	June 1
Валéрія (F)	Valerie	June 6
Варвáра, Вáрця (F)	Barbara	December 4
Василúна (F)	Vasylyna	January 1
Васúль (M)	Basil	January 1
Вартоломíй (M)	Bartholomew	June 11
Венедúкт (M)	Benedict	March 14
Верóніка (F)	Veronica	July 12
Вíктор (M)	Victor	November 11
Вíктóрія (F)	Victoria	January 31

Ukrainian Name	Ukrainian Name or English Equivalent	Julian Calendar Date
Вікéнтій (M)	Vincent	November 11
Вітáлій (M)	Vitaliy	April 22
Вітáлія (F)	Vitalia	April 22
Владислáв (M)	Vladyslav	June 14
Владислáва (F)	Vladyslava	November 30
Володúмир (M)	Volodymyr	July 15
Володимúра (F)	Volodymyra	July 15
Володислáв (M)	Volodyslav	September 24
Вячеслáв (M)	Vyacheslav	March 14
Гавриíл, Гаврúло (M)	Gabriel	March 26
Гáнна, Галúна, Гáля (F)	Ann, Hannah	March 10
Гервáсій (M)	Gervase, Jervis	October 14
Гéрман (M)	Herman	May 12
Гілярій (M)	Hilary	July 12
Гнáт, Ігнáтій (M)	Ignatius, Hnat	March 26
Горгóнія (F)	Georgina	December 29
Григóрій (M)	Gregory	January 30
Давúд (M)	David	January 1
Данúло (M)	Daniel	December 17
Дáрія, Дарýся, Дарúна (F)	Daria, Darusia, Daryna	March 19
Денúс (M)	Dennis	October 3
Денúсія (F)	Denise	October 3
Діодóр (M)	Diodor	March 10
Дмитрó (M)	Demetrius	October 26
Доротéя, Дóра (F)	Dorothea, Dorothy, Dora	June 5
Едвáрд (M)	Edward	January 28
Емíлія (F)	Amelia, Emily	August 8
Еміліян (M)	Amelian, Emil	August 8
Éва (F)	Eva, Eve	December 21
Євгéн, Євгéній (M)	Eugene	January 21
Євгéнія (F)	Eugenia	December 24
Євдокíя (F)	Evdokia	March 1
Єлисавéта (F)	Elizabeth	September 5
Захáр, Захáрій (M)	Zachary	September 5
Зенóн (M)	Zenon	January 30
Зенóна, Зéня (F)	Zenonia, Zenia	January 30

Ukrainian Name	Ukrainian Name or English Equivalent	Julian Calendar Date
Зінаі́да, Зі́на (F)	Zinaida, Zina	October 11
Зо́я (F)	Zoia, Zoe	February 13
Іва́н (M)	Ivan, John	June 24
Іва́нна (F)	Yvonna, Johanna, Joan, Jean	June 24
Ігна́тій, Гна́т (M)	Ignatius, Hnat	March 26
І́гор (M)	Ihor	June 5
Ізабе́лла (F)	Isabel, Isabella	April 24
Іларіо́н (M)	Ilarion, Larry	October 21
Іла́рія (F)	Ilaria, Laria	March 19
Іла́рій (M)	Ilary, Larry	July 12
Ілля́ (M)	Elias	July 20
Іри́на (F)	Irene	May 5
Ісидо́ра (F)	Isidora	March 10
Йо́сип (M)	Joseph	December 26
Йван (M), see Іва́н		
Кали́на (F)	Kalyna	June 13
Калисти́на (F)	Celestine, Celeste	May 25
Канди́д (M)	Candid	January 21
Канди́да (F)	Candida, Candace	January 21
Катери́на, Катру́ся, Ка́тря (F)	Katherine, Katerina	November 24
Киприя́н (M)	Cyprian	October 2
Ки́р (M)	Cyrus	January 31
Кири́ло (M)	Cyril	January 18
Кіндра́т (M)	Conrad	January 4
Кла́ра (F)	Clara	June 1
Кли́м, Кле́ме́нт (M)	Clem, Clement	January 23
Клеме́нтія (F)	Clementine	January 23
Костянти́н, Ко́сть (M)	Constantine	May 21
Костянти́на (F)	Constance	May 21
Кузьма́ (M)	Kuzma	November 1
Крисце́нтія (F)	Krystsentia	June 15
Ла́вра (F)	Laura	August 18
Лавре́нтій, Лаврі́н (M)	Lawrence, Lavrin	August 10
Лари́са (F)	Larissa	March 26
Ле́в, Левко́ (M)	Lev, Levko, Leo	February 19
Лео́н (M)	Leon, Leo	June 18

Ukrainian Name	Ukrainian Name or English Equivalent	Julian Calendar Date
Леона́рд (M)	Leonard	November 1
Леони́д (M)	Leonid	August 8
Лі́дія, Лі́да (F)	Lydia	March 23
Лука́, Лука́ш (M)	Luke	October 18
Лукі́я (F)	Lukia, Lucia	December 13
Лукія́н (M)	Lucian	October 15
Луї́за (F)	Louise	December 13
Любо́в, Лю́ба (F)	Lubov, Luba	September 17
Любоми́р (M)	Lubomyr	August 13
Любоми́ра (F)	Lubomyra	August 13
Людми́ла (F)	Ludmilla	September 16
Ма́вра (F)	Maura, Moira	October 31
Магдали́на (F)	Magdalyna	July 20
Макси́м (M)	Maksym, Max	August 13
Максимілія́н (M)	Maximilian, Max	October 22
Маргари́та (F)	Margaret	February 27
Марі́я, Мару́ся, Марі́йка (F)	Maria, Mary	September 8
Марія́н, Мар'я́н (M)	Marian	December 10
Мар'я́на, Марія́нна (F)	Marianna	February 16
Ма́рко (M)	Marko, Mark	April 25
Марке́л (M)	Marcel	August 1
Маркія́н (M)	Markian, Mark	August 9
Ма́рта (F)	Martha	June 4
Марти́н (M)	Martin	April 14
Мари́на (F)	Maryna	March 12
Матві́й (M)	Matthew	November 16
Ма́я (F)	Maya, May	January 26
Мела́нія, Мала́нка (F)	Melania	December 31
Мето́дій (M)	Methodius	July 5
Мечесла́в (M)	Mecheslav	December 19
Мечесла́ва (F)	Mecheslava	December 19
Мики́та (M)	Mykyta	September 15
Мико́ла (M)	Nicholas	December 6
Ми́на (M)	Mina	November 11
Миро́н (M)	Myron	August 18
Миросла́в (M)	Myroslav	May 5

Ukrainian Name	Ukrainian Name or English Equivalent	Julian Calendar Date
Мирослáва (F)	Myroslava	May 5
Михáйло (M)	Michael	November 8
Михайлúна (F)	Michaelina	November 8
Мóніка (F)	Monica	April 1
Мстислáв (M)	Mstyslav	April 15
Мстислáва (F)	Mstyslava	April 15
Надíя (F)	Nadia	September 17
Натáлія, Натáлка, Натáля (F)	Natalia	August 26
Натанаíл, Натáн (M)	Nathaniel, Nathan	April 22
Нéстор (M)	Nestor	October 27
Нúкін, Нúкон (M)	Nykon	March 23
Нíна (F)	Nina	January 14
Нóнна (F)	Nona	August 4
Оксáна, Ксеня (F)	Oksana, Ksenia	January 23
Олéг (M)	Oleh	September 20
Олéкса (M)	Oleksa	March 17
Олексáндер, Олéсь, Лéсь (M)	Alexander, Oles, Les	August 30
Олексáндра, Олéся, Лéся, Сáндра (F)	Alexandria, Olesia, Lesia, Sandra	August 30
Олéна (F)	Helen	May 21
Óльга, Óля, Олюся, Люся (F)	Olha, Olia, Olusia, Lusia	July 11
Онóпрій (M)	Onopriy	June 12
Орúна, Орúся (F)	Irene, Oryna, Orysia	April 16
Óсип, Йóсип (M)	Joseph	December 26
Осúпа (F)	Josephine	December 26
Остáп (M)	Ostap, Eustace	August 20
Павлúна (F)	Pauline	June 3
Павлó (M)	Paul	June 29
Палáгна, Палáжка (F)	Palahna	May 4
Паллáдій (M)	Palladiy	November 27
Петрó (M)	Peter	June 29
Петронúлла, Петрýня (F)	Petronella, Petrunia, Petrina	May 31
Пилúп (M)	Philip	November 14

Ukrainian Name	Ukrainian Name or English Equivalent	Julian Calendar Date
Пили́пія (F)	Phillipa	April 21
Полія́нна (F)	Pollyanna	May 19
Пота́п (M)	Potap	December 8
Присці́ля (F)	Priscilla	July 14
Про́кіп, Про́коп (M)	Prokip, Prokop	July 8
Радосла́в (M)	Radoslav, Rad	April 2
Радоми́р (M)	Radomyr, Rad	November 28
Раі́са, Ра́я (F)	Raisa, Raya	September 5
Рафаі́л (M)	Raphael	November 8
Рахи́ля (F)	Rachel	April 30
Реве́кка (F)	Rebecca	October 9
Регі́на (F)	Regina	February 22
Роэа́лія (F)	Rosalia, Rose	May 18
Роксоля́на, Рокса́на (F)	Roxoliana, Roxanna	January 24
Рома́н (M)	Roman	November 18
Рома́нна, Ро́ма (F)	Romanna, Roma, Romona	November 18
Ростисла́в, Сла́вко (M)	Rostyslav, Slavko	March 14
Ростисла́ва (F)	Rostyslava	September 24
Ру́та (F)	Ruth	July 16
Саві́на (F)	Savina	March 16
Самі́йло, Самуі́л (M)	Samuel	August 20
Са́ра (F)	Sarah, Sara	July 26
Світла́на (F)	Svitlana	February 20
Святосла́в (M)	Svyatoslav	April 20
Святосла́ва (F)	Svyatoslava	April 20
Севастія́н (M)	Sebastian	February 26
Севери́н (M)	Severyn	September 9
Серафи́м (M)	Seraphim	July 29
Серафи́ма (F)	Seraphina	July 29
Сергі́й (M)	Serhiy	October 7
Си́дір (M)	Isidore	May 14
Си́ла (M)	Syla	July 30
Сильва́н (M)	Sylvan	July 30
Сильве́стер (M)	Sylvester	January 2
Си́мон, Семе́н (M)	Simon	February 3
Соломі́я (F)	Salome	August 1
Соломо́н (M)	Solomon	December 2

Ukrainian Name	Ukrainian Name or English Equivalent	Julian Calendar Date
Софı́я, Со́ня (F)	Sophia, Sonia	September 17
Степа́н (M)	Stephan, Steven	December 27
Степани́да, Стефа́нıя (F)	Stephania	November 11
Суза́нна (F)	Susanna	August 11
Тама́ра (F)	Tamara	May 1
Тара́с (M)	Taras	February 24
Теодо́р (M)	Theodore, Ted	February 16
Теодо́ра (F)	Theodora	September 11
Теодо́сıй (M)	Theodosey	May 3
Теодо́сıя (F)	Theodosia	May 29
Теодо́т (M)	Theodot	June 7
Те́кля (F)	Thekla, Tecla	September 24
Тео́н (M)	Teon	January 5
Теофа́н (M)	Teofan	September 29
Теофı́ль (M)	Theofil	February 6
Теофı́ля (F)	Theofila	February 6
Тере́за (F)	Teresa	January 31
Тетя́на, Та́ня (F)	Tetiana, Tania	January 12
Ти́мон (M)	Tymon	August 28
Тимофı́й, Тимоте́й, Тимı́ш (M)	Timothy, Tim	January 22
Тома́, Фома́, Хома́ (M)	Toma, Thomas	October 6
Три́фон (M)	Tryfon	February 1
Ула́с, Вла́сıй, Влас (M)	Ulas	February 11
Уля́на, Юлıя́нна (F)	Ulianna, Julianna	March 4
Фе́дıр (M)	Fedir, Theodore	August 8
Фе́лıкс (M)	Felix	July 6
Филимо́н (M)	Philemon	November 22
Филимо́на (F)	Philemona	November 29
Фıя́лка (F)	Fialka, Violet	September 11
Фла́вıя (F)	Flavia	March 9
Фло́ра (F)	Flora	August 18
Фло́рентıй (M)	Florent	August 22
Флоре́нцıя (F)	Florence	August 22
Харити́на, Хари́тя (F)	Charita	October 5
Хома́, Фома́ (M)	Thomas	October 6
Христофо́р (M)	Christopher	May 9

Ukrainian Name	Ukrainian Name or English Equivalent	Julian Calendar Date
Христи́на, Хри́стя (F)	Christine	July 24
Христия́н (M)	Christian	May 24
Цеци́лія (F)	Cecelia	November 22
Юди́та (F)	Judith	June 6
Юлія́н (M)	Julian, Julius	June 21
Юлія́нна, Уля́на (F)	Juliana, Uliana	December 21
Ю́на (F)	Una, Eunice, June	May 4
Ю́рій, Ю́рко (M)	George	April 23
Юсти́н, Усти́н (M)	Justin	June 1
Юсти́на, Усти́на (F)	Justina	October 2
Юхи́м (M)	Yukhym	August 16
Яки́м (M)	Joachim	September 9
Я́ків (M)	Jacob	April 30
Яре́ма (M)	Jeremiah, Jeremy	May 1
Яри́на (F)	Irene	September 18
Ярода́р (M)	Yarodar	May 15
Яроми́р (M)	Yaromyr	April 11
Яропо́лк (M)	Yaropolk	November 22
Яросла́в, Сла́вко (M)	Yaroslav, Slavko	January 21
Яросла́ва, Сла́вка (F)	Yaroslava, Slavka	April 13

GERMAN CUSTOMS IN NAMING CHILDREN   PRE CHRISTIAN

Christianity brought saints' names to the Germanic lands. Many parents gave their children a saint's name, while some pagan names were used until the Counter-Reformation in the sixteenth century. About this time, Lutherans began to use only the names of saints found in the Bible or Old Testament names.

Beginning in the sixteenth century the parents sometimes added a secular name to the Christian name, giving the child two first names (*vornamem*), for example, Wolfgang Amadeus Mozart; Wolfgang is a saint's name. In the seventeenth century most Protestant and Catholic German infants were given two baptismal names. Late in the eighteenth century single names were again popular, but by the end of the nineteenth century double names were back in vogue. When a person had two given names, it was customary to call the person by the second name. However, in church records the person may have been identified by either the first or second name, or both.

By giving their children two names, parents may have kept a favorite name in their family. Sometimes all the boys in the family were named Johann: Johann Wilhelm, Johann Karl, Johann Friedrich, etc.

Children were often named after a godparent, who might also have had the same name as one of the grandparents.

JEWISH CUSTOMS IN NAMING CHILDREN

Jewish children were traditionally named after one of their ancestors. Ashkenazic Jewish children were never named after a living ancestor, for religious reasons. Sephardic Jews followed their own tradition of naming children after particular ancestors, both living and deceased.

The tradition of giving Biblical names began in the tenth century, but the custom of dual names did not begin until the thirteenth century. A child was given a religious name to be used in the synagogue and a non-Jewish name to be used on secular occasions.

Most Jews in northern and eastern Europe traditionally used only their personal name and father's name, having no surnames, until the nineteenth century, when they were forced to adopt surnames. Thus, names changed with each generation.

Ben means "son of," as in David ben Abraham, or "David son of Abraham." *Bar* also means "son of." *Ben rab* followed by the father's name is "son of the worthy (father's name)." "Son of" in Arabic is *ibn* or *abn*, and can be a clue that the person was a descendant of a Sephardic Jew. *Bat* is the "daughter of."

A Jewish custom still popular today was the renaming of a seriously ill person in the hope that the Angel of Death would not be able to find that person. If you are trying to find the birth record of an ancestor and find a different name, this renaming practice might have been the reason.

SOURCES AND ADDITIONAL READING

Johnson, Arta F. *Origins, Development, and Meaning of German Names.* Columbus, Ohio: published by the author, 1984.

Kurzweil, Arthur. *From Generation to Generation: How to Trace Your Jewish Genealogy and Personal History.* New York: William Morrow & Co., 1980.

Chapter Thirteen:

BREAKING THE
LANGUAGE BARRIER

A TIMETABLE

1480   Polish became the official state language, and the literary language after Latin.

1514   The first books were printed in the Polish language.

1523   Roman letters began to replace Gothic letters, making print easier to read.

1582   The Gregorian calendar was adopted in Poland.

1612   The Gregorian calendar was adopted in Prussia.

1618   There were 11 million people living in 1 million square kilometers of land in the Polish Commonwealth. Languages spoken by the habitants of the Commonwealth at this time:

Polish	40 percent
Ukrainian	30 percent
Byelorussian	15 percent
Lithuanian	5 percent
Others	10 percent

One-and-a-half million people spoke these other languages (listed in descending order): Yiddish, German, Latvian, Russian, Estonian, Armenian, Prussian, Tatar, Livonian, Slovak, Czech, Romany (Gypsy). (450,000 Jews spoke Yiddish; 300,000 lived in towns, the rest in rural villages.)

1918   The Russian Empire adopted the Gregorian calendar. The Russians used the old Julian calendar until 1918. In the nineteenth century the Julian dates were twelve days behind the Gregorian dates. Some records from Russian areas show double dates side by side—the old Julian and the new Gregorian. The Russian Orthodox Church still uses the old Julian calendar.

Source: Pogonowski, Iwo Cyprian. *Poland, A Historical Atlas.* New York: Hippocrene Books, 1987.

THE POLISH LANGUAGE

The letters *ć, ń, ś,* and *ź* are used only before a consonant or at the end of a word. When these sounds appear before a vowel, the *ć* is replaced by *ci, ń* is replaced by *ni, ś* is replaced by *si,* and *ź* is replaced by *zi.*

The Polish language has no *Q, V,* or *X. Ks* is substituted for the *X* sound in words such as *Ksawery,* "Xavier." Because Latin uses the letter *X,* priests in particular were likely to mix *X* into their Polish handwriting. For instance, *X* in front of a priest's name represents *ks.* (*ksiądz*), meaning "Reverend (Priest)."

There are no diacritical marks *ą ć ł ĩ* in the English language as there are in the Polish. These marks are often ignored completely when words or names are written in another language, especially English. Occasionally a phonetic translation occurs, such as *Dębiński* to *Dembinski* or *Stanisław* to *Staniswav.* Be careful not to confuse a *ł* with a *t.*

Some Polish consonants change their pronunciation at the end of a word. *Kolbug* is pronounced *Kolebuk* and may eventually appear as such or even changed to *Kolebuck. Rzeszów* is pronounced "zhe-shoof."

There are exceptions to these general rules. For more information about pronunciation and word endings, consult a book for beginners on learning the Polish language. And, as you have probably noticed, there are no articles *a, an,* or *the* in the Polish language.

Language and Regional Differences

When a word begins with *ch-* the *c* is silent, only the *h* is pronounced. Consequently you may find a name like Chorzępa or Chełmiński written *Horzempa* or *Helminski.* Another example of a name that might evolve into one that is spelled the way it is pronounced belongs to Lech Wałęsa, "Va-wen-sa."

In central Poland the *h* sound and *ch* sound are sometimes given the Russian pronunciation *kh.* So Chorzępa may be pronounced *Khorzempa* or *Horzempa.*

THE POLISH ALPHABET			
Letter	**Sound**	**Pronunciation Notes**	**Variations**
a	short a	c*a*r, m*a*ma	
ą	ah'own		
b	b	*b*ook	at end of a word = *p* sound
c	ts	ba*ts*	
ć	ch	*ch*eese	
d	d	*d*ad	at end of a word = *t* sound
e	short e	l*e*t, p*e*n	
ę	eh'own		before b or p = *em* sound
			at end of a word = *eh* sound
f	f	*f*or	
g	g	*g*ood (hard *g*)	at end of a word = *k* sound
h	h	*h*ave	
i	long e	m*ee*t	
j	y	*y*es	
k	k	*k*ite	
l	l	*l*ook	
ł ĺ̃	w	*w*in	
m	m	*m*om	
n	n	*n*o	
ń	ny	o*ni*on	
o	short o	t*o*rte	
ó	oo	g*oo*se	
p	p	*p*at	
r	rolling r	as in French, German, and Scottish: tip of tongue repeatedly vibrates against the palate	
s	s	*s*et	
ś	sh	*sh*eep	raise tongue slightly
t	t	*t*op	
u	oo	g*oo*se	
w	v	*v*at	at end of a word = *f* sound
y	short i	p*i*t	
z	z	*z*one or watche*s*	at end of a word = *s* sound
ź	zh	Rhode*s*ia	raise tongue slightly
			at end of a word = ś (*sh*) sound
ż	zh	plea*s*ure	lower tongue slightly
			at end of a word = sz (*sh*) sound

PRONUNCIATION OF COMMON LETTER COMBINATIONS			
Combination	**Sound**	**Pronunciation**	**Notes**
ch	h	Scottish lo*ch*	c is silent when words begin with ch
ci	ch	*ch*air	
cz	ch	*ch*air, ca*tch*	
dz	dz	a*dz*e	at end of a word = c (*ts*) sound
dź, dzi	j	*j*am, *g*entle	at end of a word = ć (*ch*) sound
dż	dg	bri*dg*e	at end of a word = cz (*ch*) sound
li	lyih	va*l*ue	
ni	ny	o*ni*on	
-ów	oof	pr*oof*	-ów is found at the end of a word
rz	zh	plea*s*ure	lower tongue slightly at end of a word = sz (*sh*) sound
ść	shch	fre*shch*eese	
ści	shchy	fre*shch*eese	
si	shee	*shee*	
sz	sh	*sh*ow	lower tongue slightly
szcz	shch	fre*shch*eese	
zi	zhee	Rhode*si*a	raise tongue slightly

In Russian-influenced areas the h sound is replaced by a g sound. Halicz becomes Galich/Galicia. As mentioned before, there is no *h* in the Russian alphabet.

The Polish, Byelorussian, and Ukrainian languages have both the letters *g* and *h*. Czech has no *g*, and substitutes an *h*.

All of the above changes and pronunciations may influence the spelling of names and other words you will find in records. Write your surname down and use the alphabetical guide and the above information to phonetically sound out your surname. You will also see the unlimited number of ways to spell your surname. A hint for decoding the handwriting in old records: look at other letters in the text that you are certain you know, and try to match them up with the unknown letter(s).

Cases in the Polish Language

In many languages, including Polish, the endings of words change according to their use in a sentence. These different uses are called cases. Two of the most commonly used cases in Polish language records are nominative and genitive. The nominative case is used when the noun (name) stands alone or acts as the subject of a sentence, the genitive when the noun (name) is used to show possession.

There are two types of surnames in Polish:

1. Noun (Nominal)—*Bór*, "forest"

2. Adjective (Adjectival)— *Kowalewicz*, "son of the blacksmith"; *Borski*, "dweller of the forest."

Feminine names almost always end in -*a*. Surname endings are -*cka* and -*ska* for the feminine versions of -*cki* and -*ski*. Most first names end in -*a*: *Róża, Józefa*, and *Władysława*. Many feminine names are derived from masculine names, for example, *Józef* and *Władysław*.

Most men's names are fairly easy to identify in written records. Women are usually identified "of (the family name)" in the same way that we use the word *née*. The Polish phrase *z domu* and Latin *de domo*, both meaning "from home," also are used to indicate the maiden name.

NOMINAL SURNAMES				
Case	**Mr.**	**Mrs.**	**Miss**	**Mr. & Mrs. or Family**
nominative	Bór	Borowa	Borówna	Borowy, Borowie
genitive	Bór	Borowi	Borównej	Borów
"	Boru	Borowej		
"	Bora			

ADJECTIVAL SURNAMES				
Case	**Mr.**	**Mrs.**	**Miss**	**Mr. & Mrs. or Family**
nominative	Borski	Borska	Borska	Borscy, Borsci
genitive	Borskiego	Borskiej		Borskich

Examples:

Stanisław syn Jana Bór i Katarzyny z Adamczaka—"Stanisław the son of Jan Bór and Katarzyna from (home) Adamczak"

Marya córka Stanisława Górskiego i Stanisławy Komorowskiej—"Marya the daughter of Stanisław Górski and Stanisława Komorowska"

It is easy to become confused because of the changing word endings and assume Stanisława Górskiego and Jana Bór are women, or mistake the mother's name for the father's name. Although -*a* is a feminine ending, it is also the masculine possessive (genitive case) in a few instances!

Sometimes people also misinterpret their ancestor's name. Looking at the second example above, you might assume that *Stanisława Górskiego*, as spelled, is your ancestor's true name when, in fact, the true name is *Górski*. Be careful—watch name endings!

The following list is provided as an example of the surname endings you can expect to find in just one Polish parish of the period 1760 to 1850.

Name as Found in Register	Surname
Zofia de Kazmierczǫka	Kazmierczak (son of Casimir)
Zofia de Kazmierczonka	" "
Hedwig Przybyizantka	Przybysz (newcomer)
Agnieszka Jędrzeyiotka	Jędrzejczak (son of Andrew)
Catharina Kędzierzyna	Kędziora (curly-haired)
Jadwiga Bratkowa	Bratek (pansy)
Marianna Bratkowna	" "
Catharina de Hirsców	Hirsch (stag)
Catharina Hirszowna	" "
Cunegunda de Daierlingowna	Daierling, Dajerling, Deyerling
Margaretha de Daierlinczǎka	" " (son of a worthy man)
(The above two names appeared in the same entry: one is the mother of the child being baptized, the other is the godmother.)	
Marianna Tylezonka	Tyll
Marianna Tylerowska	"
Margaritha Deszczyna	Deska (board or plank; not Deski)
Margaritha Deskowa	" "
Agnetis de domo Pokrywczaka	Pokrywka (lid of a pot)

All these surnames are in the genitive (possessive) case. Sometimes the same person's name is seen in more than one variation in the same register. Evidently, the registrar used whatever variation he thought was appropriate at the time.

Not only do the female surname endings vary, but the surnames themselves change over a period of time. In 1767 a surname was *Kryszak*. In the next several decades *Kryszak* and *Ryszka* were both seen in the registers. By 1813 the name was exclusively spelled *Ryszka*. The surname variously appeared as *Ryska, Ryszkowiak, Riszka, Krzyozka,* and *Kryska* in between. Another surname from a different area of Poland was spelled *Insadowski* in early records, and slowly changed to *Sadowski*.

Numbers and Dates

Numbers and dates are often written out in vital records that use the narrative form: "On this day, the twenty-eighth of July one thousand nine hundred ninety-two I baptized . . . " *Tysiąc dziewięćset dziewięćdziesiąt dwa* is "one thousand nine hundred ninety-two."

CARDINAL NUMBERS					
0	zero	zero	20	twenty	dwadzieścia
1	one, once	jeden, raz	21	twenty-one	dwadzieścia jeden
2	two	dwa	22	twenty-two	dwadzieścia dwa
3	three	trzy	23	twenty-three	dwadzieścia trzy
4	four	cztery	24	twenty-four	dwadzieścia cztery
5	five	pięć	25	twenty-five	dwadzieścia pięć
6	six	sześć	30	thirty	trzydzieści
7	seven	siedem	40	forty	czterdzieści
8	eight	osiem	50	fifty	pięćdziesiąt
9	nine	dziewięć	60	sixty	sześćdziesiąt
10	ten	dziesięć	70	seventy	siedemdziesiąt
11	eleven	jedenaście	80	eighty	osiemdziesiąt
12	twelve	dwanaście	90	ninety	dziewięćdziesiąt
13	thirteen	trzynaście	100	one hundred	sto
14	fourteen	czternaście	101	one hundred and one	sto jeden
15	fifteen	piętnaście	1,000	one thousand	tysiąc
16	sixteen	szesnaście			
17	seventeen	siedemnaście			
18	eighteen	osiemnaście			
19	nineteen	dziewiętnaście			

ORDINAL NUMBERS

1st	first	pierwszy	22nd	twenty-second	dwudziesty drugi
2nd	second	drugi	23rd	twenty-third	dwudziesty trzeci
3rd	third	trzeci	24th	twenty-fourth	dwudziesty czwarty
4th	fourth	czwarty	25th	twenty-fifth	dwudziesty piąty
5th	fifth	piąty	30th	thirtieth	trzydziesty
6th	sixth	szosty	40th	fortieth	czterdziesty
7th	seventh	siódmy	50th	fiftieth	pięćdziesiąty
8th	eighth	ósmy	60th	sixtieth	sześćdziesiąty
9th	ninth	dziewiąty	70th	seventieth	siedemdziesiąty
10th	tenth	dziesiąty	80th	eightieth	osiemdziesiąty
11th	eleventh	jedenasty	90th	ninetieth	dziewięćdziesiąty
12th	twelfth	dwunasty	100th	one hundredth	setny
13th	thirteenth	trzynasty	101st	one hundred and first	sto pierwszy
14th	fourteenth	czternasty			
15th	fifteenth	piętnasty			
16th	sixteenth	szesnasty			
17th	seventeenth	siedemnasty			
18th	eighteenth	osiemnasty			
19th	nineteenth	dziewiętnasty			
20th	twentieth	dwudziesty			
21st	twenty-first	dwudziesty pierwszy			

MONTHS

styczeń, stycznia	January	I
luty, lutego	February	II
marzec, marca	March	III
kwiecień, kwietna	April	IV
maj, maja	May	V
czerwiec, czerwca	June	VI
lipiec, lipca	July	VII
sierpień, sierpnia	August	VIII
wrzesień, września	September	IX
październik, października	October	X
listopad, listopada	November	XI
grudzień, grudnia	December	XII

The first word for a Polish month is the nominative, the second word is the genitive (possessive). Sometimes months are written in roman numerals.

POLISH TERMS FOUND IN VITAL RECORDS

The following terms are frequently found in vital records from the eighteenth and nineteenth centuries.

agaria: diarrhea (from Latin *agaricus* = agaric, which is a cathartic/laxative)
akta małżeństwa: marriage register
akta urodzin: birth register
akta zejścia: death records
akta zgonów: death register
akuszerka: midwife
apopleksja: apoplexy
ayaria: diarrhea

babcia: grandmother
biegunka: diarrhea, flux
blednica: chlorosis, greensickness
bliźniaczy: twin
błonica: diphtheria (from *błona* = membrane)
bracia: brothers
brak danych: lack of evidence, unknown
brat: brother
bratanek: brother's son, nephew
bratanica: brother's daughter, niece
bratowa: brother's wife, sister-in-law
bronchit: (chronic) bronchitis
brzemienny: pregnant, with child

chałupnik: farmer with a small cottage but no land
chłopy: peasants
cholera: Asiatic cholera
choleryn(k)a: sporadic, English, bilious, or summer (infantile) cholera
choroba: disease, illness
choroba angielska: rickets, "the English disease"
choroba serca: heart disease
chrosty: pimples, measles (same as *krosty*)

chrzest: baptism
ciąży: pregnant, with child
ciocia: mother's sister, maternal aunt (though often used generically)
ciotka: mother's sister, maternal aunt (though often used generically)
cmentarny, cmentarz: cemetery, burial ground, churchyard
córka: daughter
czerwonka: dysentery, bloody flux

data i miejsce: date and place (of)
data ślubu: date of marriage
data urodzenia: date of birth
dekanat: decanate
diecezja: diocese
dnia: day
dolne: lower
drugi: second
dwór: manor house
dyfteria: diphtheria
dyzenteria: dysentery, bloody flux
dziadek: grandfather
dzieci: child
dziedzic: heir (seen as the occupation of a nobleman)
dzień: day
dzierżawca: a lease-holder, tenant

ewangelickie: Evangelical (Lutheran)

familia: family
farny: parish
febra: fever
folwark: working farm

gangrena: gangrene
garncarz: potter
gmina: county
godny: patriciate of a very large city
godzina, godz.: hour, o'clock
gorączka: fever
gorączka połogowa: puerperal fever, childbed fever
gospodarstwo: household, homestead, farm
gospodarz: farmer
gościec: gout, arthritis

gościec stawowy: rheumatic fever, rheumatism
górne: upper
grecko-katolickie: Greek Catholic
gruźlica: tuberculosis, phthisis, consumption
gruźlica skóry: lupus

Höllander: Dutchman, Dutchwoman

i: and
imię: name
imię chrzestne: Christian/baptismal name
imiona: names
imiona rodziców: names of parents
influenca: influenza

jad: virus

kaszel: cough
katar: catarrh, rheum, head cold
katar kiszek: enteritis
katar oskrzeli: bronchitis
kawaler: bachelor
kątnik: laborer, poor person who lives in someone else's cottage
kiła: syphilis; also hernia
kmieć: self-supporting farmer
koklusz: whooping cough, pertussis
kolka: colic
komornik: farmer who owned no land or cottage and lived in someone
      else's house; also may refer to elderly parents after they retire and live
      in their child's house
konwulsje: convulsions, fits
kościół : church
krew: blood
krosta: pustule, pimple
krosty: pimples, rash, measles
królestwo: kingdom
krwawa biegunka: dysentery, bloody flux
krwawiączka: hemophilia
krzywica: rickets
ksiądz, ks.: priest, Reverend Father
księgi hipoteczne: mortgage books
kumornik: see *komornik*

kumoszka: godmother
kumoter: godfather
kumy: godparents
kupiec: merchant
kuratel: ward (child)
kurcz: spasm, contraction
kuzyn: cousin

lata: years old, age
leśnik: forester, woodsman
łowca: hunter
lub: or
luźny: vagabond, a person with no possessions; a "street person"

malaria: malaria
mała, małe, mały, mł.: little
małżeński: married (as in married couple and married life)
małżeństwo: marriage
małżonek: husband
małżonka: wife, consort
marazm: marasmus, infantile debility; due to malnutrition
martwo urodzony: stillborn
matka: mother
matka chrzestna: godmother
mąż, męża: husband, husband's; also a man
metryka: original record (of birth, marriage)
miasto: city
miejsce: place
miejsce urodzenia: place of birth
młodzian: young (unmarried) man
myśliwy: hunter

narzeczona: fiancée
narzeczony: fiancé
nazwisko: surname
nazwisko panieńskie: maiden name
nazwisko po mężu: married name
neofita: neophyte, convert
nerka: kidney
niepełnoletni: a minor, an infant
nieprawny: illegitimate

nieślubny: unwed, illegitimate
nie-szlachcic: a commoner ("not noble")
niewiadomy: unknown
nowa, nowe, nowy, nw.: new

oberżysta: innkeeper
oblubienica: bride
oblubieniec: bridegroom
oboje: both
odpis: copy, transcript
odra: rubeola, measles
ogrodnik: farmer with a house and garden, but no cropland
ojciec: father
ojciec chrzestny: godfather
ojczym: stepfather
około: about, circa
olęder, olędry, olęderski, olender: Hollander, Dutch
opatrzny: poor burgher
operarzy: workman, laborer (from Latin *operarius*)
opiekun: guardian
opuchlina: dropsy, edema, swelling
ospa: smallpox
ospa dziecięca: chicken pox
ospa wietrzna: chicken pox
ożeniony: married

pan: literally, lord, sir, Mr.; in modern usage, a man
pani: lady, mistress, Mrs.
panieńskie nazwisko: maiden name
panna: girl, maiden, miss
parafia: parish
pas: row (in a table of printed matter)
pasierb: stepson
pasierbica: stepdaughter
pasterz: shepherd
piasek moczowy: gravel (a kidney disorder)
piekarz: baker
pierwszy: first
pitoce, pytochie, pytochij: phlegm, rheum (from Latin *pituita*)
plamisty: spotted, rash; probably spotted fever
płuco: lung

pochować: bury
pochówek: burial
pogrzeb: burial
połogowy: puerperal fever, childbed fever
położna: midwife
poronienie: miscarriage
powiat: county
pół brat: half-brother
północ: midnight
półrolnik: farmer with cropland, a house, farm buildings, and animals
pół siostra: half-sister
prababcia: great-grandmother
prababka: great-grandmother
pracowity: peasant
pradziad: ancestor
pradziadek: great-grandfather
prawnuczęta: great-grandchildren
prawosławne: Orthodox
przednazwiska: middle name, nickname
przydomek: surname
przyjaciele: friends
przy połoga: puerperal fever, childbed fever
pthysis: phthisis, consumption, tuberculosis of the lungs
puchlina: dropsy, edema, swelling

rachityzm: rickets, rachitis
rataj: serf dependent on the village lord
reumatyzm: rheumatism
rodzic(e): parent(s)
rodzina: family
rodzony: own (brother, sister, etc.)
rodzony brat/siostra: full brother/sister, brother/sister german
rok: year (abbreviated r. after a year, for example, 1875 r.)
rolnik: farmer
ropne zapalenie: quinsy, cyananche, tonsillitis
rosyjski: Russian
róża: erysipelas; also known as "the Rose," "St. Anthony's Fire," and "phlogosis"
różyczka: rubella; sometimes rubeola
ruski: Ruthenian, Ukrainian

rzeżączka: gonorrhea
rzymsko-katolickie: Roman Catholic

samic(zk)a: female
samczy: male
sinica: cyanosis
siostra: sister
siostrzenica: sister's daughter, niece
sklepikarz: shopkeeper
skrofuły: scrofula (tuberculosis)
skryba: scribe, clerk
slup: column (in a table of printed matter)
słabość, słabosi: debility, weakness, illness
sławetny: average resident of a big city or rich burgher in a small town
sołtys, szołtys: administrator of a village (equivalent to Latin *scultetus*)
stara, stare, stary, st.: old
starość: senility
stetryczały: bilious
stryj: father's brother, paternal uncle (often used generically)
stryjenka: father's sister, paternal aunt (often used generically)
suchoty: consumption
syfilis: syphilis
syn: son
synowa: son's wife, daughter-in-law
synowie, syny: sons
szambelan: chamberlain
szeryf: sheriff
szewc: shoemaker
szkarlatyna: scarlet fever, scarlatina
szkorbut: scorbutus, scurvy
szlachic: nobleman
szos: house tax
szwagier: brother-in-law
szwagierka: sister-in-law
ślub: marriage
średnie: middle
świadectwo: certificate
świadectwo chrztu: baptismal certificate
świadectwo ślubu: marriage certificate
świadectwo śmierci: death certificate

świadectwo zgonu: death certificate
świniopas: swineherd

taniec św. Wita: St. Vitus Dance
tężcowy: tetanus
tkacz: weaver
trzeci: third
tyfoidalny: typhoid
tyfus: typhoid, typhus; the distinction between the two was not made until
    mid-nineteenth century
tyfusbrzuszny: enteric fever, typhoid
tyfus plamisty: spotted fever, typhus

uczciwy: village craftsman, inn owner, or people living outside the town
    walls
udar paralityczny: paralysis
ułan: Polish cavalryman armed with a lance, a Polish lancer
umarł : died
umarł dnia: day of death
umrzeć śmiercią naturalną: natural death, natural cause of death
unrodzony: nobleman possessing land
urodził, urodzony: was born, birth
urząd stanu cywilnego: civil register office

wagabunda, wagus: vagabond, person with no possessions, a "street
    person"
wdowa: widow
wdowiec: widower
wiek: age
wielka, wielki, wielkie, wlk.: great
wielmożny: literally, powerful (a respectful form of address, still used);
    owner of several villages and/or holder of an important regional office
wieś, wsie: village, villages
wietrzna: chicken pox
wnuczęta: grandchildren
wnuczka: granddaughter
wnuk: grandson
wodna puchlina: dropsy, edema
wodogłowie: (chronic) hydrocephalus, dropsy of the brain
wojak: soldier

województwo, woj.: province, voivodeship

wól, wole: goiter

wuj: mother's brother, maternal uncle (though often used generically)

wujenka: wife of mother's brother, wife of maternal uncle (though often used generically)

wymienica: trader

wyniszczenie: marasmus, infantile debility; due to malnutrition

wyrobnik: laborer

wyrobnik rolny: farmhand

wyznanie: religion

zacny: richest merchant

zagrodnik: farmer who owned a house, farm buildings, and animals, and farmed a small plot of land

zagrodnik z roli: literally "a farmer with land"; farmer who owned a house, farm buildings, and animals, and farmed a medium-size plot of land

zamieszkanie: place of residence

zapalenie: inflammation

zapalenie mózgu: encephalitis, brain fever

zapalenie nerek: nephritis

zapalenie opłucnej: pleurisy

zapalenie opon mózgowych: meningitis

zapalenie otrzewnej: peritonitis

zapalenie płuc: pneumonia

zatrucie krwi: septicemia, pyemia, blood poisoning

z domu: "from home," maiden name, father's surname

zgonu: death

zmarł : died

żołciowy: bilious

żołnierz: soldier

żółtaczka: jaundice

żona: wife

żonaty: married

żydowskie: Jewish

THE LATIN LANGUAGE

After one year of Latin in high school I wanted to switch to German but the principal wouldn't let me. Latin is a dead language, I thought; even the

Catholic Church was changing its policy and dropping Latin in exchange for using the vernacular of the people participating in its services. I studied Latin for two years, and then German in college. I wanted to learn Polish also, but the university no longer taught it. Now I am very grateful for studying both Latin and German—I never imagined that I would be putting them to use for many years to come.

The Latin found in Polish church records is not exactly textbook Latin. The Polish priests were not as well versed in Latin as they were in their native Polish. The priests often mixed Latin and Polish in the same record entry, probably when they were unfamiliar with the correct Latin word or form. The Christian name may be in Latin followed by a surname in Polish, because Polish surnames do not translate into Latin.

Compounding the problem is the incompatibility of the Polish and Latin alphabets. There is no *w* in Latin, whereas *w* is frequently used in Polish. *K* is almost never seen in Latin and is usually replaced by a *c*. *J* does not exist in classical Latin, but in many Latin records in Poland it is used to represent the consonant *i/j*. An example is the word for "young person": in classical Latin it is *iuvenis*; in Polonized Latin it is *juvenis*.

U was originally written *v*, but is seen as a *u* in Polonized Latin records. There is no *y* in Latin, except for words of foreign origin. *X* is used in Latin; in Polish *ks* is substituted: *Ksawery* for *Xavier*. Latin also does not use the articles *a, an,* and *the*.

Proper Names

CASE	MR.	MRS./MISS	MR. & MRS. or FAMILY
nominative	-us, -um -er, -es	-a,-ne	(the name)
genitive	-i, -is	-ae	-orum, (-um, -ium)

The following are examples of names as you might find them in Polish church records:

Stanislaus filium Joannis Bori et Catherinae de domo Graserow—"Stanisław the son of Jan Bór and Katarzyna from home Graser" (Note: *Graserow* is Polish, the rest is Latin.)

Catharina uxor Joannis Bor tabernatori—"Katarzyna the wife of Jan Bór the tavernkeeper"

Petrus Bor maritus Mariae—"Piotr Bór the husband of Marya"

Numbers and Months

For every pair of words below, the first is the masculine (example: *unus*) and the second is the feminine (example: *una*).

Numbers		Age (in Years)
1	unus, una	annotinus, annotina (1 year old)
2	duo, duae	biennius, biennia (2 years old)
3	tres, tres	trimus, trima (3 years old)
4	quattuor, quattuor	quadrimus, quadrima (4 years old)
5	quinque, quinque	quinquennis, quinquennis (5 years old)
6	sex, sex	sexennis, sexennis (6 years old)
7	septem, septem	septuennis, septuennis (7 years old)
8	octo, octo	octiennis, octiennis (8 years old)
9	novem, novem	noviennis, noviennis (9 years old)
10	decem, decem	decinnis, decinnis (10 years old)
11	undecim, undecim	
12	duodecim, duodecim	
13	tredecim, tredecim	
14	quattuordecim, quattuordecim	
15	quindecim, quindecim	
16	sextusdecim, sextusdecim	
17	septemdecim, septemdecim	
18	duodeviginti, duodeviginti (2 before 20)	
18	octodecim, octodecim (8 plus 10)	
19	undeviginti, undeviginti (1 before 20)	
19	novemdecim, novemdecim (9 plus 10)	
20	vicensus, vicensa	vicennis, vicennis (20 years old)
20	vicesimus, vicesima	vigesimonarius, vigesimonaria (20 years old)
20	viginti, viginti	
25	quiniviceni, quinivicenae	quinivigesimonarius, quinivigesimonaria (25 years old)

continued

Numbers		Age (in Years)
30	triginta, triginta	trigesimonarius, trigesimonaria (30 years old)
40	quadraginta, quadraginta	quadragenarius, quadragenaria (40 years old)
50	quinquaginta, quinquaginta	quinquagenarius, quinquagenaria (50 years old)
60	sexaginta, sexaginta	sexagenarius, sexagenaria (60 years old)
70	septuaginta, septuaginta	septuagenarius, septuagenaria (70 years old)
80	octoginta, octoginta	octogenarius, octogenaria (80 years old)
90	nonaginta, nonaginta	nonagenarius, nonagenaria (90 years old)
100	centum, centum	centenarius, centenaria (100 years old)

Latin Terms Found in Vital Records

The following terms are frequently found in vital records from the eighteenth and nineteenth centuries.

abiit: he/she died
abitus est: he/she departed/died
abluo: I baptized
ablutus est: he/she was baptized
accatholica: non-Catholic
accola: local resident
acquiescat: he/she died/reposed
adolescens, adolescentis, adol.: a youth, young man or woman, one not previously married
adnotatio: annotations, additional remarks; there usually is a space reserved for additional comments in a vital register
advocatus: administrator; representative of a municipal landowner who exercised judicial authority given to him by the feudal lord
aeger, aegra: sick or ill, physically or mentally
aetas: age

MONTHS		
Januarius, Ianuarius	January	I
Februarius	February	II
Martius	March	III
Aprilis	April	IV
Majus, Maius	May	V
Junius, Iunius	June	VI
Julius, Iulius, Quinctilis	July	VII
Augustus, Sextilis	August	VIII
Septembris, 7bris	September	IX
Octobris, 8bris	October	X
Novembris, 9bris	November	XI
Decembris, 10bris	December	XII

agonia: cramps

agricola: peasant farmer; nineteenth-century term for a land-owning peasant

agrippo: pneumonia

alias: also known as; nickname

ambo: both, also; used to indicate the person(s) came from the same location

amita: paternal uncle, father's sister

ancilla: maid-servant; female slave

annus, anno: year

antesuscepto: before having a child; while pregnant; from *ante* (before) and *suscipio, susceptum* (of a parent having a child); seen as a cause of death or in birth records; a miscarried or stillborn baby

anucella: an old woman

anulla: aged, elderly, "up in years"

apoplexia: apoplexy; stroke

apothecarius: storekeeper, shopkeeper

audtem, autem: but, however, now, on the other hand

auriga: (wagon) driver

avia, aviae: grandmother

avilis: shepherd; see *ovilio*

avunculus: maternal uncle, mother's brother

avus, avi: grandfather; an ancestor in general

baptisator: to baptize

baptisma: baptism

baptizatus: baptism

bapt. ab obstetrix: baptized by the midwife

biduum: two-day period

binominis, binom.: having two given names, such as a first and a middle; not to be confused with a twin birth

borussia: Prussia

brasiator: brewer

caelebs: unmarried person, usually a bachelor

camerarior, camerarius: chamberlain

capitis: large head; seen as a cause of death, probably hydrocephalus

capitus dolor: head pain

carnarius: butcher

catarrhus: catarrh, inflammation of the mucous membranes, especially the throat

catholica: Catholic

cauponarius, cauponis: tavernkeeper, shopkeeper

censuani: "of wealth," meaning the person had wealth

cetarius: fishmonger

cholera: jaundice or Asiatic cholera

cholericus: bilious, jaundiced

circa: about

circumspectus: poor burgher

civis: citizen; subject (under the king); burgher or town dweller

coelebs: unmarried person, usually a bachelor

cognomen: surname, family name

colicus: colic

colonus, colonorum: (tenant) farmer; colonist; peasant

combustum, combusti: injury from burning or scalding

commater: godmother

compater: godfather

concepta est: she was pregnant

conditio: status in society; occupation

conjugatus: married

conjuges: married couple

conjugo, conjugium: marriage

conjugum: of/from a married couple

conjux: spouse

consors, consortis: consort

consorte sua/suus: her/his consort (partner) in marriage, usually the wife

consuarior legitt. conjugae: "advised that this is a lawful/legitimate marriage"

contagio, contactus: infection

copulatio, copulationis: marriage

cor, cordis: heart

coram: in the presence of

cruditas: indigestion, overloading of the stomach

cum: with

curatio medici: doctor

curator: guardian, overseer

custos: guardian, custodian (as in guardian of a minor child); custodian (of an estate); also watchman, jailer

d., de., decessus: death, die, deceased

de: from

decanatus: deanery, part of a diocese

de domo: maiden name; "of the house of," "from home"

defunctorum parentum: deceased parents

defunctus: die; "to finish life"

denatus: death

destitutio: "abandoning" (the survivors); he/she leaves behind (the survivors)

dicto, do.: ditto, "to say over"; as previously stated

dies: day

dies vitae: age; "day of life"

dolor: pain

dolore stomachi: stomach pain

domesticus: peasant who possessed only a cottage and garden, no cropland

eadem: likewise, the same, also

ebdomada: week

ecclampsia: convulsion

ecclesia: church

ejusdem: the same, also

eodem: the same, also

et: and

ex, e: from, of; as in "son or daughter of"

ex I voso (name), e prime voso (name): "from the first sacred vow (name)";
  literally "from the first marriage to (name)"; seen in cases where a
  woman was married more than once
ex aqua baptis ab obstetrix: "of the baptismal waters by the hand of the
  midwife"; baby was baptized by the midwife and was in danger of im-
  mediate death or was stillborn
ex loco: "from the place"; birth place or former residence
extremum munitus: (sacrament of) "last rites provided"

faber, fabri: craftsman
faber tignarius: carpenter
famatus: well known; average resident of a big city or a rich burgher in a
  small town
famula: female slave; handmaid
famulus, famulum: male slave; servant
febris: fever
febris nervosa: strong fever; febrile seizures
fecunda: pregnant
femina: feminine, female
ferrarius: blacksmith
figulus, figularis: potter
filia: daughter
filius: son
fili__ major__: adult son (-us, -um); adult daughter (-a, -am)
fili__ minor__: minor son (-us, -um); minor daughter (-a, -am)
filius fratris, filius sororis: nephew; "son of the brother (or sister)"
flusor sanguinis: flow of blood; bled to death
fornal: serf dependent on the village lord
frater: brother
frater germanus: own (true) brother
fratres: brothers and sisters; siblings

gemelli: twins
generosus, generosa: nobleman/noblewoman possessing land
genitores: parents
genitus, genita: birth
gnatus: birth; same as *natus*
gravedo: catarrh, head cold

graviditas: pregnancy
guttur: throat, windpipe; raspy sounds

hebdomada, hebdomas: week
heres, hares, haeres: village owner, owner, proprietor, heir/heiress
honestus, honesta: a title: "the Honorable"; denotes a social class above
    peasants; village craftsman, inn owner, or people living outside the
    town walls
honoratus, honorata: richest merchant
hora: hour
hortulanus: farmer, with land and buildings
humatus, humata: burial
humatio: burial
hydrops: dropsy, edema, accumulation of fluid in a part of the body

icterus: jaundice
ictus: stroke
iecur: liver
igne combusta: injured or died from a burn or scald
ignis, igneus: fire
ignotus: unknown
illegitimatus (-a) thori: illegitimate birth status, parents not married to each
    other
imbecillitas: weakness; as a cause of death it is failure to thrive
impubes, -beris: youthful, unmarried; also below the age of puberty
incertus, incerta: uncertain, unknown
incola: inhabitant, native; sometimes a foreign resident
infans, infanta, infantus: literally "speechless," usually means an infant or
    child
inquilinus, inquilina: landless or tenant farmer; one who farms for another
    landowner; possibly a person of foreign origin, sometimes a local
    resident
interitus: enteritis
in vivus, in viva: "at birth"; usually means an infant who died at birth

jecur: liver
juvenis: young person; also refers to an unmarried man, regardless of age
juvenis liberi: independent minor person

labes: stain, blemish; rash; spotted fever

laboriosus: used as a title with a person's name, a hard-working person or peasant

laborius: worker, laborer

lanarius: wool worker

laniarus, lanius: butcher

legitimatus (-a) thori: legitimate birth status; child was born to parents married to each other

liacus: person with no possessions, vagabond; a "street person"

liber: freeman

liber: book, register

liber bannorum: register of marriage banns

liberi, liberum: children

liberi (libr.) non sunt: "there are no children" surviving

libero conditiones (condiciones): released from the marriage contract

locus: location, place

locus nativitatis: place of birth

magnificus, magnifica: a title; owner of several villages and/or holder of an important regional office

mane: (early) morning

marita: wife

maritus: husband

masculus: male

massa: mass, lump

mater, matris: mother, of the mother (mother's)

matertera: maternal aunt, mother's sister

matrices: original (birth) records

matrimonium: marriage

matutina, matutinus: of morning; early in the morning

medicus: doctor

mendicus: beggar

mensis: month

mercator: merchant

miles: soldier

miles (milites) limitaneus: frontier troops

molitor: builder

morbus, morbi: disease; often used to mean the "cause of death"

mori, morior, moriturus: to die

mors, mortis: death; often used to mean "cause of death"

morte in aqua embrio: "died in the embryonic water"; miscarriage or stillbirth; miscarried and stillborn babies were often baptized

morte naturali: natural death; death by natural causes

mortuus, mortua: dead

mortuus (mortua) est: "he/she is dead"; "he/she died on (date); usually used to indicate the date of death

mulier, mulieris: woman, wife, matron

munitus, munita: fortified, protected, secured; "fortified" with the sacrament of the last rites

nascor: to be born

nata: "so born"; née; usually precedes a woman's maiden name

natus, nata: born

nativitatis locus: birth place

neophita, neophyta: female neophyte or convert; newly baptized member of the church

neophitus, neophytus: male neophyte or convert; newly baptized member of the church

neosponsa: newly betrothed woman, bride

neosponsus: newly betrothed man, bridegroom

nepos, nepotis: grandson, sometimes a nephew; in general, a descendant

neptis: granddaughter

nihil: nothing

n. n.: see *nomen nescio*

nobiles, nobilis, nobilium: nobility, of noble birth; also "well known"

nobilitas: nobleman, nobility

nocte, noctis: night

nomen: name

nomen nescio: unknown; "I do not know the name of (person)"

non: not

non exant: deprived of life

non munitus, non munita: not protected with the sacrament of the last rites

non uxoratus: unmarried man; "not married to a wife"

non vivus, non viva: "not alive"; usually means an infant was stillborn

nothus: illegitimate child

notificat: notify; (name) notified (the recordkeeper of the event); refers to the person who notified the recordkeeper of the event

nox: night

nubo, nubere (nubam, nubum): said (of a woman) to be married to; to marry

nubilis: (said of a woman) of an age suitable for marriage
nulloque detecto impedimento matrimonio: "no hindrance to the marriage is
    found"; the couple is free to marry
numerus: number
numerus domorum: "number of the house"; house number
nuptiae: marriage

obitus, obit.: death
obstetrix: midwife
operarius: workman, day laborer
oppidum, oppidio: town
orbus: orphan, "deprived of parents"; also "deprived of children"
organicus: musician
oriendus, oriundus: birth; born in (place)
ortus: birth; origin
ovilio: shepherd

pagus, pagi: village
papula: pimple
parens: parent; sometimes a grandfather or an ancestor
parenti: parents
pariter: also, equally
pariter, paritor: an occupation: apparitor or beadle; messenger or summoner
    of a court; parish officer with various subordinate duties, such as
    waiting on the clergy, keeping order in the church, etc., similar to a
    modern usher or parish councilman
parochia: parish
partus: birth
pastor: shepherd
pater, patris: father; father's, of the father
patrini: godparents
patrini et eorum conditio: godparents and their occupations or status
patris viro ignoti: "father—the man—(is) unknown"; the father is not
    named in the birth record because it is an illegitimate birth
patruus, patrui: father's brother; paternal uncle
pauperus, pauperis: pauper, poor person
pectus, pectoris: chest or breast
phthisis: consumption, tuberculosis of the lungs
pictor: painter

piscator: fisherman

pistor: baker; miller

plebus, plebes: commoner; one not of noble birth

pleuritis: pleurisy

post: "after"; leaves behind, surviving, deceased; usually refers to the surviving members of the deceased person's family

posthumus: "after the burial"; the child was born after the father's death

praeceptor schola: schoolteacher

praefectus: overseer; mayor; judge; superintendent of a small government, such as a town

predefunctus: previously deceased; used, for example, in cases where the father died before his child was born

procurator: manager; bailiff; administrator

providus: poor burgher

pudica, pudicans: virtuous, chaste, modest; usually indicates a virgin or an unmarried man

puella: girl

puer: boy

puerperium: childbirth

puerperus, puerpera: of childbirth

pulmonis: lungs

pupillaris: ward; child

pustula: pox, blister

recte: correctly; properly

relicta, relictus: forsaken, abandoned; may refer to a widow or widower

religio: (name of the) religion (practiced by the person/s)

relinquit, reliquit: "he/she leaves behind"; surviving family members

remex: oarsman, rower

renes, renum: kidneys

rerrus, rerra: from *res, rerrum*: thing, object, matter, circumstance

rheumatismus: rheumatism

robarata: from *roboro, robare*: to strengthen; last rites were administered at time of death

rusticus, rustico: landless farm laborer; peasant

rusticus vagus: vagabond; person with no possessions; a "street person"

sacerdos: priest

sacramentis totiis munitiis: "fortified by all the last rites" of the church

sanguis, sanguinis: blood
sanguinis flusor: flow of blood
sarcinator: cobbler
sartor: tailor
scriba: scribe, clerk
scultetus: mayor; sheriff; village administrator; representative of a
      landowner in a rural area, who exercised judicial authority given to
      him by the feudal lord
senectus, senestrus (-a): senility
senex, senis: an old person
senilis, senile: senile
sepultus, sepulta: burial
sepultura: burial; interment
serrum, serri: a late hour
sexus: sex (male or female)
siccus, sicca: sound of health
silvanus: forester silvculture
silvicola: forest dweller; one who inhabits the woods
silvestris: "of the woods"
sino libr., sino liberi: leaves no children
soror, sororis: sister; sisters
sororis filia: niece, daughter of the sister
spectabilis, spblis: patriciate of a very large city
sponsa (-ae): bride
sponsus (-i): groom
status: social status; condition, state
stomachus: esophagus or throat; stomach
structor: mason, builder, carpenter
struma: scrofulous tumor
stuprata: pregnant out of wedlock
suarius: swineherd
subcamerarius: chamberlain
substantia indeterminata: indefinite means of subsistence or property; it is
      not known how the person was able to feed, clothe, and shelter him-
      self/herself; unknown social class
subulcus: swineherd
sutor, sutoris: shoemaker

tabernarius: shopkeeper
tabernator, tabernatoris: tavernkeeper, innkeeper, shopkeeper

tabes: consumption, tuberculosis

testes, testis: witness(es)

tetanus: tetanus; cramps; lockjaw

textor, textrix: weaver (male); weaver (female)

thori: "status of birth" (legitimate or illegitimate)

thussis: cough; whooping cough

thyfus: typhus fever

treme (or any *trem-* word): tremors, trembling

trigeminus, tergeminus: "three at birth"; triplets

trucido: murder, slaughter, massacre

tuber, tuberis: swelling

tumor: swelling

tussis: cough; whooping cough

tutor: guardian

tyfus: typhus fever

uhlanus, ulanus: Polish or German cavalryman armed with a lance

ulcus, ulceris: sore, ulcer, wound; also seen as *ulieri*

ultima, ultimus: extreme, either original or last

ultra, ultere: advance, excess; sometimes refers to a disease in an advanced
     state

uterus, uteri: womb, uterus, belly; also a womb with its contents:
     an unborn child, a pregnancy

uxor: wife

vagabundus (-a), vagantus (-a), vagus (male), vagatrix (female): vagabond,
     person with no possessions; a "street person"

venator, venatoris: hunter

venenatus (-a): poisoned, drugged

venter, ventris: stomach, belly, wound

vermis: worm

vertigo: dizziness

vesper, vesperis, vesp.: evening

vespere: in the evening

vicinus: neighbor

vicus, vici: village; street; part of a town

vidua: widow

viduus: widower

villa: usually an estate; also a country house or farm

vilicus, villicus: steward, bailiff, overseer of an estate

vir: man, male person, husband

vir excellens: title used with the name of an intellectual such as a teacher, lawyer, doctor, professor

virgo: virgin, unmarried girl; abbreviated *vir* and *vrne* (*virgine*) and *vrm* (*virginam*)

vocitatus: "called" or "known as"

volnus: wound, injury

vomica: abcess, ulcer, boil; plague

voso, votus: from *voveo*, a vow or sacred promise, as in the sacred wedding vows; *ex I voso* indicates the first marriage

vulgo: common person, commoner; used as a title with a person's name

vulgo: nickname; "commonly known as"

vulnus, vulneris: wound, injury

THE GERMAN LANGUAGE

A lot of German words are easy to translate as many are almost the same in English. Unfortunately the old-style German handwriting is often very difficult to read—many letters are formed very differently than ours are now, and there were many ways to draw an individual letter itself. Good books for translating German records are Edna Bentz's *If I Can You Can Decipher Germanic Records* and Ernest Thode's *German–English Genealogical Dictionary*.

PROPER NAMES			
Case	**Mr.**	**Mrs./Miss**	**Family Names/Mr. & Mrs.**
nominative	(name)	(name)	(name)
genitive	*-s*	*-s*	*-s*
dative	*-em, -e*	*-er*	*-en*

The dative case is used with *von*. For example:

Wilhelm der Sohn von Johanne(m) und Magdalener Schmidten— "Wilhelm the son of Johann and Magdalena Schmidt"

Wilhelm der Sohn Johanns Schmidts—"Wilhelm the son of Johann Schmidt"

German Terms Found in Vital Records

alt: old
Alter: age; old age
ältest: eldest, senior
am: on the
Aufgebot: proclamation; marriage banns; conscription

Bauer: farmer
Beerdigung: burial
Begräbnis: burial
Bemerkung(en): remark(s)
Beruf: occupation, trade
Bezirk, Bez.: district
Bezirksamt: local government office
Braut: betrothed, fiancée; bride (only on wedding day)
Bräutigam: fiancé; bridegroom (only on wedding day)
Bruder: brother

Datum: date
der älter, d. a.: the older, the eldest, senior
der jünger, d. j.: the younger, junior
deutsch: German
Dorf: village

Ehe: marriage
Ehefrau, Ehegattin: wife
Ehemann, Ehegatte: husband
Eltern: parents
Enkel: grandson, grandchild
Enkelin: granddaughter
etwa: approximately
evangelisch, ev.: Evangelical

Familie: family
Familienname: family name, surname
Frau: woman, wife
Fräulein: girl, unmarried woman

Gatte: husband
Gattin: wife
geboren, geb.: born
geborene: "was born," maiden name
Geburt: birth
Geburtsort: birth place
Geburtstag: birthday
Geburtsurkunde: birth certificate
Gemeinde: parish
gestorben, gest.: died
getauft, get.: christened, baptized
Gewerbe: occupation, trade
griechisch-katholische Kirche: Greek-Catholic Church

Heirat: marriage
Heiratsschein: marriage certificate

im: in the
im alter von: aged, "in the year of"

Jahr: year
Jude: Jew
judisch: Jewish

katholisch, kath.: Catholic
Kind: child
Kinder: children
Kirche: church
Kirchenbuch, k. b.: church book, church register
Kleinkind: infant
Knabe: boy
Kreis, Kr.: "circle," province, county

Land: state, country
Lebensalter: age; literally "age of life"
Litauen: Lithuania
litauisch: Lithuanian
lutheranisch, luth.: Lutheran

Mädchen: girl, maiden
Mädchenname: maiden name
Mann: man, husband
Militär: soldier, the military
Monat: month
Mutter: mother

Name: name

Ort: place
Osterreich: Austria
österreichisch: Austrian

Pate: godfather
Patin: godmother
Pfarrbezirk: parish
Pfarrer: pastor, priest
Polen: Poland
polnisch: Polish

russisch: Russian
Rußland: Russia

Schein: certificate
Schwester: sister
Sohn: son
Sohn von, S. v.: son of
Staat: state, country
Stadt: town, city
Stammbaum: genealogical tree, family tree, pedigree chart
Stand: condition, occupation, status in society
Standesamt: registrar's office
starb: died
starb kinderlos: died without children
Sterben: death

Tag: day
Taufbuch: baptismal register

Taufe: christening, baptism
Taufgesinnte(r): Mennonite, (ana)baptist
Taufname: Christian name
Taufpate, Taufzeuge: godfather
Taufpatin, Taufzeugin: godmother
Taufschein: baptismal certificate
Tochter: daughter
Tochter von, T. v.: daughter of
Tod: death
trauen: marry
Trauschein: marriage certificate

un der, u. d.: and the
unbekannt: unknown

Vater: father
Veheiratung: marriage
verstorben: deceased
Vorname: first name, given name, Christian name

Wiedertauffer: "again baptized"; Mennonite
Witwe, Wwe., Witfrau: widow
Witwer, Wwer.: widower
wohnen: live, reside
Wohnort: dwelling place, legal residence

Z. militär: prepared for military conscription
Zeuge(n): witness(es)
Zuname: surname, family name
Zurüstung: preparation (for military service through conscription)
Zwangsaushebung: conscription

THE RUSSIAN LANGUAGE

After 1868 in the Russian-occupied areas of Poland, vital records were required to be kept in the Russian language. Most of the these records have an index. Use the alphabet below to search the indexes, then photocopy or pho-

RUSSIAN ALPHABET

Printed	Cursive	English
А, а	*А,а*	*a*
Б, б	*Б,б*	*b*
В, в	*В,в*	*v*
Г, г	*Г,г*	*g*
Д, д	*Д,д,д*	*d*
Е, е	*Е,е*	*ye*
Ё, ё	*Ё,ё*	*yo*
Ж, ж	*Ж,ж*	*zh*
З, з	*З,з*	*z*
И, и	*И,и*	*i*
Й, й	*Й,й*	*y*
К, к	*К,к*	*k*
Л, л	*Л,л*	*l*
М, м	*М,м*	*m*
Н, н	*Н,н*	*n*
О, о	*О,о*	*o*
П, п	*П,п*	*p*
Р, р	*Р,р*	*r*
С, с	*С,с*	*s*
Т, т	*Т,т*	*t*
У, у	*У,у*	*u*
Ф, ф	*Ф,ф*	*f*
Х, х	*Х,х*	—
Ц, ц	*Ц,ц*	*ts*
Ч, ч	*Ч,ч*	*ch*
Ш, ш	*Ш,ш*	*sh*
Щ, щ	*Щ,щ*	*shch*
—, ъ	*-,ъ*	--
—, ы	*-,ы*	--
—, ь	*-,ь*	--
Э, э	*Э,э*	*e*
Ю, ю	*Ю,ю*	*yu*
Я, я	*Я,я*	*ya*

tograph the entry you need. You may also want to make a copy of the names in the index that you think might be yours. If you can't translate the Russian cursive script well enough to pick out names and dates, have the entry translated for you.

The preceding alphabet is a modern version. Become familiar with the Russian alphabet and it will be easier to "read" the names.

GENEALOGICAL RESEARCH IN RUSSIA

If you are conducting research in areas of Eastern Europe that were once under Soviet domain, you may wish to write directly to the new Commonwealth of Independent States. In the past it was difficult, if not impossible, to obtain records from the Soviet government. In 1988 the government announced it would allow genealogical inquiries, but not much is known about the success of this method of research yet. The Commonwealth of Independent States will probably take a long time to organize itself, but the new openness should guarantee access, and the favorable rate of exchange between U.S. dollars and Russian rubles should be attractive to individuals who have the spare time to answer genealogical queries.

It may take a long time, more than just a few months, to receive a reply, but translating your inquiry into Russian will undoubtedly speed up the research process. In your letter of inquiry include the complete name of your ancestor, specific town and region of his birth, marriage, or residence, date of the event, and his religion and ethnic group. Send your inquiries to:

> Glavnoe Arkhivnoe Upravlenie pri Sovete Ministrov SSSR
> 11943—Moskva
> ul. Bolshaya Pirogovskaya, 17
> Rossia (Russia)

Still more avenues for Russian research are opening up. The National Archives Volunteer Association (NAVA) and the AROS Society, Ltd. (Archives of Russia) recently signed an agreement to form the Russian-American Genealogical Archival Service (RAGAS). This service will handle requests from Americans who wish to have genealogical research done in areas of the former Soviet Union.

The American agency will accept inquiries, using a bilingual form, and send them to AROS to be processed and forwarded to the proper archives. This system will operate in the Commonwealth of Independent States (Russia, Ukraine, Byelorussia, etc.). For more information, contact the following:

NAVA
National Archives
Washington, D. C. 20408

RAGAS
P.O. Box 236
Glen Echo, Maryland 20812

To contact AROS directly, write or phone:

AROS Ltd.—The Archives of Russia
SU-103821—Moskva
15 Pushkinskaja ul.
Rossia (Russia)
Telephone: 011-7-095-9579
Fax: 011-7-095-200-4205

Family History Services of Moscow is another new organization that can search genealogical materials from Russia, Ukraine, Byelorussia, and all the other areas of the former Soviet Union. Urbana Technologies handles inquiries from Americans and sends them to Family History Services in Moscow. Write to them for more information about services and fees: Urbana Technologies, 2011 Silver Ct. E., Urbana, Illinois 61801.

ADDITIONAL READING

Bentz, Edna M. *If I Can You Can Decipher Germanic Records*, 1982 (9th printing, 1991); Edna Bentz, 13139 Old West Avenue, San Diego, California 92129.

Bulas, Kazimierz and Francis J. Whitfield. *The Kościuszko Foundation Dictionary.* 2 vols.: English-Polish, Polish-English. New York: Kościuszko Foundation, 1983.

Frazin, Judith R. *A Translation Guide to 19th Century Polish-Language Civil-Registration Documents*: *Birth, Marriage and Death Certificates.* 2nd ed. Jewish Genealogical Society of Illinois, 1989. (Available from: Hamakar Judaica, Inc., 6153 Mulford, Unit D, Niles, Illinois 60648.)

Mikos, Michael J. *Computer Programs for First and Second Year Polish.* (Computer programs that teach vocabulary and grammar, designed for use with Apple II (R), Macintosh, and IBM.) Available from: University of Wisconsin–Milwaukee, Language Resource Center, CRT B-31, P.O. Box 413, Milwaukee, Wisconsin 53201-0413.

Shea, Jonathan D. and William F. Hoffman. *Following the Paper Trail*: *A Multilingual Translation Guide.* New Milford, Connecticut: Language and Lineage

Press, 1991. (Available from the publisher: Language and Lineage Press, 60 Old Northville Road, New Milford, Connecticut 06776-2245.) Translates German, Swedish, French, Italian, Latin, Portuguese, Romanian, Spanish, Czech, Polish, Russian, Hungarian, and Lithuanian documents.)

Thode, Ernest. *German–English Genealogical Dictionary*. Baltimore: Genealogical Publishing Company, 1992.

Chapter Fourteen:

WRITING LETTERS
TO POLAND

Writing letters to Poland asking for records or assistance can be very fruitful. You can write to churches, civil records offices, libraries, and institutes. Perhaps you can request a photograph of your ancestor's church, homestead, or village. By writing to the parish priest or civil records office you can even find out if there are any of your relatives left in the ancestral village. You may be able to begin a correspondence with descendants of your long-lost relatives.

My American-born mother-in-law, Helen, and her first cousin Stanley in Poland corresponded in French during their high school years in the 1930s. Just two months before my husband and I left for our trip to Poland in 1985 we began to write to Stanley's son Andrew. We met Andrew and his son Przemysław in Poznań and found out that Przemysław and our daughter Rebecca share the same birthday, March 19. Przemysław and Rebecca began writing letters—the third generation to do so!

The following are a few guidelines you should follow when writing letters to Poland:

1. Write in Polish, as letters in English are usually not answered. Parish priests and civil registrars will generally not respond if they don't know what you are asking for, and will not take the time to find a person who can read English. Your relatives, moreover, will be more likely to respond to a letter written in Polish.

Use the "Polish Genealogical Letter-Writing Guide" (page 233) to compose letters in Polish. Failing that, find someone who can read and write Polish; try parish priests, language teachers, professional translators, or friends and relatives. They may be able to write things that are not in the Guide, or translate the reply you will receive from Poland.

Be polite when composing your letter. Poles have extremely good manners, and *proszę* (please) and *dziękuję* (thank you) will go a long way toward a prompt response.

Polish handwriting is slightly different from American, so type your letter, then add the Polish diacritical marks where they are needed. Be sure to include your own return address on the letter itself.

2. Send as much information as you have on your ancestor and be specific. Include the maiden names of the women and birth dates and places, if known. It won't do to say that your ancestor was "born about 1870 to 1880," but you can probably ask for a search within a three-year period. Many records are not indexed, and an archivist will not spend time looking through every entry for a ten-year period. You must also be specific about the names of towns and villages, so do your homework to find out exactly where your ancestors originated.

3. Always include a donation when requesting a document from a parish or church archives; however, do not ask for more than three items at a time. At least $5.00 per document requested should be included with your letter, but ask what the standard fee is for a record from the civil registrar's office.

If you send money with your request, always say so in the letter and state the amount. Send cash, not a personal check, because checks are difficult to cash in Poland. If it makes you feel safer, find a business that sends parcels to Poland. These businesses are often associated with Polish travel agencies and can send cash to Poland for you. There was only one instance in my correspondence in the past fifteen years in which the parish priest wrote back and said that there was no money in the envelope, but that was during the period when mail was being opened up and censored.

4. Include one or two International Reply Coupons, available at most U.S. post offices, with each letter you send to Poland. As a substitute for a SASE outside of the United States, IRCs can be exchanged at a Polish post office for return postage. Postal rates in Poland have increased dramatically in the last few years, as has everything else, while salaries have stayed the same or been lowered, so be sure to include enough IRCs to assure a reply.

While you are at the post office, find out the cost of postage for letters to Poland, as international rates increase with every *half-ounce* of weight.

5. Reply time may be anything from a month to a year, but you can usually expect a reply in two to four months. In general, mail from Poland arrives in the U.S. in five to fourteen days.

6. Send a "thank you" note after you have received your reply. It can't hurt, and it may help you in obtaining information in the future. If you are espe-

cially pleased with your reply from a parish, you can send an extra donation to be used for a Mass for your ancestors or as a gift to the church.

A short letter in English may be acceptable when writing to the National Library for help in locating your village or to find out its proper mailing address:

> Biblioteka Narodowa
> 00-973 Warszawa
> ul. Hankiewicza 1
> Polska (Poland)

To find the name and address of a Roman Catholic parish for a specific village or town, write to the University Library, Catholic University of Lublin:

> Biblioteka Uniwersytecka
> Katolickiego Uniwersytetu Lubelskiego
> 20-950 Lublin 1
> ul. Chopina 27
> Polska (Poland)

You can also write in English to the Directorate of State Archives, who will forward your request to the appropriate local civil records office:

> Naczelna Dyrekcja
> Archiwów Państwowych
> ul. Długa 6, skr. poczt. 1005
> 00-950 Warszawa
> Polska (Pozland)

Polish Genealogical Letter-Writing Guide
Adapted from the LDS Genealogical Library Patron Aid,
Series C, no. 302

The following letter-writing guide is provided so that you can select the appropriate ideas and construct a letter that will be easily understood. First, however, you must take care to address your letter in the manner set out below:

Local Parish:

> Catholic: Parafia Rzymsko-katolicka
> Orthodox: Parafia Prawosławna
> Lutheran: Parafia Ewangelicka
> (Name of Town), woj. (województwo = name of province)
> POLSKA
> POLAND

Local Civil Records Office:

> Urząd Stanu Cywilnego
> (Name of Town), woj. (województwo = name of province)
> POLSKA
> POLAND

Example:

> Parafia Rzymsko-katolicka
> Sokolów Małopolska, woj. Rzeszów
> POLSKA
> POLAND

The above format can be used when the exact address is not known. If you know the Polish "zip code," it is not necessary to include the name of the województwo (province).

GENEALOGICAL TERMS AND SENTENCES*

1. Greetings:

Dear sir,	Szanowny Panie,	[Civil Records Official]
Dear Father,	Drogi Ojcze,	[Catholic or Orthodox]
Reverend Priest,	Szanowny Księże,	[Catholic or Orthodox]
Dear Pastor,	Drogi Pastorze,	[Protestant]

2. I live in the U.S.A., but my ances-   2. Mieszkam w Stanach Zjednoczo-

*Reprinted by permission. Copyright © 1983, 1985 by Corporation of the President of The Church of Jesus Christ of Latter-day Saints.

try is from Poland and I would like to know more about my Polish ancestors.

nych, lecz jestem polskiego pochodzenia i chciałbym [chciałabym, if you are female] dowiedzieć się więcej o moich polskich przodkach.

3. I am preparing a history of my ancestors in Poland and need information from your vital records.

3. Spisuję historię moich przodków z Polski, i dlatego potrzebne mi jest pewne dane z Waszych ksiąg metrykalnych.

4. The following individual is my ancestor who was born in Poland. I have given all the vital data about this person that I have.

4. Następująca osoba, która urodziła się w Polsce, jest moim przodkiem. Podaję wszystkie dane jakie o niej mam.

5. The following individuals are my ancestors who were born in Poland. I have given all the vital data about them that I have.

5. Następujące osoby są moimi przodkami którzy urodzili się w Polsce. Podaję wszystkie dane jakie o nich mam.

6. [Give as much *pertinent* information as possible. Use only those items below for which you can give accurate information relevant to what you are requesting. Do not give information about events that occurred after the ancestor left Poland.]

name and surname:
date of birth (approximate):
place of birth:
full name of father:
full maiden name of mother:
first name of mother:
full name of husband:
full maiden name of wife:
first name of wife:
date of marriage:
place of marriage:
date of emigration:
religion:

Orthodox = prawosławne
Jewish = żydowskie

imię i nazwisko:
data urodzenia (w przybliżeniu):
miejsce urodzenia:
imię i nazwisko ojca:
imię i panieńskie nazwisko matki:
imię matki:
imię i nazwisko męża:
imię i nazwisko panieńskie żony:
imię żony:
data ślubu:
miejsce ślubu:
data emigracji:
wyznanie:

Roman-Catholic = rzymsko-katolickie
Greek-Catholic = grecko-katolickie
Evangelical-Lutheran = ewangelickie

7. Please send me a complete extract of the birth or christening record (1) of this person. (2) of these persons.

7. Proszę o przesłanie mi pełnego odpisu świadectwa urodzenia lub chrztu (1) tej osoby. (2) tych osób.

8. Could you please check your birth records from _(year)_ to _(year)_ for the birth record of this person?

9. Please send me a complete extract of the marriage record (1) of these persons. (2) of this person's parents.

10. I would like to know more about the family of this person and if you would provide the names and birthdates of the brothers and sisters and an extract of the marriage record of the parents, I would be very grateful.

11. I believe that _(name)_ died in your area about _(date)_. I would like a complete extract of the death record.

12. If you do not have the necessary records, I request that you provide the address of the place where such records can be found.

13. Please let me know the cost for your help and how I can pay.

14. Please let me know how I can make an offering to your parish in exchange for your help.

15. I enclose $ _(amount)_ as an offering for your parish.

16. I need information from the parish register of the Evangelical Lutheran parish in _(Polish name of parish/_

8. Proszę sprawdzić w Waszych aktach od roku _(year)_ do roku _(year)_ , czy macie świadectwo urodzenia tej osoby.

9. Proszę o przesłanie mi pełnego odpisu świadectwa ślubu (1) tych osób. (2) rodziców tej osoby.

10. Interesuje mnie rodzina tej osoby i byłbym wdzięczny [byłabym wdzięczna, if you are female] za podanie mi imion, nazwisk, oraz dat i miejsc urodzenia rodzeństwa, jak również przesłanie mi odpisu aktu ślubu rodziców.

11. Myślę że _(name)_ zmarł [zmarła, if it is a female who died] w Waszej okolicy około _(date)_ . Proszę o przesłanie mi pełnego odpisu aktu zgonu.

12. Jeśli te akta nie są w Waszym posiadaniu, proszę o podanie mi adresu, gdzie się one znajdują.

13. Proszę także o poinformowanie mnie, jakie są koszta Waszej pomocy i w jaki sposób mogę je uregulować.

14. Proszę także o poinformowanie mnie, w jaki sposób mogę przesłać ofiarę pieniężną dla Waszej parafii by podziękować za Waszą pomoc.

15. Załączam _(amount)_ dolarów jako datek na Waszą parafię.

16. Potrzebuję dane z ksiąg metrykalnych ewangelickiej parafii w _(Polish name of parish/town)_ , po

town) ; in German, (German name of parish/town) . I will be most grateful if you would inform me where the records of this Evangelical parish are presently to be found.

17. My ancestor was a Greek-Catholic in (parish/town) . I would like to locate the christening and marriage records of the Greek-Catholic parish. Are these records available in your (1) parish office? (2) archive? Has an Orthodox church taken them? If the records are not available to you, could you provide the address where the records may be found?

18. In order to prepare a history of my family, I need information from the Jewish records of birth, marriage, and death from your community. If you know where such records were kept and where they are presently located, would you please inform me?

19. I would like to locate any relatives who may live in your town. My ancestor was (full name) . He resided in (place of residence) before he left for America in (year) . If you know any persons of this name or relatives of the family, I would be grateful if you would give this letter to them so that they can contact me.

20. If you could answer in English or German, I would be very grateful as I am better able to read and write in these languages.

21. I thank you in advance for your assistance.

niemiecku (German name of parish/town) . Będę bardzo wdzięczny [wdzięczna, if you are female] za podanie mi, gdzie można obecnie znaleźc księgi metrykalne tej parafii.

17. Mój przodek był wyznania grecko-katolickiego w (parish/town) . Potrzebne mi są dane z akt chrzcin i ślubów tej grecko-katolickiej parafii. Czy są one dostępne w (1) Waszej parafii? (2) Waszym archiwum? Czy kościół prawosławny ma je w swoim posiadaniu? Jeśli nie macie tych akt, to czy możecie podać mi adres, gdzie się one znajdują?

18. W celu uzupełnienia historii mojej rodziny, potrzebne mi są dane z żydowskich ksiąg urodzin, ślubów i zgonów z Waszej okolicy. Jeśli wiecie gdzie takie akty były prowadzone i gdzie się obecnie znajdują, proszę uprzejmie o poinformowanie mnie.

19. Pragnę odnaleźć krewnych żyjących w Waszej miejscowości. Mój przodek nazywał się (full name) i mieszkał w (place of residence) przed swym wyjazdem do Ameryki w roku (year) . Jeśli znacie ludzi o tym samym nazwisku lub ich krewnych, proszę o przekazanie im tego listu, aby mogli się ze mną skontaktować.

20. Jeśli możecie odpisać w języku angielskim lub niemieckim, to byłbym wdzięczny [byłabym wdzięczna, if you are female] gdyż lepiej władam tymi językami.

21. Z podziękowaniem.

22. Closings:	22.
with regards, respectfully,	z szacunkiem, z poważaniem,
23. My address:	23. Mój adres:

The following sentences may be used in writing follow-up letters.

24. Thank you for the information you have sent. It has helped me very much.	24. Dziękuję za informacje, które mi przesłaliście. Bardzo mi one pomogły.
25. I need further information about one of the individuals you mentioned in your letter. This is __(name)__	25. Potrzebne mi są dalsze dane o jednej z osób o której mi napisaliście. Jest to __(name)__ .
26. I have already received from you the following data about this person:	26. Już od Was otrzymałem [otrzymałam, if you are female] następujące dane o tej osobie:

[see number 6]

Chapter Fifteen:

WHEN YOU VISIT POLAND

"Should I go with a tour group or on my own?" is the first question you will ask when planning a trip to Poland. Your answer depends on several things: What do you expect to do in Poland? Visit relatives or sightsee or both? Do you plan to do research in archives and libraries? Can you understand Polish? Do you speak Polish? How long will your trip last?

My husband and I visited relatives in Poland in 1985. We rented a Polish Fiat and drove around the country using the 1944 U. S. Army Service maps and a Polish road atlas, and never got lost. My husband speaks no Polish and I understand Polish somewhat, but do not speak the language well. All the families that we visited found a relative or close friend who spoke English, sometimes better than some English-speaking Americans I know. We stayed in Poland for twelve days, but that was not long enough to do all that we wanted.

If you plan to do research in archives, libraries, or churches, write ahead to make appointments and to be sure that what you are searching for is there. Speaking Polish is helpful, but don't be afraid to travel on your own if you don't. Menus in the restaurants in cities and towns are written in at least two languages—Polish, English, and sometimes French and German as well. City maps are sold at many street corners, as are newspapers, flowers, cigarettes, and souvenirs. You can rent a car or travel on the extensive train system and then use taxis and trams to get around in the cities. Before deciding whether to go with a tour group or on your own, get information from a Polish-American travel agency and from the Polish Genealogical Society of Connecticut (see chapter 3 for address), which plans genealogical tours of Poland.

If you don't know where some of your relatives are residing in Poland, talk to your older family members or look through old letters, passports, and other documents.

Many Poles are eager to find their American cousins, so write a letter to locate your relatives in Poland. It is best to correspond in Polish, but if you can't find someone to translate your letter for you, you will have to write in English. Your English letter may not be understood, and it may take a while for your relatives to find someone who can read your letter to them. You can usually expect their reply to be in Polish.

If I were to send an inquiry to my grandfather's cousins in Poland, I would address my letter to *Rodzina Stanisława Modrzyńskiego*, "the family of Stanislaus Modrzyński," and send it to the last known address of my Polish relatives. I could also send a letter to the local parish priest, town hall, or newspaper, and tell them I am interested in finding my *living* relatives in that village or town.

When you correspond with your Polish relatives, tell them you are planning to visit Poland and would like to visit them also. Give them the exact dates that you plan to be in their town—they will be waiting for you.

Don't expect your relatives to know everything about your ancestors. Remember that they have not done the enormous amount of genealogical research that you have (you will probably overwhelm your hosts with the family history that you bring with you!). You may, however, spark their interest in family history, which may eventually assist you in researching your ancestors in Poland.

See how your ancestors lived: visit the homesteads, churches, and villages of your ancestors. Go to the *Stare Miasto*, "Old Town," section of the cities and towns. See the museums, especially the ethnographic museums, which have farm buildings and homes and articles from various time periods of Polish history.

Take photographs of your relatives and of churches, gravestones, village points of interest, and village name signs. Many churches have the history of the parish on a wall near the church entrance—copy or photograph it.

With a lot of planning, your trip to your homeland may well be the most memorable you have ever taken.